QUEEN OF THE VIRGINS

CARIBBEAN STUDIES SERIES
Anton L. Allahar and Shona N. Jackson
Series Editors

QUEEN OF THE VIRGINS

Pageantry and Black Womanhood in the Caribbean

Property of Jose E. Muñoz

M. Cynthia Oliver

University Press of Mississippi
Jackson

www.upress.state.ms.us

The University Press of Mississippi is a member of the Association of
American University Presses.

Copyright © 2009 by University Press of Mississippi
All rights reserved
Manufactured in the United States of America

First printing 2009

∞

Library of Congress Cataloging-in-Publication Data

Oliver, M. Cynthia.
Queen of the Virgins : pageantry and black womanhood in the Caribbean /
M. Cynthia Oliver.
p. cm. — (Caribbean studies series)
Includes bibliographical references and index.
ISBN 978-1-60473-242-9 (cloth : alk. paper) 1. Beauty contests—Virgin
Islands of the United States. 2. Beauty contestants—Virgin Islands of the
United States. 3. Black women—Virgin Islands of the United States. I. Title.
HQ1220.V63O45 2009
306.4'613—dc22   2009009732

British Library Cataloging-in-Publication Data available

For Autumn Oshun

CONTENTS

ACKNOWLEDGMENTS

This book has benefited from the help of many people over the past ten years. First, I thank my family; my husband, Jason; and my son, Elias; who have supported and nurtured me throughout this process. I am deeply grateful.

I owe many thanks to my professors and my colleagues who have supported this work, especially Barbara Browning, whose gentle influence kept me going. My gratitude also goes to Maryse Conde, Phil Harper, Fred Moten, Jose Muñoz, and Ngugi wa Thiong'o. Dean Mary Schmidt Campbell of Tisch School of the Arts and the Department of Performance Studies provided a dissertation fellowship so that I could do my fieldwork.

In the islands, many people helped me make contacts and supported my daily existence, feeding me both intellectually and nutritionally along the way. I thank the libraries and their staff on St. Thomas, especially the University of the Virgin Islands and the Enid Baa Library; Robert Nicholls; my family on island, Juanito and Phyllis Benjamin, Mario Greaves Jr., the late Carol Mondesire and Diane Mondesire, and Yvonne and Ecedro Wesselhoft; pageant officials and organizers, including Deborah Gottlieb, Utha Williams, and the Lions Club of St. Thomas; others who extended their help, knowledge and/or willingness to be interviewed, especially Kim Boschulte, William Chandler, Cheryl Plaskett, Rachel Riddle, Violet Victoria, Leah Webster, and Lorna Webster; and the contestants themselves, Lynda Ortiz, April Petrus, Sherece Smith, and Carolyn Wattley.

In St. Croix, my thanks first and foremost go to my mother, Mary Howell-Oliver, a queen to me always, and to my dear father, Everett Oliver. Both have always loved and supported me. I thank my sisters, Lillian and Loretta, and the numerous pageant organizers, contestants, friends, and officials who helped me along the way, including the late Jessica Tutein Moolenaar, Marjorie Brown, Stephanie Brown, Cassandra Dunn, Lisa Galiber, Tina Henle, Cherra Heyleger, Marise James, Wayne James, Claire Roker, and Janasee Sinclair. I could not have done this work without the assistance of excellent librarians on the island, especially Carol Wakefield of the St. Croix Landmarks Society and her successor, Paula Wilson.

I thank my friends, Portia B., Karen Graham, Sara Hook, and Renee Redding-Jones. I offer a very special thanks to those friends and colleagues who looked at versions of this manuscript and gave me constructive feedback. Shanti Pillai, Kate Ramsey, Nichole Rustin, and Deborah Thomas validated my pursuit of this work. Of course, any and all faults of this text are exclusively my own.

The University of Illinois Research Board assisted this project by providing humanities release time so that I could finish revisions. Special thanks go to Kal Alston, then head of gender and women's studies, for her constant advocacy; to Patricia Knowles and Rebecca Nettl-Fiol, successive heads of the University of Illinois Dance Department from 2000 through 2005; and to my supportive colleagues there and elsewhere, including Lisa Dixon, Jordana Mendelson, Tere O'Connor, Larry Parker, Kathy Perkins, John O. Perpener III, Wanda Pillow, Dianne Pinderhughes, Gabriel Solis, Arlene Torres, Gina Ulysse, and Yutian Wong.

Finally, I am deeply grateful to the University Press of Mississippi and particularly to Seetha Srinivasan, who recognized this project's worth in its early stages; Walter Biggins; and the anonymous readers whose detailed and insightful critiques helped make this a better book.

QUEEN OF THE VIRGINS

INTRODUCTION

Situating the Virgin Islands—A Caribbean Nation, a U.S. Colony

When the guy made the song Caribbean Queen, we all danced to it. But we didn't really know what it meant. I know now what it meant, exactly.

—**CAROLYN JENKINS**, *Miss U.S. Virgin Islands 1999 pageant choreographer*

On March 21, 1999, Sherece Smith, a twenty-five-year-old customer service representative for the Water and Power Authority of St. John, was crowned "The Essence of the Caribbean," Miss U.S. Virgin Islands 1999. In a full sweep, Smith took not only that title but also the numerous awards that can go along with it or serve as consolation prizes for the contestants not fortunate enough to win— Miss Photogenic, Miss Congeniality, Best Evening Wear, Miss Intellect, and Best Promotional Presentation. As each of these awards was announced, the tension in the auditorium mounted. A cheering section from St. John became more and more confident as the moments passed. The trophies were placed at her feet, and sashes crossed her shoulders. When officials finally announced that she was the queen, bedlam struck the chandeliered room. A woman ran from the rear of the space, bounded onto the stage, and squeezed Smith before photographers could snap the coveted photograph of her crowning. A wave of other men and women followed. The photographers turned from taking pictures of the stage to taking pictures of the approaching hoards of well-wishers. For the first time since 1981, the pageant had a contestant from St. John, and for only the second time ever, a St. Johnian had won the crown and the opportunity to represent the territory.[1] By the end of the first week of her reign, popular radio programs and talk on the streets had already identified Smith as one of the most popular queens to wear this title, not only ushering in what some observers believe to be a new wave of pageantry in the U.S. Virgin Islands—much as Claire Roker, former queen and current pageant organizer, did in the 1960s—by resuscitating the title of Miss Virgin Islands.

LOCATING PAGEANTRY

Pageants run riot in these islands. Queen shows have been the premiere entertainment, generating the highest attendance of all performance events in the Virgin Islands yet contradictorily suffering from dwindling audiences and needing periodic revival. Queen shows at times have eclipsed local talent shows, calypso tents, and certainly most alternative cultural events in proscenium theaters, school auditoriums, or community common rooms across the islands. No matter the ebb and flow of their popularity, pageants persist. It is possible, as the director of the largest theater space in the Virgin Islands has said, for islanders "to enter contests from the moment you are born, to the time you put your second foot in the grave."[2] From the Little Miss Sweetheart pageants, which engage toddlers and preteens, to the Talented Teen Pageant, to the island representative contests (Miss U.S. Virgin Islands or Miss American Virgin Islands), to the senior contests, women can indeed compete at every stage of their lives.

Pageantry has had a long and colorful history in the Virgin Islands, and "queen shows," or pageants,[3] have become a spectacle. The shows take place in an almost exclusively female world: with the exception of a small cadre of gay men involved in the production process, women run, compete, and view these performances. These pageants are rehearsals of intraclass politics, the place where women of the middle and upper classes have used their influence to solidify their place in local society. As coaches, image consultants, franchise owners, and organizers, they affect the ways island women imagine who they are and their capacity for self-improvement, power, and influence. These productions involve significant cross-class contact and politics as individuals from differing backgrounds engage, train, and perform notions of Virgin Island and Caribbean womanhood. Pageants encourage a cross-class investment as women pursue sponsorships from the business community to support their efforts, sometimes live with organizers to "absorb" the ambience of success, or garner grassroots support, as when young women from state-supported housing choose to participate.

While organizers' influence may at first appear to be the standard result of a Europeanized aesthetic pressure, pageants in the Virgin Islands are stunning examples of an alternative aesthetics of a celebrated black body, an aesthetics that has been both cause to celebrate and cause for conflict. Pageants are a place where these bodies, both individual and communal, exchange aesthetic information with one another through the communities of pageant organization, viewing, and performance. Their involved preparation rituals are amateur theater at its best, responding to local desires and tastes, changing with the times, and ultimately setting the U.S. Virgin Islands apart from those locations hell-bent on assimilating into the dominant Europeanized culture of pageantry.

Pageants are a transnational industry. Contests and the people who participate in them engage in intraisland commerce as they hire image consultants and agents from locales such as Puerto Rico who have circulated in the business for decades and have become experts, much like their South American and Eastern Caribbean neighbors. In participating in these circuits of style and progress, pageants in the Virgin Islands also persist in processing the women of the Virgin Islands as materials/bodies moved from raw to refined. They participate in a repetition of a history whereby colonial forces have used the Caribbean as the source of raw materials for refinement, yet pageants simultaneously disrupt the conventional power dynamics of the colonial relationship, both in the way the black woman has been designated sexually and in the perceptions and opinions of her physical appearance. Pageants are signifiers of attitudes about sexuality and womanhood related to race and class stratifications.[4] They unveil the ways in which codes of behavior are communicated and operate both visibly and invisibly within certain communities. They demonstrate physical and cultural relations to a broader Caribbean, which embraces similar spectacles of pageantry and womanhood in ever-changing formations.

Why are pageants the popular entertainment of choice in the Virgin Islands? The answer lies in the pageant's ability to transform over time to suit the needs and tastes of the populace, its ability to shape or define black womanhood differently and at different junctures, and its location as the place where women of all ages perform most. I begin the journey by looking at the survival tactics and development of a black female psyche during slavery, which functioned despite a systemic onslaught that worked against her at all fronts. In the mid- to late nineteenth century, community women took on the role of town crier and became "queens," indicating how an underclass of black women understood themselves and their possibility for becoming celebrated activist figures. I consider what pageantry and its persistence have meant for women in the Virgin Islands through the emergence of popularity contests of the 1930s, a burgeoning tourist industry and civic organizations led by prominent women during the 1950s, the introduction of franchises in the 1970s, and contemporary incarnations during the 1980s and 1990s.

In recent years, a variety of scholars have focused their research on pageants. Their work demonstrates the resonance of this form of performance in the contexts of global markets for pageantry and the ways in which pageantry is used transnationally to demonstrate local culture and its involvement in a worldwide discourse on the roles of women in nation formation and representation.[5] These studies confirm the weight and seriousness women accord to pageant culture and the ways in which notions of beauty may or may not mobilize life-sustaining and quality-of-life consequences. In other words, pageants betray the ways in which beauty and those talents associated with pageantry can serve as stepping-stones to certain social circles, with the promises of economic betterment not far behind.

Of course, beauty means different things in different locations. Pageants are the place where global models succumb to local tastes. The Virgin Islands' pageants demonstrate the disconnect between native ideas and North American notions of beauty that have dictated, with few exceptions, "the composite contestant who is 5 feet 6 inches tall, 119 pounds with brown hair, blue eyes and a fair complexion."[6] These alternative aesthetics have thus far sealed the Virgin Islands' ranking (or lack thereof) in the international battles and demonstrate a more democratic and generous view of beauty. This fact has freed the U.S. Virgin Islands to perpetuate its own aesthetic and performative standards.

LOCATING THE U.S. VIRGIN ISLANDS

To discuss the cultural particularities of this territory of islands and their practices, I must locate the U.S. Virgin Islands geographically within the Caribbean, historically in relation to its current colonizer, and politically in relation to its sister islands. The Caribbean is an area most often defined by the islands of the Greater Antilles, the larger and more studied areas of Cuba, Haiti and the Dominican Republic, Jamaica, and Trinidad and Tobago. Between these more visible and densely populated islands are the Lesser Antilles, the Bahamas, and certain coastal zones of South and Central America (Suriname, Guyana, and Belize) that share cultural and historical relations to island plantation societies.[7] The Caribbean is a world located between southern Florida and the northern edge of Latin America that sociologists and cultural studies theorists often posit as the seat of modernity, where Europe began its expansion and where globalization and transnational markets were initiated. Yet historians of the West have failed to acknowledge the Caribbean's role in these significant global movements.[8]

The U.S. Virgin Islands are located in the northeastern corner of the Caribbean region, forty miles east of Puerto Rico and southeast of Cuba, the Dominican Republic, and Haiti. St. Thomas, St. Croix, St. John, and Water Island are the four largest among the more than one hundred islands in the territory. They begin the chain of the Lesser Antilles, which includes the British Virgin Islands and continues south through current and former French, British, and Dutch colonies, geographically ending with Trinidad and Tobago. Because of the close proximity of island nations, movements of people and goods have long constituted an interisland system of formal and informal exchange. Islanders have been a part of economies that include higglers (street peddlers), small shopkeepers, and large international corporations that operate in the islands to assure their control of local products and services for export and import.

The complex inter-Caribbean relationships produced by the proximity of so many islands have been the source of ambivalence for many Virgin Islanders, in great part because of the U.S. Virgin Islands' territorial status under the U.S. government.[9] The political and economic benefits and securities of the association with the United States may appear on the surface to separate the Virgin Islands from its neighbors. Yet those apparent benefits are not enough to set the islands apart from the materiality of their condition as colonized islands subject to the same politically and economically dependent status as the rest of the colonized Caribbean. When I say that these characteristics, the ties to the United States, separate the territory from the rest of the Caribbean, this is not to say that the U.S. Virgin Islands is not a participating member of the diverse archipelago. Nor am I saying that its ties to a colonial power are unique; however, the ties to a specific colonial power—the United States—come with a particular set of advantages, challenges, and practices. While natives and seasoned Caribbean travelers acknowledge significant ethnic, cultural, and even geographic differences among islands, appealing to U.S. and European tourist markets ill-equipped to see difference in Caribbean communities drives local governments to differentiate themselves from one another. Thus, legislators, government agencies, and the cultural sector, including beauty pageants, have articulated difference as a strategy for self-definition and economic survival in a region whose capital is strongly tied to tourism and the continuing appeal to outsiders persistently looking for something new to experience. Policymakers challenge themselves to articulate difference—that is, what makes the U.S. Virgin Islands particular to itself—just as those differences make the territory protective of its perceived advantages. The complexities of a population that includes multiple races and nationalities have made articulation of difference a challenging enterprise. Thus the advantages I mention are generally but not exclusively economic. The U.S. Virgin Islands is considered by many of its neighbors as the gateway to the U.S. mainland for those in search of political, social, economic, and cultural advantages over what exists in their home countries. A glance at any of the local newspapers offers the details of these encounters: they periodically report the arrival of illegal immigrants seeking asylum from political unrest or respite from depressed economic conditions. Relationships between neighboring peoples and the U.S. Virgin Islands population become charged as local conditions remain strained in part because of corruption, fiscal mismanagement, and promises of tax relief for the wealthy and international corporations rather than for the large and predominantly black middle and working classes.

Strained relationships with Virgin Island neighbors are not the exclusive territory of the "outside." The sister islands have also had their fair share of tensions, which erupt periodically as a consequence of historical differences between the islands. St. Thomas, the capital and seat of the Virgin Islands legislature, has been a center for Caribbean trade since its occupation by European travelers. The first island in the Caribbean owned by Denmark, St. Thomas, has always featured an economy that depended on local interactions with the multiple faces of industry. While it has also been a society with a plantation economy, its topography was better suited to trade. Thus, it was also a more diverse island, harboring populations of free blacks, free colored persons, and multiple other traveling groups.[10]

St. Croix, the largest of the four major islands, had a plantation economy. Owned by five nations (the Spanish, French, British, Knights of Malta, and Dutch) before Denmark's purchase of the island in 1733, St. Croix petitioned to be included in the negotiations for the sale of the territory to the United States in 1868. Its eventual move from an agrarian economy to a tourist one has situated the island in second place in the legislative pecking order, causing many debates about political and economic equity among the islands and the distribution of resources among them.[11]

St. John, the third-largest of the four islands, also had a plantation economy and was the site of the first slave rebellion in the Virgin Islands. Neglected for many years in a standoff between the Danes and the British, who occupied nearby islands, St. John became a virtual appendage to St. Thomas after emancipation. In the 1950s, Laurance Rockefeller purchased approximately half the island, and in the middle of the decade, he sold his holdings to the Virgin Islands government, thereby reserving two-thirds of St. John as national parkland. The balance of the island is the subject of a struggle between wealthy whites who can afford to stay on or purchase the prohibitively expensive land and local black residents, who work to protect their considerably smaller interests.

Water Island, the smallest of the four islands, located a few miles from St. Thomas's harbor, has private access and is the exclusive residence of just a few Virgin Islanders. Complicated interisland politics exist among the four Virgin Islands, over and above the external negotiations the islands must conduct with their neighbors.

The ethnic makeup of these islands contributes to the complications of politics and class. In 1950, the population included approximately 74 percent native-born Virgin Islanders, 11 percent Puerto Ricans, 11 percent other Caribbean islanders, and 4 percent continentals (whites from the United States). By 1970, the population was 47 percent native-born Virgin Islanders, 6 percent Puerto Rican, 28 percent other Caribbean islanders, 13 percent continentals, and 6 percent "other."[12] And in 2003, the *Virgin Islands Daily News* reported, "14 percent of Virgin Islanders of all races identified themselves as Hispanic or Latino—15,196 people out of a total population of 108,612. That compares with 85,078 who identified themselves as black or African American, 78 percent of the population."[13] St. Croix contains significant Spanish-speaking communities originating in Puerto Rico and the Dominican Republic, and a French-speaking minority lives on St. Thomas. These residents must coexist with black native-born Eastern Caribbean and African American groups; mixed-race, white American, and European groups; and East Indian, Arab, and Persian groups. U.S. Virgin Islanders often refer to "down-islanders"—people from the Eastern Caribbean islands further south along the chain—as "aliens," borrowing the language used by U.S. immigration officials. Often discriminated against for their legal status as well as their subtle cultural differences, these individuals come to the Virgin Islands in search of economic opportunity, and the territory depends on them for much of its blue-collar and domestic labor. Cultural differences among the groups, such as food preparation and clothing, differentiate them and broaden an already racially, economically, and ethnically divided community.

The U.S. Virgin Islands are not unlike their British Virgin Island neighbors to the east, which historically created an informal system of identity markers: island of origin, skin tone, political party affiliation, and class. British Virgin Island markers have dissolved into a generalized national identity whose requirements have led to a "muting" of island distinctions that previously enabled island nationals reliably to pass judgment on strangers.[14] The U.S. Virgin Islands have suffered their own kind of cultural muting, and its citizens are frequently accused of lacking a well-defined sense of Caribbean identity, in part because of who is and is not considered local native or resident in the territory. Because of the U.S. Virgin Islands' diversity and political and economic incorporation into the United States, national self-definition is no easy task. Members of this community occupy all echelons of class and are as diverse politically as any contemporary nation, with conservative and religious groups as well as moderates, liberals, and radicals, Rastafari as well as proponents of corporate involvement in the development of island resources. This sometimes volatile mix of ethnic and cultural differences and economic disparity leads the territory metaphorically to close itself to its neighbors, to set itself apart from those on whom the local economy depends.[15]

The U.S. Virgin Islands are both Caribbean and North American. The recipients of both U.S. largesse in terms of funding of government programs and U.S. indifference to the islands' political and cultural variance, conditions in the territory call for innovative thinking and creative governance. The resulting conflicts and the ambivalence between the U.S. Virgin Islands and its neighbors and between the islands and the United States work themselves out on the beauty queen stage, on the bodies and the artistic choices made by pageant participants, professional coaches, consultants, and audiences.

Most of the territory's theatrical performances bear strong North American influences. Though not direct reproductions of American (and often African American) talent productions, plays, or music events, theater in the Virgin Islands closely resembles U.S. performances in concept and structure. Yet these performances are equally Caribbean in tone, cadence, and aesthetic sensibility. They remain anchored in local culture. There are no sharp divisions, only a mixing and mingling, a blurring of tastes, of approaches, of presentation, creating a typically Caribbean mélange of form. The queen show exemplifies this merging of this and that from North America to Antigua, Trinidad, and Latin America.

Few scholars have studied the cultural production and entertainment of the U.S. Virgin Islands. While performance events have been explored in the Greater Antilles, the Lesser Antilles has received little attention. This volume incorporates the Virgin Islands into this body of cultural analysis. The phenomenon and profusion of pageants in the U.S. Virgin Islands indicates the raced, sexed, and classed events that articulate larger sociopolitical relationships among individuals and groups in this small territory. Pageants and the abundance of these entertainments demonstrate the dearth of spaces (or the perception thereof) in which young girls and women have an opportunity to express themselves, perform themselves, and imagine a future in which they are visible, influential, and powerful. These events thus articulate a gendered national consciousness. I use *nation* here with the thorough understanding that it is a complicated relationship of territory and autonomy, of imagination and practice, of what Partha Chatterjee calls the "inner domain" of belief and matters of the spirit versus the material domain of the "outside."[16] I define nationhood and national sensibilities as that which occurs in dialogues within the territory and with the United States as colonizer of this locale. They demonstrate values, the influences of transnational movements of Caribbean people between the continent and the region, that have affected local aesthetics and performances, and they indicate the ways in which Virgin Islanders participate and imagine themselves participating in global systems and the manifestation of modernity. Like Puerto Rican identity, which Arlene Davila defines in relation to transnational Puerto Rican communities, Virgin Islanders have traversed locations within the United States and abroad since the 1950s and thus broadened the notion of what a Virgin Islander is and does.[17] This cultural nationalism remains perpetually in process and maintains the Virgin Islands' relationship with modernity.

LOCATING MYSELF

I grew up in the Virgin Islands, and for as long as I can remember, queen shows were held in honor of all occasions of any significance. Queens were our celebrities, and many retain that status. They are survivors of the harshest criticism island communities can unleash on their fellow citizens, tongue lashings that can include critiques of contestants' appearances as well as of their personal or familial shortcomings. The survivors dazzle in our broiling sun, steeled against our daily pettiness. They shine as models of poise and statuesque beauty chosen by a select few who represent us and our ways of seeing. Queen shows can offer those considered of low status or otherwise ignored the opportunity for a debutante-like coming out into the community. And participation can offer an affirmation for those already prepared to be in the public eye.

I ran for queen of my high school in 1976 and won. Like Sherece Smith, I made a clean sweep, taking Miss Congeniality and Miss Popularity as well as the overall title, Miss St. Dunstan's. As a dancer/performer, I was encouraged to run by my friends and others around me who thought I possessed talent. While that may have been true, the queen show was clearly not merely about my artistic gifts. I was not convinced of my suitability for the job, and that ambivalence grew as I experienced the exposure to and critique of the parade-going crowds who assess, often celebrate, but sometimes denounce and measure each year's queens with renewed vigor. I wondered then about what I had participated in and about its usefulness to young women and to the community. These questions have persisted.

In this volume, I explore the popular performances of the Virgin Islands and engage in larger discussions about what they do for the young women who participate in them and the larger community that supports or opposes these events. In addition, I examine their value to the Virgin Islands and greater Caribbean communities as indicators of membership in a global phenomenon and the performances of specific identities and of nation.

I consider myself a Virgin Islander. At the same time, I do not and cannot consider myself a local or a native for reasons that will become clearer in the discussion of these titles in chapter 4. Instead, I function in a middle location between these more concretized identities. The nature of the terms *local* and *native* is persistently contested and debated in the territory in efforts to determine birthrights and land rights, the balance or imbalance of power relative to the variety and size of populations inhabiting the islands, and the distribution of wealth and opportunity. I am part of a group of middle-class, black, college-educated islanders that has been conducting conversations about local practices, divisions, and sociopolitical engagements over time. I no longer live in the Virgin Islands. I have lived in the continental United States—New York and now Illinois—for more than twenty-five years. Like many individuals who now and historically have considered them-selves islanders, I travel back and forth regularly, maintaining my relationships with my family, my friends, and local goings-on. I am a part of the transnational movement that has significantly influenced and defined and been influenced and defined by numerous practices in the islands. As an established choreographer and performer, I have participated in queen shows as contestant, as entertainment, and as judge (though not of the contest I examine here), and I have developed an eye for the study of movement and its indications both on and beyond the stage.

In this ethnographic study, I seek to present that part of the Virgin Islands that has gone misrecognized historically—that is, the ways in which women control their lives and take care of those in their charge, the alternative familial set-ups that benefit a community and do not adhere to a Europeanized set of values, and sexualities that function healthfully despite or in contradiction to external pres-sures that degrade native people's values and practices. I present complexities that have been so easily and summarily dismissed because they lie within a so-called queen show or beauty pageant. I am curious about queen shows' continuing ap-peal in a community that has moved historically from slavery to democratic self-governance and yearly from carnivalesque bacchanalia to the quotidian.

I uncover the Virgin Islands' subtle equivalent of what W. E. B. Du Bois identi-fied as the "double consciousness" of black people in the United States. Du Bois uncovered those intangible "something elses" that allowed black men and women to appear in their public modes independent of who they were privately.[18] I exam-ine these differences, those realms of possibility in the lives of women in this com-munity. My analysis highlights the aspects of women's lives reserved for survival, operating outside of a system that persistently and implicitly tells them they are somehow worth less and are responsible for the ruin of their children, men of any race, and imperial systems that are larger and contain more historical baggage than women could ever carry.

I look at this material through the lenses of both performance and cultural studies. The live performance of the 1999 Miss Virgin Islands pageant is the center from which I draw out my analysis of the production. This work contributes to the scant scholarship on cultural production in the U.S. Virgin Islands, filling in the gaps left by the abundance of work on the Greater Antillean islands. I am interested in the ways the smaller Caribbean islands contribute to larger conversa-tions regarding nation, Caribbean history, gender identity, public performance, and sociohistorical developments, how the complexities of smaller nations can create a more densely woven tapestry of Caribbean identity and worldview. This work will be of interest to Caribbeanists, historians, gender and cultural studies theorists, and black performance enthusiasts of many disciplines. This project is a meditation on nation formation, the ways in which women's bodies figure in this enterprise as it is imagined by both the participants and large sectors of (black) Virgin Island society. While this project is by no means the first study of pageantry in the region, it is a comprehensive look at the practice in the U.S. Virgin Islands and as such offers an in-depth analysis of pageant's historical and contemporary implications in relation to the social and political history of the area. I ultimately argue that black women of the Virgin Islands and other Caribbean nations have used a global form of performance to determine a complex, subtle, multiply signified articulation of womanhood that reflects their values outside a Europeanized model as well as the history through which they have traveled and the contemporary world they occupy.

Something is unspoken though not secret about the multiple cultures of participating black Caribbean women and is significant both in their daily existences and within the context of pageants in the territory. Antonio Benitez-Rojo touches on this phenomenon when he calls the Caribbean

> a technologicalpoetic machine, or if you like, a metamachine of differences whose poetic mechanism cannot be diagrammed in conventional dimensions, and whose user's manual is found dispersed in a state of plasma within the chaos of its own networks of codes and subcodes. . . . [T]he notion of polyrhythm (rhythms cut through by other rhythms, which are cut by still other rhythms)— if it takes us to the point at which the central rhythm is displaced by other rhythms in such a way as to make it fix a center no longer, than to transcend a state of flux—may fairly be the type of performance that characterizes the Caribbean cultural machine.[19]

Benitez-Rojo examines the levels of meaning that exist within island cultures. I am interested in decoding behaviors among pageant participants in the U.S. Virgin Islands that locate this territory as an example of the complexities of hybridity,[20] political and social relations and contradictions that inhere in Benitez-Rojo's example and in the Virgin Islands' status as a postcolonial, transnational, modern island nation negotiating the twenty-first century.

To present these complexities, this book is divided into three parts. Part 1 looks at historical queens. I begin by tracing the history of a European system designed to subjugate and exploit black women for labor. Personnel terminologies during the slave trade prove the systematic reduction of the value of women in the slave system and simultaneously in the metropolitan centers of Europe.[21] Measured against young or adult males or articles of trade, black women eked out a place for themselves within crippling conditions and accessed and reserved some measure of power for themselves and their communities. Despite their devaluation, black women spoke out, rose to power of varying kinds, and performed for themselves and for their communities in socially and politically productive ways. Like writers of Caribbean women's and slave histories, I employ a "combination of foraging and disfiguration," raiding fragments of history to fill in the excluded narratives important to this study.[22] Black women's resistant acts and celebratory performances at tea meetings, carnival events, and dance dramas ultimately set the stage for me to ask what was psychologically and physically necessary to enable black women of the region to construct an image of themselves as queen. Black women's survival strategies were shaped by their struggles to maintain psychological wholeness and achieve social and political justice. They, thus demonstrated the extent of their journey from servant to queen, a journey embodied differently at different historical moments.

In chapter 2, I examine the U.S. relationship with the Virgin Islands and the effects of the promise of citizenship. Jim Crow's reach across the Caribbean Sea from the late nineteenth to mid-twentieth century perpetuated long-standing biases and perceptions of black women as less than whole beings, as promiscuous and infantile on one hand and as unfeminine hardworking brutes on the other. During the early years of U.S. rule—particularly between the 1930s and 1950s—black women, although aware of the U.S. government's perceptions of them, enjoyed a freedom of existence that rendered stateside judgments irrelevant. This freedom manifested itself in numerous ways, but I focus on women's family roles and participation in labor. Island pageants of the 1940s make clear that groups of island women were less concerned with U.S. perception than with their capacities for social and political movement within their immediate environments. Thus, while government reports detailed island women's failings, these women pursued their aesthetic, cultural, and political interests by choosing to participate in and manage events that offered clearly alternative representations of beauty, popularity, and success.

While no doubt influenced by North America, practices in the islands reflected the change in women's attitudes toward their autonomy and the possibilities business and civic participation offered them during the 1940s and early 1950s. Using newspaper reports, I trace the evolution of queen shows from simple May Day celebrations to popularity contests held at high schools and local businesses. These contests uncover issues of class and shade as they reveal who wields power in the communities. The contests gave rise to civic pride, and participation expanded, creating a heady new time in which new ideas regarding collectivity and nation arose. I unearth the subtleties and unstable nature of local notions of nationhood as they were expressed within performative structures and surrounding social spheres of pageantry that become identifying practices.

In the Virgin Islands territory, the ultimate fruit of toil—economic freedom—remains out of reach for the vast majority of the people. Although money and social standing are the golden ring sought by all pageant contestants, other issues are also at stake. Chapter 3 begins with the territory's quest for big business. The islands' government embarked on a campaign to involve every Virgin Islander in the belief that tourism would salve the beleaguered economy of the 1920s through 1940s. The closing of Cuba to U.S. tourists in the early 1960s motivated the Virgin Islands to sell itself even more intensely as a vacation destination. Island newspapers charted the development of a tourist board and of advertising campaigns that would assist the public and legislature in identifying and marketing "Virgin Island" or "native" behaviors. Carnival was reshaped as an official and unified event. And the queen shows shifted from the popularity contests of the 1940s and 1950s to a newer model influenced by Eastern Caribbean and South and North American aesthetic practices.

Through extensive interviews, I trace the development of pageants as they created imaginary relationships with the budding tourist industry and recast talent performance segments as promotional presentations dedicated to introducing the territory to tourists, a population rarely if ever in attendance at local pageants. I also show how U.S. Virgin Islands pageantry has changed over time, influenced by North American feminism and a burgeoning black consciousness, and probe pageantry's meaning for contemporary participants. Pageants are equivalent to carnival in that they offer the illusion of equality. They appear to be avenues where each woman comes to the stage with the same chances despite her class, ethnic, or social background, where every woman has a fair shake at greatness, real or perceived. Black women have come from devaluation to celebration, from the bamboula and queen of tea meeting and dance drama to popularity winner and civic organizer. With this ammunition—with words, influence, power—the stage is set for the twenty-first-century queen to perform herself.

Part 2, "De Jus Now (Modern) Queens," begins with chapter 4, a narrative of the Miss U.S. Virgin Islands pageant performance as I experienced it on March 21, 1999. I first recount events as I witnessed them, thereby allowing the pageant to unfold as it did for me on stage. I then read the specific performances as they relate to the politics of life in the islands and how those politics appear in the words and on the bodies of participants.

Chapter 5 argues that the contestants' promotional presentations make them cultural ambassadors in a phantom relationship with tourism and related civic projects. Miss U.S. Virgin Islands contestants negotiate their notions of island identity and announce the qualifications of "the native." By doing so, they reflect the machinations existing in a broader intra–Virgin Islands political discourse. Pageant participants reflect broad contemporary social and political issues and simultaneously express something subtler than either the historically constructed or contemporary pageant's notion of the Caribbean woman. In their multiple expressions and expressiveness of Virgin Islands womanhood, they negotiate their locations in relation to an "exploitative" practice oriented toward tourism, middle-class representations of respectable citizenship, heterosexual male desire, and political and economic powerlessness. These women are not simply oppressed by a desire to adhere to dominant U.S. determinations of beauty and success, as indictments of pageant values often contend; rather, contestants' actions demonstrate a continuation of resistance strategies grounded in Virgin Island and Caribbean history.[23]

Theirs is not a classic feminist response to the perceived exploitation of women. Pageant contestants choose to prance, dance, dip, skip, act, and/or sing onstage to "sell" their island—and indirectly themselves, in the view of some observers. Can a queen show be a feminist project? Although pageants represent the utmost in objectification, many other issues are also at play, and they take us to the heart of what is meant by *agency* as women attempt to change their lives and those of the people around them. The multiple levels at which the pageant functions—in relation to notions of beauty and its fluidity, to processes of both colonial and postcolonial identity formation, and to local and transnational negotiations of economic and political power—make this kind of project worth scrutinizing *from* a feminist perspective.

Part 3, "I Come; You Ah Come (I Have Arrived; You Too Will Arrive)," begins with chapter 6, in which I examine Miss U.S. Virgin Islands pageants in the late 1980s and early 1990s, an era during which the number of contestants waned and organizers took aggressive steps to put on entertaining shows. The drop in pageant attendance resulted from interisland politics and perceptions of fairness, an issue raised more generally as a result of the territory's political organization. Because the government seat is in St. Thomas, Crucians (natives of St. Croix) and St. Johnians feel that St. Thomians take the lion's share of the territory's resources. These interisland relationships are replayed on island stages as the fairness of judging comes into question, women and their respective islands are pitted against each other, and individual aesthetic preferences and personal politics are challenged. Though the interisland rivalries do not appear to dictate a particular idealized version of black womanhood, this chapter examines how these political relationships shape divergent perspectives of island femininities. Although pageants dictate "proper" female behavior—elements targeted for polishing or elimination by trainers, coaches, and hangers-on during the rehearsal and performance process—island women both adopt and resist these practices and values. The language of pageants offers insight into the nature of intraisland politics and organizers' attitudes as they "mold," "shape," and fine-tune the young women in their care.

Interviews with contestants and coaches, observations at rehearsals and performances, and casual conversations offered me insight into how queen shows present bodily practice in relation to popular attitudes and behaviors. They deliver the image of chastity, an image that does not correspond to the actualities of daily life in the community or to U.S. Virgin Islands gender relations more broadly. In this way, pageants express a measure of Virgin Island sensibilities, desires, and tastes, presenting the Virgin Islands self to other islanders, to the rest of the Caribbean, and ultimately to the world as participants in this very global but no less local activity.

Chapter 7 looks at audience, at the appetites that have developed for drama and at the drama that has spawned a particular kind of voyeurism. I use a narrative of the experiences of two Miss U.S. Virgin Island queens, including details of the judging process and of pageant missteps, to expose the judging as an area in which neither audience nor contestant has much influence. Instead, pageant organizers use judging to reproduce contest values, thereby supporting the status quo. As such, judging provides the island public with an arena in which to witness and air opinions about inequities within the contests and to relate these more general conflicts to those within the political life of the community. In other words, judging enables the people to come to terms with power and launch their opposition to it in a variety of formats, from local radio shows to legal battles. Judging also provides an avenue through which the aesthetics of the territory are discussed in relation to that which exists outside it. For example, the Virgin Islands notions of beauty and poise differ substantially from such notions elsewhere. In this setting, where audiences and judges confront the panorama of differences not only between contestants but also between natives and residents of the Virgin Islands and those of other nations, these differences become the subjects of heated debate. That no Miss U.S. Virgin Islands has as yet gone on to win an international contest frees organizers and participants to create an unparalleled performance experience targeted to local tastes while fueling the ongoing dialogue regarding local women's suitability for international competition.

Finally, I address how audiences are ravenously pulled by the possibility of failure—complete, absolute, public failure—the moment when the appearance of grace is ruptured. Viewers revel in minor slip-ups and offhand blunders and enjoy witnessing scandal. Both biased judging and contestant misbehavior are examples of the back side of human nature that undeniably draws island audiences. Virgin Islanders, like other Caribbean populations, love to laugh at other people and do so harshly and with vigor. Thus it is instructive to note the ways in which drama and scandal assist or deconstruct the pageant process and either perpetuate or interrupt negotiations of class, ethnic, and cultural relationships.

The performances of queen shows are more than the surface, as the Virgin Island figure of queen has evolved from cariso singer (an a capella singer who commented extempore on local persons and politics), news and culture bearer, and rebel to national figurehead in tune with global trends. She has done so in a style anchored in the Virgin Islands and aesthetically Caribbean. The Virgin Islands' condition includes a rich, diverse, yet common legacy of both colonized and colonizer, and it is apparent in a desire to codify a heritage while keeping up with the changes that make it a modern society. On this complicated stage of social and artistic convergence, political and economic weight, and reflection, the contestants for Miss U.S. Virgin Islands 1999 defied conventional standards of beauty and femininity and carved out their place in contemporary Caribbean culture, much as women have always done historically.

Part One

THE BEFORE-TIME QUEENS

Chapter One

"FAN ME"

Imperial versus Caribbean Femininities, 1493–1940

The figure of queen in Virgin Island history and mythology evolved early on in the islands' relationship with European empires. The fashioning of Caribbean governments and social systems designed to re-create small Europes throughout the Caribbean territories left little space for this image in New World ideology. In the European imaginary, any association between royalty and womanhood was in no way connected with black female subjects. The development of European settlements in the region and the subsequent creation of systems that sought to define, control, and manage groups of Africans forced into labor and subservience disallowed the notion of blacks in positions of power. Both black and white women in the territory nevertheless negotiated their conditions and identities in relation to a system that placed them at odds with one another, ultimately generating a space of resistance in which black females could regard themselves and be regarded with notions of royalty. Black women reconstituted themselves despite the psychological and physical assaults on their persons, and this chapter examines the conditions under which a black queen could be not only imagined but also created, empowered, and sustained for close to four hundred years.

Making this leap of the imagination from woman enslaved to woman enthroned requires an examination of the world conditions under which these women developed. Deleterious effects were created by the confluence of Victorian-era propriety, notions of biological determinism and scientific racism (which led to identifying the Other as a means to maintain an order exclusive of bodies existing outside the classic European model), and the language of commerce that determined the ways in which enslaved African women and children were viewed prior to their encounter with the plantation society. The responses of black women in slavery to these conditions established their evocation of agency. Here, individual and collective histories converge with the political, social, and cultural developments, such as labor disputes and violent forms of protest and early forms of carnival, to create an investment in revelry, mimicry, and performance. I discuss the emergence of a black queen and her role as resistant woman, mocking whiteness, femininity, empire, the separation of classes, and ultimately the enslavement of black people. I then use the moving body to demonstrate how dancing the bamboula and the performance of tea meetings and dance dramas served as tools of resistance and mockery that enabled the black woman of the territory to imagine herself as empowered and qualified to perform royalty. Her history is thick; it is dark, like her skin; and it begins in the Caribbean with European consternation after a long trip across the Atlantic.

THE HISTORICAL BODY

In the Virgin Islands, cultural and political upheavals were the rule for the initial two hundred years of European settlement. Like all Caribbean islands, an indigenous population (in this case the ancient Ciboney, then the Arawak and Carib groups) formed part of the territory's early landscape. According to normative historical accounts, Columbus happened upon the islands during his second voyage, encountering St. Croix, which he called Santa Cruz, in November 1493. He and his crew later sailed north and reached a cluster of more than one hundred mostly uninhabited islands, including what are now known as St. Thomas and St. John. He claimed these islands for Spain, but they remained uninhabited, neglected in favor of the larger, more lucrative Greater Antillean islands of Cuba, Puerto Rico, and Hispaniola. Spain's actions left the territory wide open for other European settlement. Battles over the territory, forced enslavement of the native populations, and a variety of illnesses decimated the indigenous peoples, and the Virgin Islands became a territory under dispute from Spain's departure until the Danish settled in St. Thomas in 1672. St. John was settled in 1717. In 1722, the English laid claim to St. Thomas and St. John, but Denmark soon strengthened its hold by placing settlements on St. John. The British then withdrew from St. Thomas, moving on to more lucrative islands further down the chain.[1] During this period, St. Croix, the first of the Virgins to be colonized, had been owned, settled, and fought over by the Spanish, the Dutch, the Knights of Malta, the French, and the British. Denmark finally acquired the island in 1733, just as the Danes were in the throes of a slave revolt on St. John, sixty-three years before the Haitian Revolution spread fear among the planter class and confidence among the enslaved throughout the region. The Danes' rule reflected their fears of the slave population, and they created a brutal system designed to deter any recurrence of unrest.

African slaves were brought into the Caribbean as early as 1510. St. Thomas received slaves beginning in 1673, and slaves first reached St. John in 1718. However, because the Virgin Islands had not been colonized officially (or permanently) until the late seventeenth and early eighteenth centuries, the Danes did not begin direct trade in slaves until persuaded to do so by the Dutch. In 1696, the governor of St. Thomas, Johan Lorenz, convinced the Danish West India Company to begin trading in slaves, and it maintained control until 1734, when trade was opened to all Danish residents of the island.[2] Prior to the Danish settlement of the Guinea Coast in the mid- to late seventeenth century, slaves were brought to the colonies by private slave traders. Spain carried few slaves under its own flag.[3] Like Denmark, Spain's need was greater than its ability to supply, opening an avenue for other groups—the British, the Dutch, and the Portuguese—to provide African labor for the territory. The demand created a lucrative space for independent traders. As the initial and most widespread colonizer of the region, Spain's actions led to some of the physical and psychological circumstances that in one way or another reverberate in the bodies of and attitudes toward African descendants to this day.

From the sixteenth to eighteenth centuries, the Spanish government used a system of *asientos* (licenses) for the importation of slave labor into the Caribbean. Foreign shippers received permission to carry a specific number of slaves to a variety of Spanish locations, creating an elaborate valuation system for both people and products (often one and the same).[4] Black women, the elderly, and children were valued at less than a *pieza*, which was defined as the value or worth of a young adult male, thereby initiating the devaluation of black women during slavery.

THE SEXUALIZED BODY

By the mid- to late eighteenth century, cultural developments in the European centers of Britain and France shifted metropolitan values about proper personal conduct, sex, and criminality. Europeans began to categorize newly encountered peoples as Others below human status, worthy of mistreatment and intrusive observation. In addition, these Others became objects of a desire that could not and would not be named outside of the spectacular and voyeuristic accounts by travel writers of the period. In the Caribbean, sexual desire across racial lines could be acted out away from the judging eyes of the European public. At the same time, the crossing of those boundaries was legitimized and excused by science and the biological "needs" of (most notably) white men, who availed themselves of their unprotected captive counterparts, black women. European empires systematically worked to create a "science" based in a desire to maintain control of economic interests, sexualities, and psyches while conquering goods and people throughout the world.[5] This science submerged and erased (or ignored) the conditions of white women and their relationships with black men and homosexual relations in the slave system.

The sexual and social control of (European) women, defined by the determination of propriety and the composition of femininity, began early in the nineteenth century.[6] Sexual freedom in Europe at the time resulted from what Michel Foucault calls "monotonous nights of the Victorian bourgeoisie," where sexuality was confined and essentially silenced and repressed.[7] Deviance was then projected on Others to make room for what came to be known as "illegitimate sexualities," leading to the emergence of the prostitute, the client, the psychiatrist, the hysteric—the Othered body. The label *promiscuous* was attached to anyone outside of the narrow Victorian bourgeois frame. The sexuality of black men and women became the model for deviant sexuality in general.[8] And class ultimately determined the proximity of bodies to respectability or promiscuity. The position of the black enslaved female body, then, could be nothing more than depraved. Black bodies were inscribed with deviance and sexual excess.[9] Catherine Hall notes that "the scientific theorising which was so strategic to understanding human variation depended heavily on an analogy linking race to gender: women became a racialised category, and non-white peoples were feminized. Similarly, class divisions were racialised, the poor constructed as 'a race apart.'"[10] Moreover, Hall continues, the "marking of difference was a way of classifying, of categorizing, of making hierarchies, of constructing boundaries for the body politic and the body social. Processes of differentiation, positioning men and women, colonizers and colonized, as if these divisions were natural, were constantly in the making in conflicts of power. The most basic tension of empire was that 'the otherness of colonized persons was neither inherent nor stable: his or her difference had to be defined and maintained.'"[11] These differences were maintained through systemic configurations and reconfigurations that produced anxieties in both genders from the colony to the metropolis and back.

White feminine anxieties motivated behaviors that sought to secure white women's position in the colony. In the Caribbean, white men's simultaneous desire for and loathing of black women displaced white women in the white male imaginary and forced both white men and women to construct themselves against the degraded image of the black woman, requiring no explanation, confessions, or apologies. Because the psychology of empire created the fictions of criminality, deviance, and promiscuity that "proved" these notions and justified colonial practices, no accountability or reconciling of conscience with practice appeared necessary. White women in the colonies depended on these "facts" to excuse their behavior and justify their mistreatment of precisely the women to whom they entrusted their lives and those of their children. On this base, black women fought to construct their identity.

THE RECUPERATED BODY

In the white imaginary, black women were capable of enduring animal-like work regimes and punishments. Black women's self-image existed in contradiction to the work they were required to do as slaves, sexual abuse by their masters, and mistreatment by white plantation mistresses. Black psychological wholeness/womanhood functioned in defiance, in opposition to a very complicated system in which powerful mythologies had been built to insure their fracturing. Black women had to rebel, whether quietly or out in the open. The search for what Hilary Beckles calls "natural rebels," he says, "begins with [Kamau] Brathwaite's claim that the slavery system impacted upon the black women in deeper and more profound ways than was the case with black men. The slave mode of production by virtue of placing the black woman's 'inner world'—her fertility, sexuality and maternity— on the market as capital assets, produced in them a 'natural' propensity to resist and to refuse as part of a basic self protective and survival response."[12]

Any action taken by a black woman to sustain herself and her family would therefore be a resistant act.[13] This survival response, the propensity to resist, was the stuff of the black woman's reconstitution and involved the figure of the queen first as leader, as a motivator of the people who mobilized crowds. Such actions later came to represent female power and attractiveness in carnival festivities. The image of this rebel woman cum queen was an oppositional response (though not merely that) to the degraded white image of the black woman. Rebel women were functional figures who were useful heads of the slave population on each plantation. These women were re-created in a black imaginary as strong, powerful, and capable, particularly in the case of the Virgin Islands, of setting things ablaze, literally and figuratively.

THE MOVING BODY

In spite of institutional categorizations that sought to identify and castigate black women, something remained untouched, remained the indestructible possession of black women, an intangible that no measure of punishment or torture could extract. In historical texts that present slave women, that presentation or representation is always associated with a body that operated sexually or that was punished for its resistance. Yet moving bodies—dancing bodies—can also be understood as resistant.

I am well aware of the inherent risk in using the image of moving bodies in relation to black people. Historical texts have oversimplified the issue and have resisted the notion of these bodies in relation to labor. I am not attempting to say that *all* black people in the West Indies danced. I know that the mention of dancing in relation to black people can be seen to reify stereotypes of black people as entertainers. However, moving the body is a complex relation that is tied to both subjugation and pleasure. When bodies expressed themselves through dance, a complicated relationship arose between black and white, woman and man, slave and master. These bodies moved to express joy, to worship, to celebrate special events, and to mimic and mock the behavior of European planters, who were, in turn, copying the behavior of their counterparts in the metropolis in efforts to prove civility and class. Bodies of both settler and laborer reinforced differences—social difference, class difference, sexual difference, racial difference.

In the history of colonialism in the New World, the first evidence of these moving bodies occurs in the logs of slave ships en route from Africa: captives were brought up on deck and forced to dance to keep them in good physical condition. Slaves' movement or dances were always treated, like other "evidence" Europeans found, as proof of an inherent depravity.[14] The movement of the hips was interpreted as a demonstration of promiscuousness, while the stomping of the feet and the accompaniment of the drum were seen as symbols of violence.[15] In the Virgin Islands, historical notes of the bamboula provide evidence of this conflict. Bamboula has been described as a dance that was wild and full of abandon, with naked black women moving until they reached an almost orgiastic frenzy. In some cases, the dancer reportedly used the tail of a snake as a phallus, exciting the mostly male audience until a child or small animal might be sacrificed and the blood smeared on all participants.[16] This is probably the most fanciful surviving description of the bamboula, perpetuating its representation as always operating sexually and violently.

Other accounts of the bamboula claim that it is a variation of the chica, while still others contend that the bamboula refers to any dance held outdoors (in contrast to an indoor dance, termed a ball).[17] Other accounts give the bamboula both a sacred and secular history. Florence Lewisohn writes that during the eighteenth and nineteenth centuries, Spanish Catholic nuns in St. Thomas and Puerto Rico performed what she believed to be a bamboula that originated on the Guinea coast.[18] The only difference between what the nuns performed and what the lay-women performed was the absence of men at sacred ceremonies.[19] For the most part, this was a dance of social commentary. While much of the attention centered on the movement of women's hips and the contrasting and mesmerizing immobility of their torsos, the accompanying songs were described as very unsensual and therefore received less attention. These songs were, in fact, avenues for transmitting information, enabling women to communicate local events. The fact that the music received so little attention eased the sharing of news.

The song or commentary of the bamboula dance was performed by a selected woman, while the dance was performed by selected teams of slaves. The commentary was leveled at higher-ups in the community, expressing the voices and opinions of the common folk.[20] The dance "served both as local tabloid and scandal sheet."[21] The woman who provided this commentary was a chief singer, often called the queen.[22] Her songs were composed on the spot, much like those of calypso singers (kings). The songs were repeated by a chorus of dancers standing in the circle that marked the performance area. The songs included local gossip (*melee*) as well as politics—whatever was relevant to slaves' lives.[23] The process by which this queen, known as a cariso singer and a predecessor to the calypsonian, was chosen is unclear, but the position required a rare talent, that of the poet extempore. This was a valued craft, as orality was the only means by which to communicate with the masses.

One of the first labor protests on the island of St. Thomas occurred in the postemancipation period when a bamboula dancer, Queen Coziah, led a group of coal workers marching through Charlotte Amalie in September 1892. Coal women, cheated by a system of tokens that was ordinarily based on silver, demanded payment in gold after the exchange was refused as a consequence of a drop in the value of silver. Queen Coziah headed a group of two hundred women who marched, sang, and ultimately gathered by the market square, brandishing sticks and other weapons until a sudden downpour and the threat of gunfire dispersed the crowd. Steamship managers responded by agreeing to increase the women's wages.[24]

Resident Europeans treated dance quite differently than creoles (persons of either African or European background born on Caribbean soil), requiring order and instruction regarding proper angles, expression, occasion, and dress. White creoles used dance to differentiate society's haves from its have-nots. Those whites with more sophistication and connections to the European metropolis kept up with the latest information on style and practice in the old country. They were eager to demonstrate their civility and class by demonstrating proper performance. White creoles imported dance masters from Europe to provide an education in current European fancy, thereby enabling those of high status to mark themselves as contemporary and civilized and set themselves apart from the mixed-race population and whites of lower social standing.[25]

Dance became a necessary social requirement and, as Caribbean cultural historian Lisa Lekis argues, no longer expressed joy or love but was reduced to an exercise in pedantry.²⁶ Therefore, while the white residents of great houses learned proper quadrilles, jigs, and the like, the black and colored populations were revising the material at hand. African elements such as criss-crossing steps and postures were incorporated into the standard European forms, ultimately creating what is now known as Caribbean dance. The vision through the greathouse windows was, in Lekis's words, "of beautifully gowned women gracefully extending their right hands to their impeccably tailored escorts, the women making a low curtsy, the gentlemen bowing gallantly over their ladies hands." She continues, "Slaves and mulattoes watched . . . and tried to imitate both the costumes and courtesies of the ballroom. So while planter children imitated the bamboula, slaves and colored imitated quadrille."²⁷ The bamboula becomes the platform for synthesis, for the adoption and adaptation of a movement language in both directions and with both groups using this physicality to say perhaps opposing yet very culturally specific things.

While many scholars have maintained that these behaviors of slave populations were merely mimetic actions, historian Neville Hall explores the possibility and likelihood of mimicry and exaggeration as an outlet for poking fun at the rigidity and formality of the high classes: "It might just as probably have been ridicule, and there is the third alternative that the slaves could have been investing the occasion with special significance by the adaptation of European styles of address and usage in contemporary 'society.' At any rate, the adaptations were subject to the slaves own sobering sense of the appropriate, an eye for the absurd, and a capacity to poke fun at each other."²⁸ Thus, born of mimicry, ridicule, or some combination of the two and nurtured through commentary and social action, the black queen emerged on New World soil and was invested with special significance.

A QUEEN APPEARS

The physical criteria for becoming a queen are unknown, although descriptions of queens' dress, manner, force, and defiance have survived. These qualities may have been essential to make a queen but tell us little about the masses' aesthetics in choosing a leader. Because the queen emerged from villages inhabited by field slaves, she was probably not, at least not initially, a mixed-race woman. She must have possessed certain talents, most prominently the ability to speak to the issues at hand, to communicate effectively with her people and presumably members of other communities. According to Lewisohn, one mid-nineteenth-century visitor to the islands noted the selection during Christmas holiday masquerades of a queen of each estate (or plantation). The visitor described the queen as "a very good looking girl" wearing satin, flowers, and jewels and preceded by two maids who danced well. Moreover, queens were elected for life, and their decorations and jewels were provided by the slaves.[29] Travel accounts of the Virgin Islands devoted much more attention to such masquerade queens than to revolutionary leaders such as Queen Coziah, perhaps in part because of visitors' preference for natives during holiday events over slaves in revolt. The former were much more pleasant and unthreatening, easily described with the fancy so many travelers reserved for the tropics. Revolutionary leaders invoked such fear and dread that any description of them would never include notions of beauty, only horror, as historical accounts of Caribbean rebellions prior to and after the St. Johnian and Haitian revolutions attest. Writing of Christmas festival royalty on St. Croix in 1845, Thurlow Weed recorded,

> The laborers on each estate elect their Queen and Princess, with their King and Prince, whose authority is supreme. These have their Maids of honor, Paiges etc. A Queen retains her rank until by age or otherwise she voluntarily retires as Dowager.
>
> The dance is opened by the King and Queen. The Prima Donna sings ballads, while the whole gang unite in the chorus, to which the drums furnish a very base, but truly appropriate accompaniment. When the royal pair are exhausted, they introduce the Prince and Princess, who in turn call up those of inferior rank . . . and thus the revelers consume the day and night.[30]

Urban slaves conducted these celebrations, while both urban and rural whites were engaged as spectators. The darker-skinned performers paid tribute to their audience, whose members were expected to reciprocate with money, foodstuffs, or trinkets, thereby reversing the usual pattern whereby whites were the subject of black scrutiny or mockery.[31] White observers of the islands did not accord substantial value to these seemingly chaotic events, which ran thoroughly against the studied, formulaic structure of the era's white dance forms. At the same time, masquerades represented the potential for white loss of control of the black masses and thus were edgy events. Operating on the border of safety and danger, they crackled with an air of excitement and drew crowds no matter how chaotic, base, primitive, or formless they appeared to white society. Danish sentiment and law may have reflected similar opinions, as black participants used the role of queen and her cariso songs as commentary in what may have been the first portents of an emancipatory event.

Even the celebratory prima donna did not merely meet and greet passers-by and accompany the queen and king; in some circumstances, she could offer social commentary on current events and could compete against other areas' prima donnas or insult masters and coloreds. Danish officials warned that slave songs could incite revolt, and according to Weed, one prima donna sang a song that may have told of impending events:

> All we girls must keep our heads together; King Christian have sent to free us all; Governor SHOLTEN had a vote for us; King Christian have sent to grant us all; we have signed for liberty; our Crown Prince had a vote in it; Our Gracious had the highest vote; King Christian have sent to say he will crown us all.
>
> oh yes! oh yes! hurra! hurra!
>
> All we girls must keep head together.[32]

This song informed listeners that the Danish government had voted to free slaves and appealed for calm and unity so that all could be crowned with freedom. Such commentary was instrumental in spreading news and in helping to organize island social and political movements.

REBEL QUEEN

During the late nineteenth century, the plantation society was in steady decline. The Haitian Revolution began with a series of uprisings in 1789 and led to the victory of the underclass with leadership of Toussaint-Louverture in the early nineteenth century, motivating black populations across the Caribbean to demand their freedom.[33] Events in Haiti instilled fear among the region's white rulers and confidence among its black populations—they, too, could become masters of their own destinies. They could be royalty. Social changes in the fabric of Virgin Island plantation society reflected these modern sentiments and threatened the status quo. The mixed-race offspring who occupied the emergent middle class were poised between the elite European creole planter society and the African-descended slave underclass. Social occasions and legislative concerns were no longer issues of black versus white but involved a wide range of those in between. Easy distinctions could no longer be drawn between the grand balls of the great houses, which excluded blacks, and village slave fetes that excluded whites. Town taverns and grand balls offered opportunities for mixing between the groups, places where the hybridization of the culture was evident in the bodies and practices of the people. Abolition had come to the nearby British Virgin Islands in 1833, and its effects reached the Danish Virgin Island underclass and its sympathizers. Denmark appointed Peter von Scholten as governor of the islands in 1827. Though his policies were more lenient than those of earlier rulers, they were not radical enough for the area's slaves, who united behind a black man named Buddhoe and forced the issue, receiving emancipation on July 3, 1848.

According to Neville Hall, this revolt succeeded in gaining blacks only the narrowest freedom, the "legal termination of servitude."[34] The end of servitude with no plans for black self-rule contributed to an already declining economy and a serflike existence, as many people, including the newly free, those manumitted by their owners, or the even fewer who bought their own freedom, remained obligated to work under contract labor conditions similar to slavery.[35] Unlike those who had been emancipated, free blacks and free colored exhibited no sense of involvement in the revolt, maintaining their patterns of separation from the black masses. Little had changed in planter society. In the words of Gordon K. Lewis, "The social legacy of slavery remained, after Emancipation, to frustrate the growth of a liberal free enterprise economy. The Labor Act of 1848 revealed how deeply the planter still thought of the laborer in chattel terms, for despite its intent of codifying the mutual obligations of estate proprietor and laborer much of it perpetuated the old outlook, seeking to hold down the worker, by contractual obligation, to work on one estate only, and legalizing the power of management to fine workers for trifles and to determine their private lives."[36]

Laws tightened conditions on black laborers' private and public lives, causing some persons to seek refuge on nearby islands. When unable to recruit locals, planters copied a strategy used by their counterparts in Trinidad and Tobago, Guyana, and Jamaica, bringing in workers from India on five-year contracts. After enduring terrible treatment, some refused to renew their contracts and returned home. With the persistence of such conditions, tensions on the islands again reached the boiling point. On October 1, 1878, when all laborers were to renew or rescind their contracts, the mood of an "apparently joyful crowd" in Frederiksted, St. Croix, "suddenly . . . turned to anger."[37] A minor disorder quickly erupted into a full-scale revolt, and the crowd perceived the police response as brutality. According to William Boyer, "The crowd besieged the fort, where they were held off by the few police on hand. Then they turned to burning and pillaging the shops and houses of the town while the white residents took refuge in local churches and on board a ship in the harbor." Although the revolt, known as the Fireburn Unrest, was perceived as "spontaneous and disorganized," involving multiple independent groups, the participation of Mary Thomas entered the cultural mythology of the Virgin Islands.[38] One cariso song heralds her bravery:

Queen Mary—tis where you going to burn,
Queen Mary—tis where you going to burn
Don't ask me nothing t'all
Just fetch me match and oil
Bassin jailhouse
tis where I'm going to burn.[39]

Three other women—Bottom Belly (Susanna Abrahamson), Queen Agnes (Axeline Salomon), and Queen Mathilda (Mathilda McBean)—joined Queen Mary in the revolt, comprising what Harold Willocks calls the "Queens of the Fireburn."[40] All were in their teens, with Mattie the youngest at sixteen, and all were imprisoned in Denmark, although Mattie returned to St. Croix as an old woman.

That whites were surprised by the revolt indicates that slaves hid their feelings and plans, and that whites misperceived black behavior. The revolt's apparent spontaneity and disorganization may have aided its success, as the diffuse and female leaders escaped white elite suspicion until the resistance was well under way. The presence of female leaders may also have led to the perception that the revolt was "spontaneous" and "disorganized" and that the participants shifted quickly from "apparent joy" to anger, in alignment with the colonial construction of women as inconsistent and untrustworthy, erratic and unpredictable.

Willocks claims that the concept of queen is based on the African concept of family, which is matriarchal: "The woman/mother was the nucleus of the family. She was the revered, and was in charge of all the social activities." During slavery, Willocks argues, the concept of woman as queen was broadened further: "She was usually noted for her skill, bravery, and intelligence, and presided at Christmas and New Year's celebrations. She was responsible for organizing the social affairs, and quelling domestic and estate problems among the slaves. She also exhibited great influence over not only the slaves of her own estate but those of other plantations as well." Their status as plantation queens gave these women authority that they used to persuade people to participate in the revolt.[41]

Near the end of the nineteenth century, Queen Mary led a Christmas procession in Charlotte Amalie, St. Thomas. One observer described her as "the most ferocious rioter during the Negro Rebellion of 1878," a "colossal female" who "proceeded, in solitary majesty, in front of her petticoated regiment, dancing as if on the same spot. The other Negro women followed in wide, regular ranks, every one of them had on light green dresses with pink aprons and snow white turbans covering their black hair. . . . She and her waving female gang took up their ambiguous song in which the words 'fan me' were accompanied with spiteful and sarcastic looks. 'Fan me' came from the rebellion days when Queen Mary [allegedly] forced a high-born white woman to wait upon her and fan her."[42] The mythology of Queen Mary not only retells the story of her resistance but emphasizes her level of power as high enough to force whites into subservience. "Fan me" thus becomes not only a playful and typical carnival reversal of societal power and a demonstration of queenliness but a sly referral to a prior historical moment of real (or imagined) power and the threat of its recurrence. At the same time, the queen delicately parades in garb completely in keeping with traditional (white) feminine beauty. The boundaries between queen as revolutionary and queen as reveler and masquerader clearly were permeable. These queens fought and celebrated with equal vigor.

CEREMONIAL QUEEN

During the U.S. Civil War, the federal government began negotiating with Danish leaders to purchase the Virgin Islands. Fifty years passed before the deal was consummated in 1917. During this period, new forms of performance emerged, reflecting the island public's sense of being besieged by "talks" surrounding the future. These forms, too, had a place for a queen.

The territory remained in crisis. Despite attempted reforms in the wake of the 1878 rioting, poor working conditions persisted. The island population changed rapidly, as Virgin Islanders emigrated in search of better opportunities and workers from nearby islands sought refuge and better working conditions on Virgin Island soil. Interisland traffic modified the islands' social and ethnic texture, as migrants brought additional kinds of cultural performances with them. As Olivia Cadaval writes of St. Croix in particular, "Migrants from Nevis, St. Kitts, Barbados, and Antigua brought with them dramatic and narrative traditions including 'tea meetings' and 'masquerade jigs' which were incorporated into the Crucian cultural repertoire." According to Cadaval, the tea meeting was a "community social event that included an oratory contest and talent show" and was "charged with pomp and humor. Participants challenged each other's oratorical skills and knowledge of history and current events."[43] Mimicking the elites' education and speech mocked their self-importance. At the same time, the atmosphere of the tea meeting also lent itself to the informal education of large groups of people regarding events within and outside the community, the complexities of language, and the intricacies and creativity of conversation.

In this setting, black women were less engaged in the dialogue of the community than was the case with the bamboula dance. Because most educators, show-offs, and of course kings were male, the women who participated as queens simply presided over what Lewisohn calls the "popular amusement of the period."[44] Originating as a European creole art form that touched on topics ranging from the Greek classics to Europe's political and social events, the tea meeting was adopted and changed by the islands' black population, creating another synthesized form that gave voice to the local underclass. Eulalie Rivera, a retired educator, witnessed a tea meeting in the early 1900s that included a king and queen representing British royalty. The chairman, or master of ceremonies, introduced each performer, who then saluted the king and queen, showing deep respect. This king and queen apparently presided over the meeting but did not participate directly, and their presence was clearly important.[45]

Such "royalty" was present at many historical entertainments documented in the Virgin Islands, including dance dramas, which told fairy tales and stories of the fantastic. As groups paraded through the streets, they reenacted biblical tales and miracle plays of the Middle Ages. Historian Antonio Jarvis believes that these forms developed in response to occasions that excluded the lower classes. As in the tea meeting, participants recited lines or made speeches. They danced the jig for hours, demonstrating endurance, skill, and improvisational prowess. In contrast to the tea meeting, however, the queen took on an active role. According to Lekis, in the King George Dance Drama, pages "announce the arrival of the Queen. The jig now becomes more lively and the dancing is faster and more exhausting. The Queen enters, and in all her glory stands before the others and slowly recites: 'Good evening, both ladies and gentlemen, Not forgetting my countrymen and my own banner, Trot out your music without any drum, I'se the new queen and I just now come!' Now the Queen dances a violent jig. When she regains her breath, she adds: 'If I were the Queen of France, And you were the Pope of Rome, I would have no fighting men at war, and no weeping maids at home. So trot your music without any drum, I'se the new Queen and I just now come!'"[46]

These dramas occurred from the 1930s through the 1950s, when the islands were attempting to recover from depressed economic conditions. Labor remained at odds with management and business owners, but an air of optimism prevailed. Tourism was being hailed as the new savior of the territory, and the United States seemed to be taking a more active role in the future of the territory after years of neglect. The refrain quoted by Lekis signifies the black woman's arrival in a place of power, her confidence in her abilities and potential. This parading queen figure has remained present in Virgin Island processions. Although positioning as queen may at one time have indicated mockery of the European community, it could also demonstrate feelings of empowerment and the right to reverence. The insistence that the musicians "trot [their] music without any drum" recalls the era when the ban on drums limited people's forms of expression and communication. Her pronouncement reinforces queens' power and influence and draws attention to a moment that confined and subsequently defined pivotal developments in island music, not only recalling the historical weight of white power and the limits placed on black expression but suggesting that the queen's power does not require drums.

Queens have thus been crucial participants in determining the path of black women's influence in social and political movements as well as cultural practices in the territories. Queens have helped to articulate black women's image of themselves in both their own and the conflicting European imaginary. Willocks's and

Beckles's revolutionary island queens became conflated with Smith/Lewisohn's and Weed's beautiful queens, thereby combining black and white versions of femininity and exposing an ambivalence, a contradiction that the role requires. This ability to be two perhaps opposing things at once follows the performance of black womanhood through time. That these women have moved from the degradation inflicted by severely oppressive structures to positions of power and reverence says something about human capacity and endurance. Black women found and kept something stored away, in reserve, and used it when the opportunity arose. Such moments may have required a persistent duality, a multiple consciousness beyond the double consciousness of the sort W. E. B. Du Bois describes in regard to the Negro position in America—that is, "two souls, two thoughts, two unreconciled strivings; whose dogged strength alone keeps it from being torn asunder."[47] The black Caribbean woman cum queen embodies Du Bois's argument.

Black slave women maneuvered in multiple ways to survive and were not historically voiceless. The bamboula, the cariso, and the numerous other performances by queens also demonstrate black women's outspokenness. The queen maintained power by expressing and representing the black woman's voice. Joining a meditation on black female degradation and survival to the stories of black queens' performances offers a glimpse of royal black woman's psychological triumph and an understanding of whence she may have come to sit on her throne.

Chapter 2

THE NEW QUEEN

Pageantry and Policy, 1930–1950

Queens in Caribbean black slave communities who were valued because of their assumptions of power, their honed craft, and overall smarts seemed little concerned with white notions of beauty and appearance. Even slave women's mimetic performances of the white planter class engaged less notions of beauty and more the accoutrements of class status. European adherence to metropolitan fashions of the day denoted an up-to-the-minute style consciousness important to and affordable by only the most affluent. European-valued appearances held sway in the travelogues of visitors, themselves exemplars of the leisure set. Descriptions from rebels to revelers may have mentioned the women's looks, but the territory's black population valued talent, political savvy, and communication ability.

This is not to say black people of the islands had no visual or aesthetic preferences or codes. Rather, these phenomena simply went unrecognized by contemporary writers. As renderings by artists of the period show, the queens were by no means bedraggled. The ways in which black people adorned themselves (with a head tie or the like) were not recognized as elements of style or beauty until centuries after the fact. Nevertheless, "beauty" in European terms was something to which blacks could aspire if they possessed an economic location in society. These associations resulted from the emerging U.S. women's movements of the late nineteenth century. In North America, entrepreneurship created a class of women who sought to carve out a market dependent on female needs and interests. As white women fought for the right to enter the workplace, universities, politics, and a new public sphere, these social issues were marked on the face and body.[1] Women's faces and bodies became the landscape against which their suitability for entering and competing in the professional arena was measured. Physical appearance could essentially determine the capacity for a particular enterprise.

While white women struggled to determine the positive social changes on their faces and bodies, black women engaged in a threefold struggle: to combat the racial determinations that had been historically etched on their bodies, to assume a contemporary social posture, and to take advantage of women's advances within the culture. Black women had been making small advances for some time, although, as Kathy Peiss points out, "no one defined the antipode of the dominant American beauty ideal more starkly than African-Americans. Kinky hair, dirty or ragged clothing, apish caricatures, shiny black faces: White men and women had long evoked these stereotypes to exaggerate racial differences, dehumanize African Americans, and deny them social and political participation."[2] White Americans were committed to sustaining a visual distinction between black and white and masking what Peiss calls "the uncomfortable truth that Africans and Europeans were genealogically mixed, and their histories irrevocably intertwined."[3] Black women, however, participated in beauty culture at the same time that white women sought to gain economic freedom and class mobility in a decidedly different fashion.

This chapter traces larger issues subsumed by the "beauty industry"; its relation to economics, entrepreneurship, and political emergence for women of the Virgin Islands; and the ways in which class came to dictate what islanders determined to be not so much beautiful as powerful. "Beauty" per se had little currency in the territory, perhaps a residue of colonial perceptions and subsequent historical struggles for self-worth. As the Virgin Islands became embroiled in negotiations regarding their autonomy, their governance, and the ways in which women participated in perceptions of islanders' capacity for self-rule, the U.S. government systematically reproduced racist colonial language. The regard for women's worth, their supposed moral predispositions, and their roles within and without the conventional family unit all became matters of great concern for the United States. Instead of being limited by colonial assignments, women of the Virgin Islands were more interested in intraisland and intragendered relationships. Members of the newly formed Women's League produced pageant events that served the Virgin Island public and continued the territory's tradition of pageantry as they ushered in a new aesthetic and performative direction. From the early development of seemingly innocent middle and high school May Day celebrations to the emergence of the popularity contests dependent on the accumulation of the most donations for charitable causes, money determined the popular and, by extension, the powerful. Linked to labor, to significant changes in governance for the Virgin Islands and their relation to the United States, to charitable causes within the territory, and to mass support, these fund-raising events ultimately influenced the way women, class, and power were regarded. In this way, class and its inevitable link to skin tone, or "shade" in the black community became undeniable factors in the equation of women, civic engagement, and pageantry.

WOMEN AND CULTURAL EVENTS IN THE ISLANDS

Prior to 1940, extant Virgin Islands documents do not mention women's concerns or entertainments. Island periodicals of that era were vehicles of industry, a collection of announcements about work, commerce, and trade that had not yet linked the business of beauty or pageantry to a labor market, as was beginning to be the case in the United States. White women in the States had been fighting for a measure of visibility, using the beauty industry to further those efforts. Black women stateside, however, were fighting different battles, less concerned with the beauty issues that occupied white women and more concerned with social uplift.[4] Similarly, Virgin Island populations had economic and political priorities, focused on white men's business interests, and between the U.S. purchase in 1917 and the late 1930s, Virgin Island newspapers reported little of cultural events attended by blacks and even less on the lives of women. Such publications provided outlets for elite complaints and notified members of the upper class of events significant to them—for example, ship arrivals and departures, vessels accepting freight, and occasionally particular families onboard.

In the late 1930s, when local newspapers began reporting on cultural events involving the black masses, they focused on general community news rather than on "women's events" and restricted such articles to the local section of the paper, typically in a single column on the second or third page with no byline. On December 27, 1938, for example, the *St. Croix Avis's* local section informed readers that

> Christmas 1938 is now numbered in the past and we are turning our attention to the closing days of 1938 and the opening of 1939. The noisy way of celebrating Christmas Eve seems to be fast disappearing. The noise of the "fog" horns and heavy sounding thunderbolts was missing, perhaps this was due from some people not having enough money to spare for these "artillery salutes" or the people are realizing now that Christmas should be the real "Silent Night, Holy Night" and yet joyful. There was music on the streets certain hours on Christmas Eve. During the early morning hours the local carol singers were out and visited the homes of some people. These beautiful Christmas numbers were very appropriate and some persons appreciate this form of celebrating Christmas by singing

the carols during the early morning. Good carol singing on Christmas morning always meet with fine reception.[5]

The article does not indicate whether these musings commented on black practices of the day, but caroling represented the continuance of a well-known island practice from the days of enslavement.

No organized singular carnival event occurred for fourteen more years. Christmas was celebrated as it had been for centuries. Having historically coincided with the ripening of cane, Christmas celebrations provided blacks with a midcrop holiday.[6] Through the 1930s, these celebrations included masquerades, events to which Virgin Islanders had long become accustomed, with groups parading through towns and neighborhoods, engaging in what educator and historian Robert Nicholls calls a "distinctive form of street theater."[7] The revelers donned masks and costumes, dressing up as Indians, animals, moko jumbies (spirited African stilt dancers), and royalty. Participants would sing, drink, play games, dance, and generally engage in merriment. The term *carnival* was mentioned in the newspapers of the time, but only as "A Night of Fun Attractions for Everybody."[8] Carnival was a minor event, often put on by a school or charitable organization, with small entertainments and door prizes.

By the late 1930s, community leaders had begun public discussions to decide which of the many wintertime holidays would be observed—Christmas, Christmas Second Day, New Year's Day, and Three Kings Day (the Catholic holiday of the Epiphany, celebrated on January 6 and introduced to the island by Puerto Rican immigrants). The business community had long been at odds with the number of holidays Virgin Islanders honored, periodically calling for a restructuring of the holiday season. No significant shift in holiday practices occurred until the 1950s, and newspapers during the 1920s and 1930s generally continued to present biased elite condemnations of the practices of the territory's poor and working classes, allotting no space to the views of the masses.

By and large, business leaders retained a pervasive and racist attitude that islanders were lazy and eager to take advantage of any opportunity to have a holiday. Moreover, the editorial neglect of cultural practices relevant to poor and working-class blacks may also have resulted in part from the educational levels and living conditions that prevailed for the vast majority of islanders. The U.S. purchase led to battles over Virgin Islanders' status as citizens of North America, as residents of the territory both coped with the realities of daily sustenance and engaged in negotiations with the empire to the north. Many resident as well as nonresident whites had little respect for the black cultural activities that now came under North American scrutiny.

SOCIAL AND POLITICAL DEVELOPMENTS

Under U.S. Navy rule for many years, subject to overt and systematic racism, and denied basic rights as citizens, Virgin Islanders occupied a unique position during the 1920s; as William Boyer argues, the islands belonged "to America without their people knowing just how American they were."[9] The United States dragged its feet in granting citizenship to Virgin Island residents, infantilizing the Virgin island public and denying the community participation in U.S. governing policy as well as local policy. The *New York Times* reported that an act, passed on March 3, 1917, and designed to expand the scope of citizenship in Puerto Rico and the Virgin Islands during the confusing time of the transfer from Denmark, was "liberal in its allowance for self government." U.S. suffragists also believed that the act enfranchised the islands' women.[10] In reality, however, U.S. officials continued to appoint leaders to govern the Virgin Islands, and residents of the territory, always considered a weak appendage to the United States rather than a member of the union, never received the right to vote for the U.S. presidency. Although Virgin Islands residents received U.S. citizenship in 1927, not until 1968 did the territory gain the right to send a delegate to Congress.[11] Women were at the bottom of that heap, as indicated by their absence from documentation of the political process and official reports on local social conditions.[12]

The islands' local government consisted of two colonial councils, one of which ruled jointly over St. Thomas and St. John and one of which had jurisdiction over St. Croix. In February 1920, a commission was established to investigate the mounting pressure toward self-rule, the first time that U.S. officials began seriously to consider residents' needs. In February 1924, a federal commission of Negroes (to use the terminology of the period) from the U.S. mainland appointed by the secretary of labor spent a few weeks in the Virgin Islands investigating industrial and economic conditions. The group's findings reflected what historian Harold Willocks calls black and liberal media support for citizenship for Virgin Islanders and the abolition of naval rule, bringing residents' plight to the attention of the rest of the world.[13] The commission supported the centralization of municipal governments so that they might be "brought into closer touch and harmony with the masses and be more largely responsible to their particular needs."[14]

However, these needs would receive consideration only in their direct relation to economic growth and the U.S. interest in putting the Virgin Islands on their feet to alleviate the perceived burden to the North American economy. Whereas officials considered Puerto Rico valuable to the United States for its military and medical testing capacities, the Virgin Islands' use value to the United States was less clear, and the United States evinced a correspondingly less clear commitment to assisting the development of the Virgin Islands. U.S. assistance also suffered from a series of blunders that Gordon K. Lewis contends resulted from a general cultural ignorance that led the islands' appointed governors and other officials to attempt romantic solutions to problems: "American officials had to learn to come to terms with an amazingly complicated set of class-color correlates rooted in constitutive principles and historical background quite different from those of their parent society."[15]

Both natural and international events exacerbated these problems, as a hurricane hit the islands in 1928 and the American stock market crashed a year later. Both events reinforced island powers' orientation toward economic and infrastructural rehabilitation.[16] In March 1930, President Herbert Hoover visited the Virgin Islands and called them an "effective poorhouse."[17] Islanders were incensed by the president's harsh criticism, which demonstrated a continued colonial attitude toward the territory and its peoples and a lack of acknowledgment of the global causes of the territory's economic problems, and their relationship with the States continued to suffer.

The global causes of the depressed local economy included factors over which Virgin Islanders had no control: the mid-nineteenth-century shift from sailboats to steamships, the increasing substitution of beet sugar for cane sugar, and Prohibition, which deprived the Virgin Islands of one of their economic staples, the production and sale of rum.[18] These conditions encouraged Virgin Islanders to migrate elsewhere (including North America) in search of greater economic opportunity. This migration and the territory's high death rates significantly decreased the Virgin Islands' population and changed the demographics, as women, children, and the elderly were overrepresented among those who remained. Continentals derided residents, characterizing local behavior and attitudes toward work as "one-fifth to one-half less efficient than the average laborer on the mainland" and thereby continuing the devaluation of women that had begun under the slave system.[19] Such attitudes led to the presumption that women lacked the moral aptitude to increase their productivity and labor. In addition, the departure of so many men left women to maintain the local community and to preserve local customs and lifestyles. Nevertheless, white North Americans continued to label the islands' women as lazy and ineffectual and as contributing adversely to the rearing of proper territorial citizens and to the larger American public.

WORK, RESISTANCE, AND THE CHANGING ECONOMY

Work-related behavior remained a contentious subject as whites continued to resist the masses' observance of holidays. While the white/elite public saw Virgin Islanders as lazy and persisted in accusing blacks of slacking off, the reality was much more complex. As Robin D. G. Kelley notes, unorganized working people find small ways to resist working conditions, control the pace and amount of work they are required to do and carve out a modicum of dignity in the workplace.[20] These tactics can include slowing down and "lifting" product in the interest of "balancing" inequities between labor and pay. Virgin Islanders employed such tactics to distance themselves from subservience, often in agricultural settings. As a consequence of their origins in a slave society, Virgin Islanders have always been class-conscious and, by extension, color-conscious. In the Caribbean, African, Chinese, South Asian, and Middle Eastern peoples have historically mixed, creating a picture more complicated than the North American black/white binary. Many of these groups have developed class consciousnesses based on the promise of prosperity and the availability of work. Nevertheless, observers have often taken a reductive view toward the multiple ethnicities in the Virgin Islands. In 1988, for example, Paul Leary argued, "The pattern of race and ethnic relations that prevails in the Virgin Islands today, after seventy years of U.S. rule, is quite similar to that of the sovereign power and is daily becoming more so. Terms such as 'mixed' are practically passé; one is either black or white (except for Asians, who are designated as 'Other' in census reporting). Except for a small percentage of persons and public events, social life is largely marked by racial separateness."[21] Leary appears to have missed the breadth that the term *blackness* carries in the territory. Members of the Virgin Islands community have not adopted the white American penchant for terms determining gradations of color. Instead, island residents' conception of blackness includes a panorama of shades. For islanders, difference has much more to do with nation and culture than with color. Thus, while ethnic and racial separation clearly remains a factor, and the dominant ideology is that class is more important than race, these are inextricably related terms. Money—inevitably linked to relative whiteness—can be the Caribbean's equalizer, to at least some extent. A person's relation to the source of money—most often, work—is the means by which power (however little of it one holds) is exercised. Thus developed the application of what Kelley calls the idea of a "moral economy," whereby indignities of the system are managed by small rebellions in the form of work slowdowns and/or petty theft. These rebellions serve as a strategy to resist "being totally subordinated to the needs of capital" and its predominant owners, the white elite.[22] Women were the executors of these resistant practices as the area's workforce shrank and became increasingly female-dominated.

Population was particularly important to the development (or the impossibility) of a Virgin Islands' local power base. By the 1930s, New York's Harlem had become home to an estimated twenty thousand Virgin Islanders, almost as many residents as the territory possessed at the time.[23] The population remaining in the island evinced a troubling distribution of wealth. Lewis describes the Virgin

Islands as a substantially depressed colonial society, "deeply rooted in an economy whose traditionally dominant occupations remained the same in 1931 as they had been in 1917, estate agriculture based on cheap Negro labor in St. Croix and harbor commerce based on hard pressed clerks and stevedores in St. Thomas." He continues, "The social structure remained rigidly conservative, grossly undemocratic, and profoundly inegalitarian."[24] According to Boyer, "More than 80 percent of the land in St. Croix was owned by twenty men, and 90 percent of all cultivated land of the three islands was in the hands of one percent of the families."[25] Thus, the majority of the population had no economic opportunity. Power remained in the hands of the few, who both perpetuated conditions that maintained their social and economic status and participated in the consistent portrayal of the poor as shiftless and without regard for work ethics or morality.

The U.S. Navy was finally replaced by a civilian government appointed by the president in 1931. The U.S. government was determined to move the Virgin Islands toward greater economic stability. Under the first civilian governor, Paul Pearson, a slow shift occurred in the Virgin Islands. To jump-start the flagging economy during the Great Depression, Congress offered New Deal money to the territory in the interest of homesteading projects, tourism development, and, with the end of Prohibition, the strengthening of the rum and agricultural industries.[26] Pearson identified six objectives along the road to increased prosperity for the islands: (1) increasing islanders' responsibility for their own government (to which end he appointed locals to administrative and executive positions); (2) increasing self-support by the local government; (3) improving economic conditions through such efforts as the launching of the Virgin Islands Company to operate sugar mills and rum distilleries, the creation of public works projects, the construction of low-cost housing developments, the development of homesteading projects to provide small farm production, and the nurturing of a significant tourist trade; (4) improving health and sanitation; (5) enhancing social conditions; and (6) improving education. Pearson oversaw marked improvement in the educational system, including increases in teachers' salaries and training, the provision of scholarships for students to study abroad, the creation of the islands' first senior high school, and a total enrollment of fifteen hundred persons in adult education programs by 1935.[27]

By the 1940s, therefore, a significant portion of the poor black population for the first time had access to education for themselves and their children.[28] The local infrastructure was being developed with new assistance from the U.S. government, though Pearson may have hoped to do more. The local newspaper still found "no continuity in action based on an established plan. With each new appointment the islands are jolted by new approaches to old problems, some of them very costly and detrimental to the best interests of the inhabitants."[29] Severe economic fluctuations continued through the 1940s, fueled in part by demand (or the lack thereof) for wartime products, including liquor. With the onslaught of a drought and the collapse of both the rum industry and the New Deal's homesteading projects, the Virgin Islands government sought to restructure the Virgin Islands Company. Truman's election to the U.S. presidency and his appointment of William Hastie as governor assisted the company's conversion to VICORP and a shift in its mandate. The new entity was not responsible for the production of alcoholic beverages but instead was instructed to conduct market research for product resources; to promote capital investment in the territory, land use planning, and transportation among the islands; to assist with small farms and communities; to make loans to individuals for agricultural, industrial, and commercial projects; to promote or engage in the development of these activities; and, perhaps most importantly, to promote the tourist trade.[30]

WOMEN, SEX, AND THE NEW ECONOMY

By the 1940s, the renewed U.S. commitment to the territory encouraged islanders to pay particular attention to events both in the territory and on the mainland. During and after the New Deal, North American attitudes concerning island women had remained consistent with colonial views of black women. Legislators regularly expressed their concerns about issues of sexual morality, pointing out the "high rate of illegitimacy" as they imposed a colonial interpretation onto relationships lacking legal sanction that produced children. Lawmakers thus attributed blame for the islands' pervasive poverty, placing women at the center of these discussions.

As a consequence of the population outmigration, the number of women in the territory exceeded the number of men by 16 percent during the 1930s, producing patterns of family organization more consistent with slavery-era practices (when paternity counted for little and planters were promiscuous) than with white North American mores. Moreover, during this era, 43.4 percent of female Virgin Islanders were gainfully employed outside the home, versus 22 percent of U.S. women.[31] Seemingly obsessed with local sexual practices and never considering what New Deal chronicler Luther Evans has called "the possible validity of a different standard of morality,"[32] legislators saw the absence of marriage as a burden on the system, devaluing other concepts of family, including that of extended kinship. Lower-class black families were categorized as "matricentric societies with a typically working mother and absentee father."[33] Lewis explains this type of family as inimical to family pride and unity, creating very weak parent-child ties, and describes the female slave as "the linchpin" of this system and inheritance as proceeding through the female line.[34] Such a perspective misses factors that might have mitigated the effects of paternal absence—most importantly, the strength of extended family ties. Virgin Islands children had long relied on relationships beyond the parental, depending greatly on aunts, uncles, grandmothers, and fictive kin (close friends). These relationships became particularly important to lower-class black families as working-age adults left home to earn their living.

Lewis also notes the "remarkably free status" of women, who were more likely to gain social and economic standing as a result of their own accomplishments than through the men with whom they were involved. Although some women might have preferred an alternative partnership setting—perhaps even the marital relationship North Americans so highly regarded—other patterns of behavior were at the very least accepted among locals as part of a cultural, sexual, and gendered legacy that contained its own liberties and restraints. Women maintained an autonomy under this system that marriage might have disallowed. In exchange for a level of independence, Caribbean women accepted the "burden" of raising their children in households where fathers merely "visited." According to Lewis, Virgin Islanders followed a pattern of "serial monogamy in which a woman will live with and bear children to several men, apparently without real conflict emerging from the plural relationship."[35] This fluidity enables rather than disables the women involved. Thus, contrary to the opinions of ruling officials who saw the situation as burdensome rather than liberating, women were not subservient or held hostage by their economic/cultural condition.

Women's effectiveness always retained an element of class, with poorer women considered less successful and their children seen as more predisposed to petty thievery and vagrancy than women of other classes. Better-educated and/or more privileged women adhered more closely to U.S. behavioral codes, gaining political respect and material effectiveness—as, for example, when teachers received the right to vote on local public policies in 1935. Further evidence of the size and influence of women comes from the fact that territorial newspapers begin to report on women's activities. Although such articles at first lacked substantial political impact, they were culturally significant. Editors of local newspapers and others of the social set became convinced that women would take an interest in social behaviors indirectly related to beauty and the beauty business taking off to the north.

BEAUTY, VIRGIN ISLAND STYLE

As beauty became fodder for increasing stateside audiences and judging, the Virgin Islands adopted parallel practices. Where beauty contests in the United

States evolved from May Day celebrations through national competitions to high school events by the 1930s, the Virgin Islands followed a different order. In February 1947, the *St. Croix Avis* printed a picture with the headline, "Miss Helen Francis Named 'Miss Virgin Islands of 1947.'"[36] This popularity contest was perhaps most significant because it was held in New York, a feature of the first annual bazaar and dance sponsored by the American Virgin Islands Society,[37] which kept close tabs on island developments. A year later, *Virgin Islands Daily News* ran a photo and short article on the Miss America Pageant: "In a preliminary round at the beauty pageant held in Atlantic City, New Jersey, Barbara Jo Walker, 'Miss America 1947,' presented a cup to Dorothy Jane Free, 'Miss Tennessee,' who won the talent prize."[38] U.S. events involving women had clearly become of interest to the Virgin Island community, not simply the other way around. In addition, the shaping of local women's interests had become the concern of local news outlets and policymakers. U.S. and Virgin Islands aesthetics regarding women had begun to intersect.

While the American Virgin Islands Society and others like it were conducting popularity contests stateside, pageant-like events called "queen derbies"[39] experienced a heyday in the territory. These derbies were fund-raising, grassroots civic events, distinct from the slick, refined queen shows that later developed. Friends and family members encouraged young women to participate, with the winner determined by the amount of money she brought in. Money—who had it, who had access to it, and how they had gotten it—was critical at this economically depressed time. Access to money translated into popularity. The queen derbies brought to the fore the divisions between the haves and have-nots that had existed for centuries among family lines in Caribbean communities. Historically, the financial leg up afforded the offspring of slave women and white planters relative to darker field slaves the template for the race/shade and power divide. Popularity, then, links to money, which is, in turn, undeniably connected to shade. If the depressed island conditions widely reported in official publications in fact existed and women lived in the dire conditions alleged by U.S. policymakers, how could such entertainments have flourished? And what purpose did they serve? Were they merely markers of class and culture? Symbols of the solidity of the elite? Or were they models for empowerment and an example of the availability of capital and advancement for those crafty enough to acquire it? The answer is that they clearly served multiple purposes. Local periodicals were soon flooded with announcements and accounts of the occasions.

MONEY AND THE NATION IN QUEEN PAGEANTS:
ENTER THE WOMEN'S LEAGUE

During the 1940s, the *St. Croix Avis* and the *Virgin Islands Daily News* carried a plethora of articles announcing upcoming queen contests at local high and grade schools and then provided the readers with the contest results, including the ranks of each. Based on these newspaper reports, these types of shows provided the dominant form of entertainment for young women in the precarnival Virgin Islands, much like the queen rallies of Liberia, which Mary H. Moran calls "public, competitive fundraising programs similar to the American telethon."[40] The Virgin Islands version also resembled a telethon, following a variety-show format that has always included local talent acts, music, and comedy routines. Both the Virgin Islands derbies and the Liberian rallies had a distinctively nationalistic nature: in Moran's words, "Most rallies, even when sponsored by private organizations, are explicitly nationalist events because the money they raise is earmarked for local and national 'development'; usually infrastructure like roads, schools, libraries, public buildings and so on."[41]

Because the Virgin Islands are a U.S. territory rather than an independent country, the use of *nation* in language about the community of islands is a very specific invocation. I use the term here in Benedict Anderson's sense of an imagined collectivity that is construed politically and has finite yet elastic boundaries.[42] Existence within the United States has created in the Virgin Islands what Partha Chatterjee terms "anti-colonial nationalism," which "creates its own domain of sovereignty within colonial society well before it begins its political battle with the imperial power." This sovereignty is created by dividing the world of social institutions and practices into two domains, the material (external) and the spiritual (inner), the latter of which bears "the 'essential' marks of cultural identity."[43] The domain of the outside and a nation's ability to reproduce the practices of the colonial power determine success in the material realm. The Virgin Islands were beginning the journey toward inner dominance of the outer domain, a process that would both support and undermine the territory's real and imagined notions of independence.

The Virgin Islands are persistently negotiating their boundaries of inclusion and exclusion in the pursuit of a national identity. During the 1940s and 1950s, this process included enthusiastic political participation by local people to determine the shape of the islands' future, the means by which they would operate politically, and how money would circulate among the people. Island cultural practices were becoming an official governmental concern. The intangibles of culture moved from the lived practices of the everyday to the halls of legislature. Ideas regarding who Virgin Islanders were and what they might represent for themselves and to one another were paramount. Nation was perhaps never more important than at this historical moment.

The late 1930s witnessed the passage of the Organic Act, which provided universal suffrage and "opened the political process to all classes of Virgin Islanders and broke the long-time monopoly of political power of the planters and merchants."[44] All federal taxes, municipal taxes, and other monies collected by any government agency would subsequently remain in the Virgin Islands treasury, matched by funds from the U.S. government. During this era, a group of St. Thomian men formed the Virgin Islands Progressive Guide, a civic group dedicated to the political initiation of the islands' peoples. The group's members included prominent figures in the islands' political sphere.

In 1946, U.S. officials appointed William Hastie as the territory's first black governor. Although he was not a local, his appointment, combined with the recent expansion of self-government, created a sense of pride among the islands' majority black community in spite of the lingering paternalism of the United States. While the Virgin Islands may never wage an overt battle with imperial U.S. power, Virgin Islanders have attained a level of sovereignty that both resists and embraces the colonial society, maintaining the inner domain while accepting financial benefits in the outer domain.

The inner domain includes the intangibles—the ways in which people move and speak, their sense of humor, how they cook, eat, dress, commune. Because these are cultural practices, they are also the primary domain of women. Nation thus becomes circuitously yet intimately related to womanhood, and womanhood becomes attached to nation through the equation of the inner and outer domains. Popularity contests continued to develop and later became linked with the Tourist Board and carnival (a decidedly nationalistic event), resulting in the redirected if now dated purpose of representing the territory both within and outside of the Caribbean. These are precisely the "multiple significations" Anderson claims for nations and nationalisms, coming into being and changing along with the historical setting.[45] They are products of culture, and their proliferation has created what Homi K. Bhabha calls the "narcissism of self-generation,"[46] remaining tied to the idea of nation, the territory, and the domain of women. These significations become attached to notions of beauty and are reiterated, just as Elaine Scarry contends beauty is compelled to copy itself or to be copied.[47]

Since their genesis in the 1940s, Virgin Islands pageants have been orchestrated by established middle- and upper-middle-class groups of women, largely as a means of raising money. The organizations' various interests overlap with those of the nation, providing incentives both for the continuation of the contests and for local government support. In the 1940s, the territory's most visible women's civic organization was the Women's League, established in 1946 and "dedicated to helping the sick and the needy and to civic improvement of the community."[48] Founders Elda Lindquist of St. Thomas; Irene Bayne, a recent arrival to St. Thomas and a veteran of stateside women's organizations; and Elizabeth Connor initially worked with Ianthe Blyden, chief nurse of the municipal hospital, and store owners Arthur Lindo and his wife, to stage charity events to garner much-needed clothing for hospital patients. Encouraged by this modest success, the group members went on "to the task of organizing the women of St. Thomas in an all-purpose civic and charitable organization."[49]

The Women's League held its inaugural meeting on May 15, 1946, at Bethania Hall, the parish building of the Frederik Lutheran Church on St. Thomas. More than thirty women pledged to work together to solve the common problems of their community. Joined by the Women's Club, an older organization that had lost many of its members and force to illness and retirement, the league addressed the needs of the sick, the poor, the elderly, and school-aged children. Members were women of "substance"—black, white, Latina, and mixed-race—and either came from well-known families with political and/or social clout or possessed enough money to donate significant amounts to support the league's day-to-day operations. They were civil servants, heads of departments in government, spouses of government officials, and executives of private and public charitable organizations. In short, these were powerful and very visible women within the community. The league's St. Croix Chapter was formed on May 14, 1947, and was headed by Armintha Anduze.[50]

The territory's governor often consulted the Women's League, asking its members "to express their views and opinions on matters of community importance, including proposed legislation."[51] The league evidently supported continental mores, as it worked "to institute a course in Family Life for the upper grades of the high school, in order to combat our problem of family instability."[52] Its efforts to instill certain ethics in the local youth community also included advocating for "some control over the content of the songs, movies, and records fed our children."[53] Although the league wielded a considerable amount of power, it operated in a sort of intentional obscurity: "The poor, like all of us, are proud—and the League wants only to lend a helping hand, without fanfare, to those who need its assistance."[54]

THE LEAGUE REIGNS

The Women's League's soon expanded its efforts beyond the needs of the sick, the young, and the elderly, recognizing "that there were a great many civic activities in which a women's organization should take an active interest in addition to charitable works." On July 3–5, 1948, the group sponsored a fair in honor of the centennial of the abolition of slavery in the Virgin Islands, giving the organization a more visible and politically public face. The fair was held on St. Croix, a logical choice since Danish governor Peter Von Scholten had issued the proclamation of freedom in Frederiksted. The festival's "spectacular" line-up included the raising of the U.S. and Danish flags, a parade, a "carnival," a community fair, cultural events (the singing of cariso, dances, and sporting events for young people), and a fireworks display. The event's souvenir program included the text of the 1848 letter from the king of Denmark emancipating the "unfree Negroes of the Danish West India Islands" as well as congratulatory letters from U.S. president Harry S. Truman and Governor Frederik R. of Denmark.[55]

The celebration's "gala event" was the Centennial Ball, held at Government House, and the "crowning of a queen." The Women's League sponsored a contestant, Elaine Julian, a teacher at Christiansted High School. Other contestants from prominent local families included Mariel Mackay, Gertrude James, Dorothy Motta, Beryl Armstrong, and Belem Seales, each sponsored by a family, a town, a school, or a business. Pageant organizers apparently were unconcerned with contestants' marital status (Armstrong, Seales, and Julian were married), unlike the proponents of stateside pageants. Candidates and their sponsors campaigned feverishly to win the "coveted crown," and competition was expected to be "keen."[56]

The "candidates" worked to collect votes, each of which cost the voter five cents, a sum that had been chosen to put the ballots "within the reach of all." Because the price was not printed on the tickets, the *Avis* continually warned the public to "PAY NO MORE THAN FIVE CENTS FOR EACH BALLOT for any candidate." Members of the centennial committee were prohibited from assisting any of the competing women in selling tickets.[57]

At ten o'clock on the night of the ball, a special committee selected by the secretary-treasurer and members of the Centennial Commission would announce the winner. To ensure fairness, representatives of all contestants would witness the counting of ballots. The victor would be crowned in a special ceremony, and the other candidates would be named "ladies-in-waiting." Albert Francis would lead an exhibition dance, and then the queen and her ladies-in-waiting would perform a waltz with their escorts. Finally, two orchestras, the Rhythm Makers and the Motta Brothers, would play an old-time seven-step and other familiar dances for the older patrons before moving on to more modern dance numbers for the younger crowd.[58]

This was nationalism at its finest, supported by women and symbolized in the body of woman. Whether the presence of a queen at nationalistic events such as the centennial lent validity to her position or offered a means for the inclusion of women is difficult to discern from extant documents, and both functions proved problematic. The participation of women as figures of mock royalty as well as orchestrators of that royalty complicate the picture. The queen's position and those upholding it occupy a place of ambiguity, a liminal space. Money and nation coincide with women becoming the symbol, the embodiment, and the marriage of the two. The queen is both royalty (with access to enough capital to insure a win) and servant of the nation (though her "work" for it may be little more than to stir pride within people's hearts by her appearance). She quickly becomes a necessity, an appealing face of the nation as she personalizes this imagined community for the consumption of the general public. Her means provide an invisible agent in the support of a national consciousness, promising the territory prosperity and participation in modernity.

Royalty became an important part of Virgin Islands culture, civic concerns, self-conception. In many ways, royalty was an invisible power, asserting itself through the dominance of specific families in these events, their consequent coverage in local papers, and the ultimate determination of who was not so much beautiful but "popular." Popularity and an association with aesthetic approval were unquestioned. Maxine Leeds-Craig argues that black women's "grooming"—a means by which black women could manage the dominant culture's positioning of them as outside the scope of beauty and thereby enhance their standing—was of utmost importance as they presented themselves to the waiting public.[59]

YOUNG WOMEN AND A WORLD OF INFLUENCE

The centennial celebration represented the height of nationalistic-type demonstrations in the Virgin Islands, but this atmosphere began at the level of junior high schools and high schools, both public and parochial. As with the contest sponsored by the Women's League, school derbies were fund-raising events, but they were also designed to determine or confirm the elite's position in the territory's social construction. Queen shows hosted by senior and junior high schools, as well as Tom Thumb weddings put on by grade schools as part of fairs, formed an important part of the island's educational culture.

In October 1947, Christiansted High School held a contest to select a queen. "Managers, parents and friends" of the three contestants "intensified their activities to dispose of their votes," each of which cost five cents. The winner was Rita DeChabert, who received 14,120 votes, and she was crowned in front of a large crowd at the Jungle Casino. DeChabert thanked not only locals but "friends in Puerto Rico and the United States mainland who purchased votes."[60]

In April 1952, the teachers and pupils of the Commandant Gade School on St. Thomas held an Easter fashion show, including a Tom Thumb wedding and the crowning of a queen, with proceeds to go to the school's scholarship fund.[61]

A month later, the Girl Scouts' May Festival also included the selection of queens. This festival hosted representatives from Puerto Rico and featured an international theme, with food, dances, and merchandise from other countries.[62] Puerto Rico and by extension the Spanish-speaking countries of the Caribbean and Latin America have significantly influenced pageantry in the Virgin Islands, bringing a distinct style and expertise. The aesthetics and values of beauty contests in the territory thus represent an amalgam of practices in the United States, Latin America, and the Caribbean, evidence of the transnational movement of materials and ideas initiated by the Middle Passage.

All of these events carried an underlying sense of power reinforced by the queen and an unspoken acknowledgment of access and privilege the crown imbued. The DeChaberts were and remain a powerful family in the Virgin Islands, known not only for their material wealth but also for their considerable land-ownership, business acumen, and political clout. That a DeChabert would win any contest she entered is a virtual certainty, not because her family members would exercise any unfair influence but because they have a wealth of contacts both within the islands and externally. DeChabert's expression of gratitude to her supporters demonstrated her awareness of power dynamics, an acute consciousness of the transnational currencies in which she and her family took part. While the other young women candidates may have come from well-known families as well, true social ranking was meted out in this event. These contests also seem to have provided less influential persons with access to those of greater influence. In such a small community, allegiance to winning families, however tenuous, can enhance a person's social status. These relationships offer an opportunity to break the ordinary boundaries that exist between the classes, allowing individuals and families to appear equal, to imagine themselves a part of this (nation) narration in the making.

BEAUTY'S LABORS

The Women's League and other such groups often operated invisibly but palpably. They held numerous civic and social events, choosing which governmental and or private causes to support. They honored themselves and those whom they held in high esteem. Unlike stateside Women's League chapters, which saw their role as protesting the Miss America Pageant as antifeminist and an "insult to womanhood,"[63] the Women's League in the Virgin Islands saw benefits and service possibilities in women's participation in pageants. Concerned with social uplift, the Women's League in the Virgin Islands sent cables to Congress and the National Association for the Advancement of Colored People urging support for the Revised Organic Act, which would restructure the territory's local government, its relation to the U.S. Department of Interior, and its sovereignty.[64]

The Revised Organic Act of 1954 secured a single municipal government overseeing all the islands and established an eleven-member legislature, with three representatives from St. Thomas, one from St. John, three from St. Croix, and four elected at-large.[65] The law gave voting rights to the islands' resident Puerto Rican and French minorities by eliminating the English literacy requirement. The Revised Organic Act also provided that permanent residents' taxes would go to the treasury of the Virgin Islands and that the Virgin Islands would receive matching U.S. government funds from the return of internal revenues on goods exported to the United States, a benefit enjoyed by the Commonwealth of Puerto Rico since 1917. The measure also established nine governing departments for the territory: agriculture and labor, property and procurement, education, finance, public safety, public works, health, social welfare, and tourism and trade. These changes enabled the Virgin Islands to govern themselves more effectively.

The Revised Organic Act of 1954 signaled the start of a new era featuring the increased movement of middle-class vacationers and the explosion of the tourist industry. Florida and Puerto Rico became major tourist hubs, and the Virgin Islands benefited from their proximity—just a two-hour flight from Miami and a forty-minute ride in a seaplane or small aircraft from Puerto Rico. Many visitors from Puerto Rico made day trips to the Virgin Islands.[66]

The growth of tourism affected the pageant industry. Contests in the Virgin Islands received increasing influence, both direct and indirect, from image consultants, charm school franchises, and beauty business satellites from the larger metropolitan and Caribbean centers. These groups came to eclipse the possession of capital and family status in determining winners, shaping future queens. Race or shade was merely a by-product of that equation. The contestants' access to capital was linked historically to specific families who held land. Those families were often mixed-race, and as they continued to marry within the community, some members became darker and some lighter. In the end it was not necessarily one's color but one's name that lent power to social settings. As these names appeared in the queen rallies and civic organizations of the territory, they brought into focus the class stratifications that defined the islands' distribution of power. The pageants were being actively altered from the small-time popularity contests to the larger machinery they would become, moving around more capital, more promises, more influence, and more possibilities for comparison between a Caribbean aesthetic and a global one.

Chapter 3

PROGRESS MAKES A MODEL QUEEN

The Birth of Tourism, 1950–1960s

In May 1947, the *St. Croix Avis* reported on events at the organizational meeting for St. Thomas's new tourist board. With "the complete cooperation of the public," the article announced, "a development program of considerable proportions can be instituted."[1] Civic leaders had begun their effort to convince the entire Virgin Islands population that tourism would solve the territory's economic ills, initiating the persistent and persisting theme that all Virgin Islanders needed to participate in the island's "uplift" to ensure collective prosperity.

The Virgin Islands government, in conjunction with the U.S. Department of the Interior, developed a strategic economic plan that enlisted islanders' participation and imagination in a collective effort to improve and modernize the territory's infrastructure for tourism. Tourism's discourse of collectivity, of equal participation, impact, and return, may have perpetuated the belief and the practices to which many women of the territory subscribed—that is, that queen shows and other enterprises in which women engaged affected the territory's material wealth, particularly the business of tourism, while galvanizing local communities. This civic and national improvement benefited from the packaging of the Virgin Islands culture, the marketing of its natural resources, and the participation of women's (and other) civic groups in a number of small yet significant ways. With the development of a tourist board, the shaping of carnival as a tourist attraction, and quotidian island practice elevated to the level of things identifiably "Caribbean," the eventual restructuring of what had originally been popularity contests for women came to symbolize a new time.

During the 1940s and early 1950s, Virgin Islands pageants imitated other Caribbean and South American contests, themselves versions of the European model. Adapting portions of contests that suited the aesthetics of the organizers, pageants were made up of bits and pieces of borrowed material and style, combined with local tastes and values. U.S. beauty pageants then developed their own appeal to the Virgin Islands populace as islanders moved north in search of education and opportunity. In response to the territory's modernization and newly developed closeness with white and black American aesthetic practices, island pageants became the place where nation, economy, and aesthetics converged in the body of young black female Virgin Islanders. Black women were beginning to demonstrate an interest in "beauty," with an eye toward being as fashionable as their white counterparts, not, as some observers have contended, because of self-hatred or a desire to be white. Pageants exemplified the territory's modernity in both practice and discourse, adopting specific codes of conduct and privileging some aesthetic choices over others. Virgin Islanders' economic and cultural savvy was expressed on stage with the emergence of a new black woman. She grew out of a period of poverty, when economic gain was made to appear a possibility for all Virgin Islanders even though prosperity was truly only within reach for a select few. Her appearance followed the path of the islands' long-standing colonial relationship with European nations, reaching modernity with the identification and marketing of Virgin Islands culture as a performance that could be exported for the symbolic taking.

As early as 1947, talks were held regarding a board that would oversee the creation of a tourist market in the Virgin Islands. When the tourist board really came into its own in 1952, it took steps to smooth the path for the continuation of "progress," changing the face of island festival practices, the ways in which residents presented themselves to one another, and the ways in which Virgin Islanders and the Virgin Islands were represented to the outside. The local *Virgin Islands Daily News* and *St. Croix Avis* published articles tracking the tourist board's efforts, including consultations with "experts" from Europe and other Caribbean islands and local professionals. All were recruited to advise and direct the territory's attempts to attract tourists and thereby solve the economic crises that for decades had gripped the area.

On November 9, 1948, the *Daily News* reported that German photographer Fritz Henle had been enlisted to produce a picture book on the Virgin Islands that could be used as a marketing tool. Henle's photographs showed local women in idyllic and typically tropical locations, often with hibiscus flowers in their hair, little makeup, and simple clothing. The volume ignited the colonial imagination with images of alluring, mysterious, simple, and most of all beautiful black women and ultimately became iconographic.[2]

The following year, the tourist board demonstrated that it was taking its job seriously by purchasing a thousand copies of *Virgin Islands Magazine* for distribution to sources, both on and off the islands, that could stimulate tourism. The magazine was a promotional publication, peppered with inviting and spectacular photographs. It also contained "island fashions" that had little to do with common local wear and more to do with clothing dictates from Europe or other exotic locales: one 1956 issue, for example, featured attractive young women dressed in an "Authentic East Indian Sari," a "British Hong Kong Suit," and a "Decorated Italian Sweater," stimulating images of the territory as accommodating any international group.[3] These magazines specifically sought to shape the Virgin Islands as a sophisticated tourist destination, someplace to which upscale visitors could imagine themselves returning year after year. By the 1960s, publications such as the *Virgin Islands View* paid more attention to local affairs, both historically and in the present, but did so with the polished presentation of the reigning Miss Virgin Islands.[4] The tourist board sought to provide travel agents with the image of a shellacked, safe, and neatly packaged sophisticated tropical locale, flooding the United States and European markets with information that would render the Virgin Islands familiar, make cultural differences appear intriguing rather than frightening, and make island people appear welcoming rather than indifferent or resentful.

The strategy worked. By June 1952, the tourist board's executive director reported "8,500 inquiries and requests for information which the Board had received and answered during the past ten months as a result of its advertising campaign. The board also distributed 2,000 travel agents' handbooks and 65,000 folders."[5] The major factor that opened the territory up for the proverbial taking was the establishment and performance of the Virgin Islands carnival.

THE (RE)BIRTH OF CARNIVAL

Initiated by radio personalities and St. Thomas locals Ron De Lugo and Eldra Schulterbrandt as an appeal to the people to rediscover earlier days when revelers had taken to the streets and celebrated the Christmas holidays en masse, the St. Thomas carnival quickly became the tourist board's favorite event, and the community's business and governing sectors, too, recognized the idea's potential appeal. Countless members of the general public joined in, filling the streets as both parade participants and spectators and making the 1952 carnival, which ran from August 31 to September 2, historic. The Women's League played a significant role, helping to organize aspects of the event, including the requisite king and queen show. A member of Antigua's tourist board visited St. Thomas to help organizers plan the festivities. On August 25, officials announced that Carmen Nicholson and Leo Sibilly, both sponsored by St. Thomian businesses, had received the most votes and would serve as queen and king, respectively.[6]

The carnival received advance publicity in the *New York Times*, which described the three-day event as a "revival of [a] traditional celebration" and gave credit to "Ron De Lugo, program director of radio station WSTA here in St. Thomas, whose persistence and daily plugging for a carnival helped lead the local Municipal Council and Governor Morris F. Castro to give the festivity their official sanction."[7] But the festival was not a revival. It was a creation.[8] Past "carnivals" in the Virgin Islands had generally been itinerant masquerading events with neighborhood folks touring their own communities and reveling on a much smaller scale.

On two occasions, however, more organized carnival events had occurred. On Valentine's Day 1912, the white elite held a twenty-four-hour celebration at which Casilda Durloo was chosen as carnival queen. One of her pages was Ralph Paiewonsky, who became governor of the Virgin Islands in 1961. The carnival also featured a parade, with participants dressed as Zulus, Indians, Cowboys, and Elick the Bear, all of them racially stereotypical characters in keeping with the reversal of social condition in the Bakhtinian sense. The next "carnival," held in 1914, expanded to two days and included donkey races, boat races, pie-catching contests, and a parade with various troupes and bamboula dancers.[9]

Klaus de Albuquerque suggests that the advent of World War I, the transfer of the islands to the United States, and the subsequent Americanization of the islands spelled the demise of this incarnation of carnival.[10] Whether these all-in-one carnivals, rather than the masquerading neighborhood troupes, were popular practice or occasions created to entertain the elite is unclear. Nevertheless, the "revived" carnival indicated a distinct shift in small island sensibilities and created something much larger, influenced by the practices of Trinidad, Antigua, and Puerto Rico. It was specifically designed to attract tourists while enlisting enthusiastic local support.

Although the 1952 carnival was labeled a "Virgin Islands" event, it took place on St. Thomas, the territory's economic and governmental capital, with the participation of musical groups, street performers, and viewing publics from St. Croix, St. John, and other Eastern Caribbean islands. At the same time that this new tradition was being created and celebrated in St. Thomas, another was in the making on St. Croix. Crucians were interested in the stimulation of Christmas festivities, traditionally a celebratory season for many in the community. The pre-Lenten holidays observed on islands such as Haiti and Trinidad held less appeal in the Virgin Islands, which had not been historically or overwhelmingly Catholic but rather Protestant. St. Thomas's festival demonstrated that a carnival event could succeed at any time of the year, without the religious anchor of its origins. The

1952 Christmas festival in St. Croix was the "biggest seen here": "A group of citizens, disturbed over the fact that the youth of the island were letting the old traditions die, decided it needed encouragement. The first committee, headed by Anna Brodhurst, planned a real Old Fashioned Christmas. They put up Christmas trees in Gallows Bay, in Watergut, in Sunday Market, in Freegut, on the Wharf and at the Bassin Triangle. And in Frederiksted." By 1956, the event was officially known as the Christmas Festival.[11] St. Croix's carnival attracted the support of large numbers of residents, including a who's who of local social and political notables, as well as participants from off the island.[12] As aesthetic consultants and participants in both the performing arts and the design of the Crucian festival, artists from other Eastern Caribbean islands played a great role in shaping events from the street parades and costuming to the look and design of the queen shows. In later years, St. John added its own festival to those of St. Thomas and St. Croix. The event at first commemorated U.S. independence on July 4 but ultimately became a more black-centered and culturally specific celebration of emancipation of the Virgin Islands slaves on July 3, 1848.[13]

CARNIVAL ENTERTAINMENT'S AESTHETIC INFLUENCES

Unlike the St. Thomas festival, those held on St. Croix in 1952 and 1953 lacked mock royalty. But other entertainments were aesthetically important in the festival's development. In December 1953, the *St. Croix Avis* announced that "several troupes, whip dancers, clowns, steel bands and other items of entertainment are expected to arrive from Antigua in time for the Old Fashioned Christmas Festival. . . . The Antiguans are going all out to join in the festivities."[14] Also from Antigua came the Hell's Gate Steel Band, which became a staple of the St. Croix festival, "tramp[ing] the streets nightly from the time of their arrival and [drawing] crowds of dancing people."[15] The Virgin Islands thus incorporated a Trinidadian creation into what quickly became a yearly celebration.[16]

Neighboring islands and groups thus contributed to the look and shape of Virgin Islands practices even though constructing a uniquely "Virgin Islands" identity remained an item on the national agenda. According to Evelyn Richardson, a Crucian socialite, the first moko jumbies to grace St. Croix came from St. Kitts, Antigua, and Barbados in the early 1900s.[17] Richard Schrader, a local writer and cultural historian, notes that in addition to Antigua's Hell's Gate, steel bands from Tortola (Hell Fire) and St. Kitts (Casa Blanca), came to the Virgin Islands, expanding the musical scene to include more than the traditional Crucian quelbe bands. St. Croix soon developed its own steel bands, among them Black Arrow, Moon Shiners, Trojans, and Watergonians.[18] Such mixings had a long tradition dating back well before the 1950s and the explosion of tourism. For example, labor uprisings both during and after slavery, particularly on St. Croix, featured laypersons and leaders from Antigua, Barbados, St. Kitts, and Jamaica. Carnival simply provided a unifying platform for the display of the area's expressive talents. None of these aesthetic and cultural influences were new or uniquely identified. They were simply *there*. Their influence had been so present over time as to be rendered invisible, particularly as the Virgin Islands sought to establish themselves in a world market and point up their difference as a marketing lure. Included in this process were the queen shows, which changed from the popularity contests of the past based on the Virgin Islands' relationships with other Caribbean islands, all of which reflected influences from Latin America and the continental United States.

THE APPEARANCE, REAPPEARANCE, AND TRANSFORMATION OF THE QUEEN SHOW

Beginning in 1954, the Crucian Christmas Festival added a king and queen to reign over festival events and lend grace and style to the hosts of masquerading people flooding the streets. The first royalty chosen were Harry Edwards and Jessica Tutein, a team that accumulated 2,981 votes, outpolling their closest competitors by more than 900 votes. Each vote cost ten cents.[19]

Tutein lived most of her life on the estate of Gallows Bay, and by the summer of 1999 she was its unofficial mayor. Reflecting back on her crown, the strong-willed and opinionated woman attributed her win to her popularity in the community but noted her belief that all local families at the time had been popular, since the number of island residents had dropped so much and the community had become so small that everyone knew everyone else. A member of the Women's League, married, and a well-known fisherwoman and baker, Tutein said she needed little time to amass the votes needed to assure her place before selecting Edwards to serve as her king. A pharmacist who "never missed a dance," Edwards was the island's most popular young man and thus was Tutein's logical choice to share the throne. Tutein described the festival as a grassroots event, created by the ingenuity and resourcefulness of the community's women. According to Tutein, the money raised by the contest helped to fund the festival, which paid each troupe that entered the parade and provided room and board for off-island performers.[20]

The pageant thus not only played a critical role in developing carnival but also provided entertainment for festivalgoers and prestige for participants. Tutein remembered variety-show-style performances, as at the earlier queen derbies, as well as a fashion show segment of the pageant at the prestigious Comanche Hotel.

However, for her, the far-more-important parts of the competition included her work to garner votes and her crowning at the Alexander Theater in Christiansted by Governor Archie Alexander. She also lamented the changes that had occurred over the preceding half century: in her view, the pageant had become less of a grassroots or community event, and the title carried less cachet, reflecting the influences of economic and population growth, political changes, and simply popular tastes and opinions. She regretted community members' complaints about the festival's management, although such mumblings about the administration of any major event are perhaps an unavoidable part of the Caribbean social landscape. In response to these complaints about better ways to serve all members of the community, members of the festival committee have recently attempted new strategies, and some of these strategies have affected the queen shows.[21]

It is difficult to determine precisely who is responsible for the distinct shifts in the look and the development of Virgin Island pageants, and variations exist on each of the three islands. Similarly, there was no one moment when the pageant structures and values shifted but rather a series of small adjustments. Tutein attributed some of the changes on St. Croix to Randall "Doc" James, a physician, radio personality, musician, and community leader.[22] From the 1950s through the 1970s, James spearheaded the island's most popular variety showcase, the Doc James Talent Show, whose corresponding club offered young local singers, dancers, musicians, and comedians the opportunity to perform to packed houses across the island and even toured other Caribbean islands. Such acts were perfectly suited to queen show presentations, appealing to popular tastes in music, dance, and clothing. Islanders loved to watch James's group, imagining what any talented youth might be able to attain. James unquestionably influenced the entertainment provided at queen shows as well as what was perceived as hip or fashionable. Talent Club performances relied heavily on stateside aesthetics in general and in particular on black North American performance, which itself reflected the shift from the aims and accomplishments of the civil rights movement to the urgency of the Black Power consciousness. During the 1960s, young Crucians' performances reflected a reverence for contemporary rhythm and blues music, a change from the aesthetic models of the three preceding decades, which came from the Puerto Rican and greater Latin American and Eastern Caribbean communities. Classic diasporic borrowing took place as members of the island community incorporated what they liked from the United States and discarded what they did not like, thereby creating new local practices. In addition, Doc James's shows popularized skits that highlighted local language and expression while presenting perplexing, laughable performances reminiscent of situation comedies.[23] These culturally identified moments became a marker of Caribbean and black pride and were incorporated into pageant events.

Other personalities and institutions are more directly associated with queen shows' shift away from popularity contests. Clarence "Cherra" Heyleger, one of St. Croix's premier sports-radio personalities and cultural events connoisseurs, took an active role in carnival planning from the 1950s through the 1970s and served for close to a decade on the festival committee, including a stint as its president. During Heyleger's years of involvement, the contest morphed from choosing a "festival queen" to selecting Miss St. Croix. In Heyleger's view, Antigua and Trinidad served as significant influences on Virgin Islanders' seasonal events and especially on queen shows: "Really, we adopted this queen show from . . . what we saw down island, especially in Antigua. Because at that time visits to Antiguan carnival was very prevalent for us here in St. Croix. We went down to the Antiguan carnival almost every year." There, Virgin Islanders witnessed pageant participants from not only Antigua but also Trinidad, Martinique, and Guadeloupe, returning with new ideas about how to develop a more dazzling, competitive, and world-class festival.[24]

The Caribbean Queen Show held by the Antigua Jaycees (a chapter of the U.S. Junior Chamber of Commerce) provided one of the major models for the St. Croix festival committee's design of that island's show. Virgin Island contestants were not initially invited to participate in the Caribbean Queen Show (then called the West Indian Queen Show), which featured queens from a number of islands, but Virgin Islanders' continued presence as spectators eventually persuaded organizers to invite the territory's contestants to join in. From the Antiguan queen show, Virgin Islanders adopted Trinidad and Antigua's carnival constructions—large, resplendent costumes—for the talent portion of the competition.[25] This cultural twist was important as local organizers sought to keep the pageant anchored in local, recognizable aesthetic modes.

NORTH AMERICAN PARALLELS

The politics and aesthetics of the 1950s and 1960s inevitably overlapped white lives with black, and those seemingly divisible lines blurred as Black Power and consciousness mixed with white youth rebellion. At the same time, as Lois Banner describes, the "mindless voluptuousness and domesticity of the 1950s ideal woman" was replaced by an intelligence and formality embodied by Jacqueline Kennedy, the model of the 1960s new woman.[26] Fashion designers and the wealthy consorted to create within the general public a fascination with celebrity, while "youths who in the 1950s had played football, cruised in cars, and worried about going steady now as eagerly seemed to take up uninhibited sex, drugs, mystical religions, natural foods, and a critical attitude toward the culture they had unthinkingly supported."[27] Moreover, according to Banner, the commercial beauty culture was forced to incorporate "naturalness" into prevailing styles as young women lost interest in heavy makeup and the elaborately coiffed hairstyles: "For the first time in American history, non-European models of beauty were not only extolled by writers on beauty, but were actually presented as models for cultural emulation. Donayale Luna was the first black model to be featured in ads in general circulation fashion magazines like *Vogue*. 'Black is Beautiful,' the slogan of the black rebellion, penetrated white consciousness. Decrying the traditional vogue of hair straightening among blacks and identifying with their homeland, many blacks proudly wore their hair naturally and called it an Afro cut."[28]

In this atmosphere, the pageants of the Virgin Islands made perhaps their most significant and drastic change. Although they did not adhere strictly to the codes prevalent in the North, Virgin Islanders paid attention to the rise in black consciousness, changing clothing and hairstyles in accordance with what was taking place stateside. Afros and bell-bottoms were sported on island streets, though perhaps not as often as in northern cities. But black women, particularly in the Caribbean, with their long history of work outside the home, never had to negotiate "mindless . . . domesticity." Voluptuousness, too, signified an acknowledged desire that black women were publicly denied. Nevertheless, pageants worked an alchemy to attempt to distance themselves from beauty's vacuous associations and moved women and the idea of representation by women to something that included intellect. The attention to celebrity Banner notes in U.S. culture was also present in the Virgin Islands as pageants created an appetite for young women to be more visible.

Heyleger believed Claire Brown Roker to be single-handedly responsible for restyling and rearranging the Crucian productions to suit modern tastes and desires.[29] The changes Roker made to St. Croix's pageants did not come from events she witnessed in Antigua or on other Caribbean islands. Roker, a businesswoman, community leader, and employee of the delegate to Congress during the late 1990s, had not even been familiar with the earlier queen derby events. Born in the Virgin Islands and transplanted to New York at age nine, Roker found her major influences in North American city life.[30]

Roker received her initiation into the pageant world as a contestant for Miss Andrew Jackson High in 1956. She was named first runner-up, which she recalled as quite an accomplishment for a black girl. She attributed her win to her avid participation in school activities, in accordance with pageant tenets. Her next contest, Miss Virgin Islands Voice, a popularity contest based on who could raise the most money, resembled the queen derbies held both in the islands and in expatriate communities in the United States. Brown won that crown in 1962–63 and was flown back to the Virgin Islands to appear in the Crucian festival parade.

She subsequently competed in but did not win the Miss Harlem Transit contest. The experience brought her into contact with Hal Jackson, a radio personality and founder of Hal Jackson's Talented Teen Pageant. When she later married Wally Roker, a member of the singing group the Heartbeats, and became involved in the music industry, her relationship with Jackson blossomed.[31]

Marriage exposed Roker to the glamour of the entertainment business. Arranging activities and dress coordination for artists such as Patti LaBelle and Aretha Franklin gave Roker the opportunity to "see how [black women] should look when they perform." She later worked in the shoe industry and as a hand and hair model before returning to the Virgin Islands in 1964 and meeting Heyleger a year later. In 1966, under his leadership, she first became involved in the Miss St. Croix pageant. At the time, according to Roker, only young ladies who could "represent" St. Croix were accepted as contestants. Their festival duties included participation in such civic activities as visiting the Queen Louise Home for orphaned children, working with the Girl Scouts, and participating in educational efforts. Contestants also had to appear youthful and be popular within the community.[32] Like Doc James, Claire Roker brought together the worlds of Afro-Caribbean and African American aesthetics.

According to Heyleger, Roker played an instrumental part in reshaping the Miss St. Croix contest. Relatives of members of the festival committee had previously been eligible to compete; members did not even have to inform the rest of the committee if they were familiar with or related to contestants. Roker created a screening process that prevented committee members' family members from competing and eliminated the possibility that committee members or judges might leak information to contestants. She also changed the process so that contestants' family members could not attend rehearsal and offer negative comments about other participants, affecting their confidence and performance. Roker worked to streamline and regularize an informal, porous process in which power moves, favoritism, and psychological maneuvering had played a significant role. She knew that such changes would not always appeal to the public.[33]

Roker moved the pageant away from a popularity contest to a professional competition in which presumably fair and impartial judges selected the winner. No longer would the number of votes a young woman received from the paying public determine who would reign as queen.

MISS U.S. VIRGIN ISLANDS

It seemed a natural progression that the Miss St. Croix pageant would funnel contestants into the Miss U.S. Virgin Islands contest, which selected someone to represent the entire territory, not simply one of the sister islands. But each pageant has its own particular trajectory, and while Miss U.S. Virgin Islands may be a terminal point for island pageantry, winners proceed to the Miss Universe contest.[34]

Sponsored by the Virgin Islands Hotel Association, the first Miss Virgin Islands pageant was held on St. Thomas in June 1956. For the talent portion of the competition, the winner, Miriam Edna Golden, gave a speech on Virgin Islands history. Golden went on to become a semifinalist in the Miss United States pageant, and when she returned to the territory, large crowds greeted her. According to Venetia Harvey, "The fact that [Golden] was not a winner made little difference. . . . Everyone was satisfied that the Virgin Islands was well represented by [one] as beautiful, charming and acceptable as could possibly be selected."[35]

The enthusiasm for national representation was short-lived, and the pageant was not held again until 1961, when Priscilla Bonelli was named queen. Bonelli had won the title of first runner-up at the Miss St. Croix contest a year earlier. By then, the contest's parent competition had become Miss Universe. Miss Virgin Islands pageants were held again in 1962, 1967, and 1971, when Sam King, owner of Pan American Finishing School and Career College and a member of the carnival committee, purchased the franchise from Miss Universe Inc. and reactivated the pageant and changed its name to Miss U.S. Virgin Islands.[36] The pageant has subsequently continued consistently in accordance with the reforms made by Roker and King. The islands and their pageants had become world-class, producing more "refined" and professional representatives who could compete in international pageants. With the sleek new pageantry and the availability of advisers, consultants, and trainers from the Virgin Islands, Puerto Rico, the United States, and further abroad, the contests were no longer the cozy home-grown competitions of the past.

Part Two

DE JUS NOW (MODERN) QUEENS

Chapter 4

THE MAIN EVENT

Miss U.S. Virgin Islands 1999, "The Essence of the Caribbean"

The Miss U.S. Virgin Islands 1999 Pageant, titled "The Essence of the Caribbean," took place in the grand ballroom of the exclusive Wyndham Sugar Bay resort on the east end of St. Thomas. Guests arrived at a small guardhouse, parked their cars, and were shuttled to the main building, designed to evoke a grand colonial feeling with large fans circling near the high ceilings and sloping staircases trimmed in rich mahogany. The audience members eagerly made their way to the pageant doors, scheduled to open at 2:30 in the afternoon. The pageant, run by the Lions Club of St. Thomas, a social group devoted to charity work, was to begin at 3:00. Rather than a typical theater space, the Wyndham Sugar Bay's grand ballroom was a long rectangular room, filled with seats and a makeshift stage. At one time, the Miss U.S. Virgin Islands pageants were held at the island's Reichold Center for the Arts, and a few other pageants still take place there. However, the Lions Club continually lost money at this venue, and members decided that the Wyndham would offer better returns. The ballroom was rented for three thousand dollars, and the club anticipated selling five hundred tickets at thirty dollars each.

This setting offered challenges for both contestants participating in the event and the audience. The flat floor meant that audience members lacked easy sight lines. The temporary stage lacked a rake (a slanted platform that would improve the audience's view) and had only a small space in which contestants could walk and a short runway. To compensate, organizers designed the show so that the young women would enter from the rear of the ballroom and walk down the center aisle, offering audience members a good look at the participants. The long walk also posed challenges for the contestants, walking in gowns and heels on a carpeted floor as they were measured, compared, rated, judged, and encouraged or jeered as they made their way toward the front of the room for the official judging.

This chapter recounts a portion of the events of the 1999 Miss U.S. Virgin Islands pageant in narrative form and then examines the ways in which the pageant's setting, format, and contestant presentations demonstrate the diasporic borrowings of the African American performance models discussed in chapter 3 as well as distinctly Afro-Caribbean forms. Both are incorporated into pageant performances and are absorbed and appreciated by local audiences without a second thought. In addition to these modes of performance, audiences witness interisland politics, jostling, and style borrowings as the young women of the pageant "represent" their respective islands and/or communities. The language of the pageant participants and masters of ceremony exposes individuals' negotiations regarding their identities and desires as Virgin Islanders and as young women in a very complex social and political environment. The Miss U.S. Virgin Islands pageant offers evidence of a territory searching for a definition of nation within the Caribbean and within a global economy that is conversing with its own community and working itself out on the bodies and in the performances of these young women.

THE PAGEANT

When the doors opened, the patrons who had arrived early to get good seats discovered that sections had been roped off. Seats to the right had been reserved for sponsors and family, while those to the left were designated for "other dignitaries"—reigning queens, trainers, consultants, and the like. At 3:30, the program began.

Deborah Gottlieb, chair of the Lions Club's Pageant Committee, welcomed the audience and introduced the two masters of ceremonies. Serving as fashion commentator was fellow Lion, educator, and 1971 Miss Virgin Islands contestant Vernelle S. de Lagarde. The other host was Lee Vanterpool, three-time Miss U.S. Virgin Islands master of ceremonies, former anchor for WBNB-TV, and current reporter for both radio and television. Gottlieb's introduction was lengthy and involved the reading of the hosts' biographies from the program. Vanterpool then took over the microphone. He instructed the large audience to "make sure you also let the contestants know you are here to support them. Don't hold back. Don't be restrained. Let them know you actually care. Show your appreciation." Vanterpool then identified and invited to the stand Roy Frett, special assistant to governor Charles Turnbull. Frett's opening remarks offered his best wishes to each of the four contestants vying for the title, commended them for their roles in the day's activities, and asked audience members to support the ultimate winner.[1]

Vanterpool returned to the stage, reviewed the program, and opened the introductory dance and speeches. In this segment, the judges evaluate the young women in four areas: poise, delivery, content and creativity, and originality. Each area is worth five points, with each contestant's total tallied at show's end. The choreographer of the production number, Carolyn Jenkins, organized the introductory dance, set to the theme from the movie *Rocky*, in an innovative style. In exact opposition to what Jenkins called the "ultimate femininity" of the contest itself,[2] the contestants were dressed in boxing shorts and gloves, and they shadowboxed their way to the stage, led by an ungloved Leah Webster, Miss U.S. Virgin Islands 1998. Webster was flanked by two "ring boys," John and Jay Hill, who wore no shirts and black vests and "guarded" and guided Webster to center stage. The crowd roared when she appeared at the back of the hall. The women boxed and jabbed the air in simple square and circular formations, crossing through lines and departing when their turn came to speak. The production number lent itself to an air of playfulness, though with an undercurrent of serious competition. The announcement of each contestant's name generated deafening applause, which quickly quieted: Lynda Ortiz of St. Croix, Carolyn Wattley of St. Thomas, Sherece Smith of St. John, and April Petrus of St. Thomas.

The introductory speeches ended the first segment the public saw, but they were not the first judged event. The preceding evening, the judges and the young women had attended a dinner hosted by the Lions Club at the Palm Court Harbour View Hotel, an establishment owned by Webster's family, where the judges' interview took place. The judges were first briefed by the official coach of the pageant, Utha Williams, who had advised the young women on etiquette, poise, and a uniform negotiation of the stage. Williams, a former and very controversial Miss U.S. Virgin Islands, explained to the judges what pageant officials had told contestants about rules and then asked the judges to "go easy on her girls."[3] The judges then invited each contestant into the room and asked her a series of questions that were ostensibly designed to provide insight into the woman's personality and determine how she handled herself both publicly and privately. Each of the seven judges had submitted three questions, and from this pool, each judge was permitted to ask each contestant one question. The interview lasted between fifteen and twenty minutes per contestant. The criteria for the personal interview were poise, charm, personality, expression of intelligence, and the delivery of responses, with each one worth five points.[4] Thus, contestants had already been ranked before the start of the official show before the viewing public.

After the introductory dance and speeches, the contestants made their way from the stage to the back of the room and out of view to prepare for their next segment, swimwear. During this time, Vanterpool introduced the judges, businesspeople, educators, and a former Miss U.S. Virgin Islands. He then explained to the audience the categories according to which the young women would be judged: personal interview, introductory speech, swimwear, promotional presentation, evening wear, and question and response. The personal interview and the promotional presentation are worth a maximum of twenty-five points. The other categories are valued at fifteen points each and include the elements of poise, charm, and sense of style (for swimwear and evening wear) or delivery (question and response).

The fashion commentator then took the microphone and spoke to the audience: "You've met our contestants during the introductory speeches, and I know you have your favorites out there. Is it contestant number 1 [applause], contestant number 2 [applause], contestant number 3 [a cheering section from St. John erupts], or contestant number 4 [another eruption]? Who will be Miss U.S. Virgin Islands 1999 [pause]? The judges' decision is final."

The announcer opened the swimwear competition with contestant number 1. Each young woman made her way down the aisle in a one- or two-piece swimsuit while the announcers commented on her apparel. Written by the contestants or members of their consulting teams, these descriptions offered delectable settings and flattering descriptions of the women as they moved through the public space. At the end of the segment, the commentator presented the contestants to the audience and judges for one last look, again taunting, "Who will be Miss Virgin Islands 1999? Will it be contestant number 1? Contestant number 2? Contestant number 3? Or contestant number 4? The judges' decision is final."

While the contestants prepared for the next segment, Lorna Freeman, a talented and popular local rhythm and blues singer, performed. Freeman imitates stateside artists to the note. This evening, she sang Mariah Carey's "I Still Believe" with absolute accuracy—a note by note reproduction of Carey's version of the song. The crowd loved Freeman's performance.

Next, Vanterpool acknowledged local celebrities in attendance, gesturing toward audience left and asking all "visiting dignitaries" or reigning queens to stand. One by one, they stood and waved to the audience, offering a brief glimpse of royalty and perpetuating the idea of community celebrity.

Next came the promotional presentation, the show's weightiest segment. Although it was billed as a "promotional" rather than "talent" competition, the lines between the two were deliberately blurred. The contestants used this segment to demonstrate their creativity and ability to promote the Virgin Islands and could use virtually any means to do so. Thus, the section took on the feeling of a talent segment, with contestants pulling out all the stops and choosing to "promote" the Virgin Islands with varying degrees of creativity. The section has become a commercial for the Virgin Islands, with each young woman determined to find a unique way to depict her country and herself in the most positive light.

With the first half of the show completed, the masters of ceremonies declared intermission, reminding the audience that the show's second half would include the evening wear segment. Intermission was filled with chatter and speculation about the early favorites.

When the show resumed, the fashion commentator introduced the evening wear competition by calling it the "seductive portion" of the evening. Background music filled the room. De Lagarde called the contestants to the stage and described them using scripts they provided:

> Fasten your seat belts [pause]. Contestant number 1, Lynda Ortiz, from the island of St. Croix, again known to us as Big Island, or Twin Cities. She's not only sweet, but she's also sexy. Watch out judges, there is no number high enough to score this beauty. Lynda Ortiz comes to us representing her island, St. Croix. She's is truly an "ice, ice baby" as she wears her lavishing ice-blue evening gown, just like the color of our Caribbean waters and the soft blue sky. Quality made only for royalty, this gown is 100 percent silk, with front side split with a peek at those sexy legs. A sunburst pattern on the top is accented with a sheer neck. Its crisscrossed back has a soft elegant drape. Cleopatra would have only dreamed to own such an extravagant gown. Lynda's silver heels compliment her Cinderella feet. Ladies and gentlemen, take note. She is truly a queen. Contestant number 1 vying for the title of Miss U.S. Virgin Islands 1999, Miss Lynda Ortiz. Make no bones about it, she knows what she has [pause]. As she is greeted by her date, contestant number 1, Miss Lynda Ortiz of the island of St. Croix, the essence of our Caribbean. Contestant number 1.
>
> And now contestant number 2, from the island of St. Thomas, none other than Carolyn A. Wattley . . . another essence of our Caribbean, Miss Carolyn A. Wattley. As Carolyn strolls up the aisle and approaches the stage, she brings to us the age of innocence. Calm, confident, a woman who knows herself and knows what she has in mind. The age of innocence grown up. Romantic rendering and a sensuous design by local designer Curtis Powelin, sewn by Simone Smith from Tortola, B[ritish] V[irgin] I[slands] [pause]. Regal, evening elegance in electric blue and wrapped so well in rhinestones. Make sure the slit is up the rear, and whatever room you enter the conversation must come to a halt. Diamonds must be the girl's best friend. Observe the white gold and diamond earrings and bracelet. Little Switzerland, you've done it again. Her hair is so elegantly done, by Kelly Charles, and makeup by Moira Morrow. Less is always more, and to be different is always outstanding. Contestant number 2 from St. Thomas, United States Virgin Islands, Miss Carolyn A. Wattley. The

age of innocence grows fast, romantic rendering and sensual design. Essence of the Caribbean in contestant number 2. Ladies and gentlemen, Miss Carolyn A. Wattley, from St. Thomas, United States Virgin Islands. Rhinestones, diamonds, electric blue all wrapped so well for this lovely contestant. As has been indicated, whatever ballroom she enters, the conversation must come to a halt [pause]. Our contestant number 2, Miss Carolyn A. Wattley. And her date is also on time. The lady knows what she has in mind for her special evening. Contestant number 2.

Wattley left the room amid a hail of shouts from the audience. The next contestant entered, and de Lagarde continued with her descriptive monologue extolling the virtues of the woman's gown, accessories, presence, and understated sexuality or desirability.

Contestant number 3 from the island of St. John, Miss Sherece Smith. Unfold your imagination, and let's soar into an ocean of turquoise and tranquility [pause, and the crowd erupts]. From the imagination of Claire's Collection comes Sherece Smith, a true treasure that could have only been inspired by the serene Caribbean sea. Reminiscent of the early 1940s, Sherece's bustier has been fully adorned with jumbo eight-inch stones which follow a graduated beehive [pause]. An elegantly form-fitted waist. The back of this gown has also been kissed with graduated jumbo stones. The skirt has been formed from a luxurious . . . silk that falls to an ample length. With a modest yet regal turn of the body, Sherece prepares for her flight as an unassuming caterpillar prepares to be transformed into a beautiful butterfly. Sherece spreads her four-foot chiffon wings [side panels of the dress] and reveals the true meaning of making a statement without ever speaking a word [crowd erupts]. That statement says confidence, elegance, and grace. Sherece shows silver shoes and original designed choker and earrings that have been set with silver and stones. This gown was designed especially for Sherece at Private Collection in Sub Base, St. Thomas. Sherece Smith, contestant number 3, as she has met her date for the evening with whatever she has in mind . . . knowing it will come true. Ladies and gentlemen, contestant number 3 [crowd erupts, the m.c. is inaudible].

Music filled the room, which was abuzz with excitement over Smith. The commentator forged ahead as the final contestant prepared to take her walk. There was a long pause as contestant number 4 made her way down the aisle, seeming a bit nervous with a determined yet shaky smile planted on her face. De Lagarde then resumed her commentary, accompanied by the endless looping of soft jazz by Earl Klugh:

Contestant number 4, Miss April Petrus, representing the island of St. Thomas. Stylish but elegant, poised and confident, styling from dusk till dawn whether by candlelight or starlight, this lady in fuchsia is simply awesome. We've often had ladies in red, but this is a lady in fuchsia with a statement that she needs to make, and she is going to make that statement this evening. April graces the stage in a one-shoulder fuchsia rhinestone, star-studded evening gown. The gown flows romantically into a scalloped-edge fantail train in the back.

The audience began to get noisy again as individuals commented on Petrus's stature, style, and walk, obviously comparing her to her predecessors. Unfortunately for Petrus, following Smith was anticlimactic. The noise swelled when Petrus stumbled ever so slightly on her way to the stage. The audience likes nothing better than to see a contestant make a mistake, however minor. Such anticipation undergirds all such competitions and is an important element in the excitement and tension that fills the air for contestants and audience members alike. The fashion commentator continued:

Simplicity and elegance go hand in hand when this gown and this lady make an evening affair accessorized with rhinestone earrings and fuchsia pumps, elegant and tailored from beginning till end. Beautiful designs on the back and front of this one-shouldered fuchsia, simple and elegant evening gown. Rhinestones, star-studded, and oh-so-elegant. The gown flows romantically into a scalloped-edge, fantail train in the back. Simplicity and elegance hand in hand for this beautiful contestant. [Commentator ad libs, repeating earlier descriptions.] Rhinestone accessories. Ladies and gentlemen, contestant number 4, of St. Thomas, United States Virgin Islands, vying for the title of Miss U.S. Virgin Islands. Whatever the evening calls for, April is ready and her date is on time. She knows what she has in mind. Contestant number 4, ladies and gentlemen, Miss April Petrus, St. Thomas, U.S. Virgin Islands.

The contestant and her escort made their way to the rear of the room and exited.

As the contestants prepared for the final event, for which they did not have to change clothes, the crowd was entertained by local calypsonian, event photographer, and *Flair* newspaper editor King Louis Ible Jr. King Ible, Jr.` is a calypsonian of the old school who relies on his voice and wit rather than on instrumental verve to comment on political events and personalities. He gave away a few of his CDs by challenging the audience to sing a verse from one of his a cappella songs, then made fun of former and current politicians using wordplay and unexpected phrasings of customary words that change meaning and throw into question issues in local politics. In the tradition of calypso commentary, Ible sang a medley of his own songs for approximately twenty minutes and lambasted current legislators, past governors, and other political heads with obvious high personal ambitions. The audience for the most part received these antics with laughter; Ible positions himself as a man of the people and charges the Virgin Islands government with self-serving ambitions. But the audience began to tire of the act and to become restless. At that point, the hosts returned for the show's final segment.

Vanterpool encouraged the first contestant to make her way to the front of the space. Ortiz reached the stage after a long, uncomfortable pause in which Vanterpool attempted to have the DJ fill the space and time with music, but Ortiz appeared just as the music began. Vanterpool asked her to choose a question from a glass bowl. All contestants were going to be asked the same question. Ortiz's choice of a question involved formality: to demonstrate to the audience that the process had been handled fairly, this segment had to be handled delicately. Vanterpool then directed Ortiz to her microphone and announced, "The question is—What do you think that each one of us, as concerned Virgin Islanders, can do to help our territory address its fiscal condition?" Ortiz replied, "What I think our territory should do, together, to fix our fiscal condition is to work together [pause]. Um, there is a lot of power in unity. And I believe that if we put our minds together, and we work together as a team, it will definitely come together. Stop bickering, stop fighting, come together, and just unify this one [pause]. Thank you." The audience was supportive, though Ortiz faltered toward the end of her response.

As the second contestant was called from a rear soundproof area, the audience members buzzed with their assessments of Ortiz's performance. Rhythm and blues music again filled the space at the last moment. In response to the fumbling that had been taking place with the location and height of the microphone the women were expected to use, the host instructed Wattley to speak directly into the microphone "so that we can all hear you." Wattley requested that Vanterpool repeat the question twice more as the microphone continued to have problems, and Vanterpool decided to have contestants use his microphone when answering the question. Wattley then offered her answer: "I feel that each one of us here in the territory needs to concentrate on each other. We need to be more hospitable to each other. We need to support each and every Virgin Islander, then things will be better here in the Virgin Islands."

When her turn came, Smith responded, "I think all of us as Virgin Islands, as one unit should look into our local governments and see where, if in fact, um, our governments need to be restructured in an attempt to alleviate—"At this point, the crowd erupted, and the balance of Smith's answer was inaudible. Smith's calm and use of language impressed her listeners. The content of the answer seemed relatively unimportant as long as it was delivered smoothly, with confidence, and without a hitch. Smith, like Wattley, referred to the fracturing of the islands' government and people, but her answer gratified the audience because of her finesse in delivery.

The audience had now become out of control. The time for good behavior had passed as audience members anticipated the final outcome. The din was deafening. The DJ finally played his interim music on cue, but virtually all that was audible was the sounds of the excited public. Petrus, the final contestant, made her way to the microphone and offered her answer: "I think that we should meet with the governor and the senators of the Virgin Islands and make an assessment of all the departments to see exactly where [audience noise, others tried to quiet them] the funds are being spent and how much is being spent in these departments. And secondly, I would make a list, a priority list, and work with the departments that need the most help first. Thank you." The crowd again erupted, impressed by Petrus's composure and intellect. Content seemed to matter only to the extent that the contestant *sounded* intelligent. Petrus was by far the most articulate and undaunted by the question posed. Yet the audience's enthusiasm for Smith and the similarity of the two women's responses led Petrus once again to seem to trail Smith. Petrus's position last in the lineup served her poorly; Smith consistently stole the show, making Petrus seem merely to be echoing (though improving on) her predecessor.

The young women attempted to leave the stage gracefully, no doubt assessing their performances and measuring themselves against one another, perhaps for the first time in the evening. The competition was over, and the final moment had arrived.

At this point in the program, a series of planned stalling actions made time for the judges to select a winner. The previous year's Miss U.S. Virgin Islands took her final walk. Webster had created a bit of controversy by leaving the territory, which the reigning queen is not supposed to do, and then expecting the pageant committee to foot the bill for her return. When committee members refused to do so, she asked listeners of her long-standing island radio show for their support. Despite the probable embarrassment of her well-to-do family in St. Thomas and the protests of the Miss U.S. Virgin Islands Organizing Committee, which was made to seem the villain, Webster accepted the public's pity and money and returned to the territory to complete her obligations as the 1998 queen. As she took her last walk, she like many other reigning queens, was moved to tears, as her recorded words were played over the sound system.

Her farewell message also appeared in the pageant program, as is common for both formal and informal events with accompanying programs. Her statement discussed her "spiritual adventure through time." Dressed in a dazzling off-white beaded and rhinestone dress and matching stiletto heels, she spoke of the "phenomenal things" she had experienced and those she still expected with each new day. Webster encouraged and advised the soon-to-be crowned Miss U.S.

Virgin Islands 1999, boasting, "As I continue to walk with confidence and without the fear of failure, I graciously, effortlessly, and courageously transform darkness into light." She continued, "When the moment arrives that a new Miss USVI is crowned, first should come feelings of joy, then relief, then reality. The title is what you make it. Although your new shining tiara displays that you were the best in a competition, you must now be the best at life." Webster further advised the new winner to "educate yourself . . . and behave in a way that constantly reminds those around you that being Miss USVI is not about a tiara, rather it is an attitude that it is all the people of the Virgin Islands." Miss U.S. Virgin Islands, according to Webster, provides a voice for a people who are "magnificent and strong," and she closed by thanking her St. Croix radio audiences for their support.[5]

After Webster completed her elegant walk, the current contestants were called to the stage so that members of the Lions Club could make presentations. The contestants stood in a half circle as trophies donated by the Bank of Nova Scotia as well as other gifts provided by local businesses were identified. The audience was encouraged to patronize the businesses that donated to this event. Gottlieb then presented the first award, for personal development: "Every young woman who enters the Miss U.S. Virgin Islands competition receives personal development training to help bring out her best qualities. However, individual efforts are key to attaining quality results and are worthy of recognition. This special award goes to the contestant whose attitude has been the most positive, who was sincerely willing to learn, who worked hard to make significant progress, and whose behavior was consistently above reproach. In recognition of her hard work and achievements, the pageant committee presents this year's personal development award to contestant number 1, Lynda Ortiz."

Vanterpool presented the second award, Miss Photogenic, to contestant number 3, Sherece Smith. The audience shrieked and continued to rumble as Vanterpool moved on to present the award for Miss Congeniality, selected by the contestants among themselves. I was told that Petrus was the only contestant who did not vote for herself in this category, meaning that her vote made Smith the winner. The announcement of Smith's victory in this category provoked more yelping from the ecstatic audience. The excitement level escalated even further as Vanterpool commented that the contestants had been so well trained and so cool that they were simply "taking it all in stride."

Smith won the next award as well, this one for best evening wear, and the one for Miss Intellect. Each time Smith's name was announced, the crowd's excitement surged to new levels. The final subcategory award, for promotional presentation, also went to Smith, and as Vanterpool attempted to announce the first runner-up for the overall title, he was interrupted by shouting from the audience. The first runner-up, he noted, occupies a very important position, "since if for any reason, our Miss U.S. Virgin Islands is unable to fulfill her duties, this contestant will step in. Contestant selected as first runner-up, contestant number 4, April Petrus." Petrus was visibly disappointed but gracious. The crowd cheered, certain now that Smith had won. But the suspense was not yet finished, and the host attempted to calm the crowd members, telling them to "collect yourselves" and "get a grip" because "there is gonna be a lot of noise everywhere tonight." He then personally congratulated everyone, prolonging the final moments of the show. But the crowd continued to scream, quieting only momentarily as he proclaimed the results: "It is my pleasure to announce Miss U.S. Virgin Islands 1999, contestant number 3, Sherece Smith." The result was bedlam, as the crowd rushed the stage. The loud-speaker system played calypso. Photographers turned from taking pictures of the contestants to photographing the audience, and any organized photographs of the queen and her royal court were lost in the excitement as spectators asserted their closeness to their queen by taking photographs with her. Smith won not only the crown but the approval of her fellow St. Johnians and of the overwhelming major-ity of other Virgin Islanders.

At the end of the evening, the members of the audience filed out of the Wyndham Sugar Bay Resort with a mixture of feelings but secure in the judges' decision-making capabilities. This pageant featured little drama, no controversy. The determination of this year's queen took place with little protest. Smith had been the clear front-runner from the moment the lights dimmed. Pageant at-tendees dispersed to their homes or to carnival activities in downtown Charlotte Amalie. The contestants celebrated the culmination of their long journey with a Lions Club–sponsored dinner at a nearby resort restaurant, although Smith and Ortiz did not attend. (Smith was whisked away by her team and the St. John contingent, while Ortiz spent the evening with family from St. Croix.) The din-ner ultimately proved to be brief, held in a location where mostly white tourists looked on curiously at the unusual sight of an entourage of formally dressed black women. The contestants and their handlers resumed their lives, knowing that they had done their best to capture the dream of representing the territory.

ANALYSIS

The Lions Club's choice of "The Essence of the Caribbean" as the theme for the 1999 Miss U.S. Virgin Islands Pageant exposed the territory's questioning of self while seeming to declare its status as a Caribbean entity that the contestants might be able to capture. What is the "essence" of the Caribbean? Of the Virgin Islands? The problematic nature of this terminology and the discourse surrounding it did not seem to concern the organizers. That a quest for the "essence" of the Caribbean might encourage or at least participate in a stereotyping, racialized, sexed, and gendered grouping of the participating young women and concomitant fixed and unwelcome assumptions about the territory as a whole was not an immediate issue for the Lions Club. The club and its 1999 Miss U.S. Virgin Islands pageant were not concerned about the dangers of essentialist categories of phenotype and genotype that would fix the behaviors of the diverse groups of people in the territory and region as immutable, as genetic lay theories serving to differentiate and articulate difference for groups of people.

Club members were concerned not with the gaze of external observers but with local, internal perspectives. Apparently clear that the audience for this form of performance does not include tourists or certain populations on the islands whose views might signal a reliance on confining stereotypes, the Lions Club staged an intraracial, intraethnic, intraclass, and perhaps even intragender discourse about who and what the territory comprises. Although the mission might indirectly make way for some of those dangers, its main purpose seemed to be, as Stuart Hall argues in his discussion of identity formation, that of articulating a constitutive outside.[6] Nation is thus defined not by what it is but by what it is not. As such, the Miss U.S. Virgin Islands 1999 pageant participated in a discourse that has long plagued the Virgin Islands: Who are we, and what defines us? In this discourse, identity is sought in determinations of who and what Virgin Islanders are not.

Historically, the articulation of a national identity was critical for the purposes of the tourist trade. On the platform of a burgeoning tourist economy, the Virgin Islands had to articulate itself and its relationships between the territory's multiple ethnicities, gendered and sexual identities, and cultural practices. The pursuit of an "essence" might indicate more accurately the ambivalent nature of the territory's membership in the Caribbean. The islands' status as an American territory that is part and parcel of the Caribbean is a challenging negotiation. Local notions of modernity depend on the relationship with the United States at the same time that the Virgin Islands resists those associations in the quest for an identity singular to itself. Like the other U.S. commonwealths of Puerto Rico and Guam, the Virgin Islands face limits of citizenship that force its governing institutions and the general population to reconsider their relevance, their status, and ultimately their value as human beings to the United States and to themselves. Thus, the contest's charge reflects the territory's search for a definition that comprises the multiple identities that make up not only the body of the nation but also its gender. In other words, this search for national self-definition depends on the perpetuation of the trope of nation as woman.[7] How women embody a national and regional consciousness and express it in a reductive representation of a Caribbeanness is critical to the success of the Miss U.S. Virgin Islands contest theme and its apparent mission. Identity is reduced to a sound bite. As Hall writes,

> This concept of identity does *not* signal that stable core of the self, unfolding from beginning to end through all the vicissitudes of history without change. . . . Nor—if we translate this essentializing conception to the stage of cultural identity—is it that "collective or true self hiding inside many other, more superficial or artificially imposed 'selves' which a people with a shared history and ancestry hold in common" . . . and which can stabilize, fix or guarantee an unchanging "oneness" of cultural belongingness underlying all the other superficial differences. It accepts that identities are never unified and, in late modern times, increasingly fragmented and fractured; never singular but multiply constructed across different, often intersecting and antagonistic, discourses, practices and positions.[8]

The insertion onstage of cultural costumes and talents alongside evening wear and question and answer segments colludes in the creation of this composite Virgin Island woman, like her country is both part this and that, local and American, native and cosmopolitan, fractured and multiply constructed. Pageants participate in the creation of Hall's "superficial or artificially imposed selves" as young women are trained in the behaviors and aesthetics of some fabricated and collectively imagined middle-class standard. Governing agencies, small businesses, and willing grassroots institutions conspire to identify culture and thereby create notions of fixity. Others reject those dictates and insist on their own markers, equally significant and different from the "official" signifiers. Yet this identity too becomes troubled and complicated, as Hall suggests, when Virgin Islanders acknowledge differences and an uneasy coexistence between themselves and the colonizer, between individual tastes and memories, as communities seek the stability of a cultural belongingness that the idea of nation promises.

Therefore, the contestant introductions clearly demonstrate the complications of interisland and intraisland politics. Linda Ortiz's introduction as someone from a place "known to us as Big Island, or Twin Cities," marked her as an outsider, not part of St. Thomian social circles. That Ortiz was responsible for her introduction (as are all contestants) and clearly cast herself in the role of outsider plays on the ways islanders have accorded each other nicknames and characteristics of identification. St. Thomas's nickname, "the Rock," refers both to the land's physical composition and to the island's position as the bedrock of Virgin Island commerce and international dealings. Ortiz also established her place of belonging and her competitive spirit as she claimed the title of the contest's "Essence of the Caribbean" at the end of her walk. In contrast, Wattley, a St. Thomian, chose to point out the international nature of her presentation, mentioning with pride her support from international businesses such as Little Switzerland and a seamstress from the British Virgin Islands. These young women play out the intraisland haggling in subtle performative ways through the indirect speech of the master of ceremonies, who announces their differences and provides the soundtrack for their performance of nationality. The language used in this contest portrays the complexity of interisland competition while simultaneously pointing out the value the community places on language and linguistic skills. In the classic badmouthing, (wo)man-of-words performance known in the Caribbean,[9] these young women are expected to display their linguistic gifts, bringing to mind the historical queens' demonstrations of education and nonsense as they introduce themselves and answer questions posed. As the audience's response to the question-and-answer section demonstrated, it did not matter what the young women said; it mattered that they *sounded as though* they were saying something. Their performance of intellectualism impressed the crowd and harkened back to the days of tea meetings and dance drama performances.

While these vocal expressions can embrace solid knowledge, they also are platforms for the absurd. Answering a public policy question in thirty seconds or less is impossible, but the contestants go along with the program and do their best to impress the crowd with a mouthful of language. In addition, their use of multiple languages as they perform in their promotional presentations, discussed in more detail in chapter 5, also demonstrates the value that the community places on this talent. In a territory that has historically hosted numerous nations and international flows, multiple language proficiencies are important. Such multilingualism is also no longer commonplace (perhaps another legacy of U.S. colonization), so young women who have mastered more than one language are celebrated. All of these phenomena, as well as a clear attention to U.S. performance values and stylings, are represented in the contestants' attire during the early sections of the show and the interspersed performances of local artists intent on reproducing stateside material. It is also evident in dashes, minute moments that could remain below the radar—for example, Ortiz's description of herself as an "ice, ice baby" (referring to the 1990s hip-hop song by Vanilla Ice). The aesthetic mixes of U.S. and Caribbean vocal performances, like that of King Ible Jr., produce the diasporic mix that comprises the complicated nature of nation in the territory.

Presenting a "constitutive outside" clearly can be a matter of personal choice. The Caribbean mélange of style, both historic and legendary, as global forces clash and mingle in the production of new forms, comes into play fully as diasporic borrowing is coupled with native ingenuity and performed on the islands' stages. However, these performances are only a measure of the social negotiations and political jostling that take place on a daily basis. In determining who is the native, what are national birthrights and the economic benefactors thereof, the introductory blurbs serve as a precursor to the meat and potatoes of the production, which exhibits much more of the territory's internal discourse on national identity and sovereignty. The promotional presentation is the pageant's primary site of national discourse. At the same time, it is merely one of the locations where these concerns play out publicly.

Chapter 5

PROMOTIONAL PRESENTATIONS AND THE SELLING OF THE NATIVE

The Queen Represents

With the new shape of queen in the territory, the emphasis suddenly shifted to representation, and young women were expected to stand for "not just the festival but . . . our community."[1] Yet to stand for is not the same as to be, so representing the women in the community required the construction of a fiction—consistently and coincidentally the job of tourism—to identify and create cultural "appetizers," that gesture toward something distinct/Caribbean/woman/different that could be easily identified, consumed, and understood. The promotional presentations and introductory speeches by the contestants in the 1999 Miss U.S. Virgin Islands pageant demonstrate the role of tourism in the Virgin Islands imaginary—identifying the "island woman" and the challenges that further an even larger attempt by islanders to define the native. In this chapter, I argue that pageants incorporate tourism's project of identifying all things Caribbean in general and all things "native" to the Virgin Islands in particular. On the one hand, pageant culture legitimizes the productions, while on the other it creates an ambassadorial, albeit fictional, place within the political machinery for the young female participants.

I examine the public's ambivalence toward this identity articulation and the machinations that accompany being "native," using Miss U.S. Virgin Islands pageant introductory speeches to demonstrate individual attempts at identifying the Virgin Islands' people. As with the narration of the pageant performance in chapter 4, I present the promotional presentations as they were performed that evening, with minor stage commentary based on my observations as a performer and performance analyst. The audience members' responses betrayed the ways in which they could imagine themselves defined and the local cultures circulating in new economies. This chapter links pageantry and legislative policy in local discourse on national identity. By constructing the fictional relationship between tourism and the Miss U.S. Virgin Islands pageant, participating islanders rehearse for each other representation and ideas regarding nation.

These performances not only prove to locals their modern status as they enter contests performed the world over but also keep the community engaged in discourses regarding authority, their relation to it, and the ways in which this pageant assists them in determining their values, visions, and means of communicating those concerns to one another.[2] What impresses audiences in these performances, what the contestants choose to include or exclude in their presentation of themselves, offers readings of linguistic discourse. In other words, what they say and how they say it betrays many Virgin Islanders' values regarding their political and social positions and how they see themselves as able or unable to move between economies and populations—in short, the everyday negotiations of their world.

At the moment of tourism's explosion after the 1950s, Virgin Islands' women were unwittingly put to work for the nation, set up to embody what it meant to be a Caribbean woman and represent her on stage. The process created a set of disturbing questions that continue to surface periodically on the contest stage as young women grapple with speeches designed to encapsulate themselves and a composite island woman. Who is the Virgin Islands woman? What are her attributes? What does she look like? How does she speak? How does she move? What does she do? While the subtext of these questions might delimit the diversity of Caribbean women, they are asked to consider these confining concepts in negotiating this area of representation. Shaped by pageant organizers and the values expressed within the limits of the contests, they are consistently operating on dual levels, identifying their private selves and their community, which might differ substantially for each contestant. The product of their work is offered up as fodder for the territory as a whole and as service to self and country.

The ostensibly natural outgrowth of this new role of the young contest winner as representative of young island women was a relationship with the burgeoning tourism industry. But there was no natural relationship; rather, one was created. Claire Roker approached tourism officials after an early contest and asked them to make Miss St. Croix the island's ambassador. More specifically, Roker suggested, "Once this young lady is totally groomed and understands what her role is, anything pertaining to tourism she should be involved in." According to Roker, her task was complicated by the fact that "back in those days, you had to know someone because they didn't utilize the young ladies as much as they should have"—a refrain that continues to this day.[3] But the relationship between the Miss U.S. Virgin Islands contest and tourism is often phantom or very indirect, as fleeting as the event itself or the passing of festival days. In the contemporary pageant, the direct relationship to tourism exists in the promotional presentation. Since the audience for queen shows or talent shows does not include tourists, such venues offer Virgin Islanders a forum in which to audition the tourist promo, to rehearse it for other islanders or, more accurately, for the pageant subculture. The Department of Tourism and the government's advertising ventures with off-island agencies are, at most, remote. Roker and other pageant organizers have persistently sought to interest the government in these events, but such efforts have elicited very little response unless a visible political benefit is explicit—for example, promoting the carnival queen yields visibility for the St. Thomas carnival and access to a voting public.

The Virgin Islands queen is rarely connected directly to tourism, with such instances limited to her occasional appearances on the cover of promotional magazines in local or exotic clothing or lying on a secluded beach. Nevertheless, the members of the pageant-attending public are eager to determine who deserves to reflect their constructed image, conceiving a role for the queen within the tourist industry and the national consciousness as a whole. For the most part, she does not occupy a "real" place, although a few contestants have made the leap from the imaginary relation to positions in the tourism field. Contestants elect to go through the rigors of "training," to enter as raw material and emerge as refined specimens proffered by the community as emblems of what is black and beautiful and Caribbean and woman. But for whom? Where is this queen's platform? Divested of their historical significance as a bearer of news and cultural critic, the current queens are figureheads for whom there is no automatic place of political significance and value.

Members of the islands' government do make some token gestures, however, as evidenced by the brief opening comments at the 1999 Miss U.S. Virgin Islands pageant offered by the governor's special assistant, Roy Frett: "Unlike many larger countries, this evening's activities will represent our national contest. . . . This individual will represent us as our ambassador. She is going to represent the intellect, the culture, the—the heritage of all of us. And as such we should give her the support that she so deserves." Frett stood in for the governor at this event, his presence a gesture toward the community that passionately devours these contests. At the same time, however, his attendance illustrated the governor's lack of commitment to an entertainment whose reputation may be ambiguous enough to warrant careful handling. Frett's comments, too, were ambiguous, both full and empty of meaning. He provided a stamp of approval for the proceedings yet offered no promise of further official engagement. His words *sounded* good. He reminded the audience members that they were participating in the national contest and that their queen would represent them in some larger capacity as ambassador. But ambassador to what? Without an official post, she is no more ambassador than any other member of the general public who has daily dealings with the outside world. Thus, while the community at large often recognizes her during and after her reigning days, particularly if she is one of the queens who is enmeshed in scandal, pageant organizers must fight to find a place for her. Determined to articulate her importance, organizers push to insert her in all possible matters of public notice. The men and women who design, desire, and create the pageants relentlessly pursue the queen's place in the national consciousness, in plain view, while concretizing their place of importance within, among other areas, the islands' cultural currency. Why the government chooses not to exploit the queen or to do so only sporadically remains a question, though the issue does not deter the actions of pageant insiders. These are the machinations of the new queenship of the territory, and it flourishes and comes into being during countless competitions of "representation," though Miss U.S. Virgin Islands carries the most presumptive weight.[4]

PROMOTIONAL PRESENTATIONS: MISS U.S. VIRGIN ISLANDS 1999

The first contestant, Lynda Ortiz, entered the space with a rousing popular calypso. She appeared wearing a Rasta hat complete with fake dreadlocks hanging down to her waist. The crowd laughed and was supportive. She danced down the aisle as though she were working her way down a parade route. Wheeling a suitcase behind her, she stepped up on the stage, and the music lowered. She began to speak as though she were a tourist just returning stateside from a cruise to the Virgin Islands. "Ah Lord. Oh my! Finally I'm home. But I don't want to be here." Some members of the audience began to shout because they could not hear her. Another listener quieted those complaining, and Ortiz continued. "A cruise to the Virgin Islands, that was so good. But I want to go back, I want to go back, I want to go back now. The islands were so beautiful. There are three of them. St. John, St. Thomas, St. Croix." At this point, she realized that her microphone was not working. A stagehand attempted to assist her, but she ultimately continued without amplification, competing with the persistent din of voices in the large ballroom. "I'm so lucky. I mean, I go away for one week, and I fall in love. I fall in love with John, Thomas, and Croix—the beautiful sandy beaches, the tropical flowers, the tropical fruits. They are so tasteful. They are so colorful. I want to go back. First there was Thomas." At this point, the sound system comes on, and the audience can finally hear her.

I shopped till I dropped at Magen's Bay. I shopped till I dropped at Charlotte Amalie—not Magen's Bay. Magen's Bay is a beach, one of the ten most beautiful beaches in the world. So relaxing, shaped like a heart. A seashore shaped like a heart, that's so creative. Oh my goodness! And St. John—snorkeling at Trunk Bay, brunch at Caneel Bay, that was sooo good. And St. Croix—Big Croix. That's where I first saw my first moko jumbie. Oh my goodness! And I drank alcohol. But not any alcohol. It was rum, Crucian Rum. I got addicted after a while. And then Buck Island; I picked a lot of sea shells. I want to go back. I want to go back now. I'm so in love. I don't care about this. I do care about— but it was all so good. Oh man, what should I do? It was so good. From the mango to the pomegranate. That tastes so good. I wonder if I could grow some locks? All the calypso music and steel pans. It was so sweet. Oh my goodness. One week was not enough, definitely. I want to go back. I don't think anything is going to stop me. I remember the hibiscus; ladies used to wear it in their hair. It was so pretty. And then the flamboyant [flowers] all over the street, all kinds of different colors. Oh my goodness. I want to go back. But what are my parents going to say? What will my fiancé say? Will they come with me? That's okay. I'm in love—with the Virgin Islands, and I can't take it anymore. I want to go back. And no one and nothing is gonna stop me. I'm gonna do it, and I'm gonna do it now. I'm going back to the islands, man.

The calypso music swelled again, and Ortiz danced off the stage and back down the aisle, back to the Virgin Islands in her tourist gear of ripped dungarees, t-shirt, and headphones blasting Caribbean music. Ortiz's presentation was beset with difficulties, and she made no eye contact with the audience. The listeners' enthusiasm fizzled. They had little time to ponder their feelings about this performance, however; the master of ceremonies encapsulated it as "an emotional presentation" and introduced contestant number 2.

Stagehands placed Carolyn Wattley's set onstage. It comprises two large painted boards, one with images of black mermaids and conch shells on a beach, and the other showing a blackboard and mock classroom. Wattley entered to a more classically paced calypso piece that described qualities of the Virgin Islands in a narrative style. Over this melody, a recorded voice said, "Welcome to the Wattley Institute of Hospitality and Culture. Please take your seats while our instructor prepares for today's lesson." Wattley made her way to the stage, wearing a beige suit, hair swept up in a tall French twist, clipboard in hand, and glasses on her nose. The music continued for a long time before Wattley finally said, "Good afternoon [pause]. Lesson number 1. When you're in the Virgin Islands and someone says 'Good afternoon,' your response should be likewise." She repeated, "Good afternoon," and the audience replied with good humor, "Good afternoon," and applauded vigorously. She continued, "Thank you, class. I see some very new and familiar faces. Hi, Sinbad. Welcome to the Virgin Islands again. Buenos tardes, Tito Puente. Nice to see you." Someone in the audience answered, "De nada," and

Nineteenth-century drawing of the Festival of Twelfth-Night, or Three Kings Day.
Photo courtesy of the St. Croix Landmarks Society Library and Archives.

Jessica Tutein and Harry Edwards, St. Croix Festival Queen and King, in Christiansted
parade, 1954. Photo by Fritz Henle. Newspaper reproduction reprinted with permission.

Early Queen Street. Photo courtesy of the St. Croix Landmarks Society Library and Archives.

Miss Utha Williams, disqualified Miss USVI, seen with Governor Melvin Evans, in 1971.

MISS U.S. VIRGIN ISLANDS PAGEANT

MARCH 21, 1999 - WYNDHAM SUGAR BAY HOTEL
sponsored by the
CHARLOTTE AMALIE ST. THOMAS LIONS CLUB

Program booklet cover for the Miss USVI 1999 pageant.

Program booklet cover for the Miss Big and Beautiful 1999 pageant.

Sherice Sharmaine Smith, Miss USVI 1999.
Photo by M. Cynthia Oliver.

Paula Smith, Miss Big and Beautiful 1999.
Photo by M. Cynthia Oliver.

Unidentified Miss St. John 1999.
Photo by M. Cynthia Oliver.

Clienta Samuel, Miss St. Croix Education Complex 1999.
Photo by M. Cynthia Oliver.

Unidentified Miss French VI 1999.
Photo by M. Cynthia Oliver.

Latoya Serrano, Miss Talented Teen 1999.
Photo by M. Cynthia Oliver.

Stephanie Chalana Brown, Miss Heritage VI
1999. Photo by M. Cynthia Oliver.

Unidentified queen. Photo by
M. Cynthia Oliver.

Shirley Richardson, Miss Virgin Islands/American Classic Seniors
1999. Photo by M. Cynthia Oliver.

Unidentified queen. Photo by M. Cynthia Oliver.

Kim Boschulte, Miss USVI 1995.
Photo courtesy of Kim Boschulte.

Unidentified senior couple. Photo by M. Cynthia Oliver.

Marise James, Miss USVI 1981. Photo courtesy of
Marise James.

Marise James (left) with unidentified queen.
Photo courtesy of Marise James.

Marise James (middle) with unidentified queens. Photo courtesy of Marise James.

Wattley then pretended to identify and greet a local attorney before launching into the meat of her presentation. "Today's class, we're gonna be talking about our Virgin Islands, so y'all just listen very, very closely. Especially you, Sinbad, cause I don't want you to get lost here in the Virgin Islands. There's some—There's some people out here that want to hold onto you. All right. First of all, we have four Virgins of which seven flags have flown over. Okay? These Virgins have a various [and] unique culture. We have Spanish. We have French." Wattley then named four of the flags that have ruled the Virgin Islands and spoke of the islands' attributes and of carnival.

And then there's St. John, the island of natural treasures. Be sure to stop by Trunk Bay and take a dip, because those oceans are the bluest that it gets. Then there's St. Croix, with Frederiksted and Christiansted. Don't get afraid when you get to St. Croix and hear people habla en español. That's like half of St. Croix. St. Croix, when you go, you can see rain forests. You can see some of the ruins.

Finally our island capital, St. Thomas, United States Virgin Islands. Over three hundred years ago, ships used to come and dock here. They used to come with their goods and trade their goods. Today ships still come, but now they are coming as cruise ships bringing thousands and thousands of visitors here.

Wattley took a long pause before continuing.

Ladies and gentlemen, we would like to [take] this time to congratulate Sinbad for having his—his ball. We would like to congratulate Sinbad for having his fiesta here in the Virgin Islands. Let's give Sinbad a hand. Class, come on. Congratulations Virgin Islands. And of course, let's not forget that carnival is coming up. We have St. John that has their Fourth of July carnival. We have St. Croix that has their Crucian festival, and of course St. Thomas, the Virgin Islands carnival. At this time, I would take a minute to show you what our Virgins think of carnival.

The music swelled, and Wattley retreated behind her set and changed into a carnival costume, replete with feathers and sequins. She danced and paused before finishing her performance with the words, "Don't forget—the Virgin Islands is the only place that you can have four summers—summer, next summer, last summer, and summer. Don't forget—contact your travel agent. You can call 777-USVI. Thank you."

Wattley's presentation was perhaps the most wordy and the least confident. She started out smoothly but quickly lost the audience as she continually paced the stage, referred to her clipboard, and turned her back on the crowd. Wattley's presentation had dead space—for example, during her costume change. Nevertheless, the audience members responded warmly to her, demonstrating their support for all the contestants and eagerness to see the show continue.

After Wattley left the stage, Lee Vanterpool, the master of ceremonies, and Vernelle S. de Lagarde, the fashion commentator, filled the time before the next contestant was ready with comments on Wattley's performance material. Vanterpool corrected omissions from Wattley's presentation of the territory's colonial history, vexing the audience by saying, "She made a mistake." He then pointed out that the St. John "carnival, or festival . . . encompasses Emancipation Day, July 3, a date important to this territory, as well as the American Independence Day, July 4." Vanterpool quickly gave up on the history lesson in the face of audience grumbling and moved on to introduce Sherece Smith. The loudspeaker system announced, "This is the last boarding call for all passengers aboard the SS *2000*, the official Virgin Island cruise line cruising you into the new millennium." Steel pan music began to play, and Smith entered in a white and gold nautical suit. The audience began to cheer. The music changed to funk, and Smith saluted the crowd and exhorted, "Come on, let's go." She took the stage and began: "Ladies and gentlemen, I am your destination director, the sensational Sherece Sharmaine Smith, and we are about to embark on a wonderful journey from Virgin Islands present to Virgin Islands future. I'll take you to a place where the shades of blue water flow into the next [lights changed to a deep blue], one more vibrant than the other, where brilliant white beaches meet oceans of turquoise waves and the soothing sounds of the shore." Ocean sound effects began to play. Audience members began to shout but were hushed by other listeners, and Smith resumed her monologue.

> I'll take you to a place where the brilliance of the sun creeps into your windows with a gentle calling [lights changed to deep orange] that [inaudible because of audience cheering]. I'll take you to a place where you can [inaudible because of audience cheers as Smith began to show slides of the Virgin Islands]. Whether Buck Island or beautiful St. Croix, or explore ancient ruins at the Annenberg plantation. Take in the sights from the beautiful Charlotte Amalie. Take a tour of Whim Greathouse plantation on St. Croix. Enter paradise in the Caribbean. Take in a birds-eye view of our beautiful islands, learn the history of St. Croix's past, like the—the home of the famous petroglyphs. Take a dip in one of the top ten most beautiful beaches in the world. Take a walk in Fort Christian on St. Croix. Visit Caneel Bay plantation on beautiful St. John. Enjoy the St. Thomas carnival, and taste the food of the Caribbean with our agricultural fair. Beyond your scope of imagination lies the potential of the Virgin Islands.

Ladies and gentlemen [loud exploding sound and audience screams] to introduce to you the grander vision of the new millennium. Imagine Island Disney
where you can be none other than Mickey and Minnie Mongoose. Experience
the supercalifragilisticexpialidocious Atlantis underwater roller coaster. Or set
your eyes on the spectacular sunset ruin[?] of mystical moko jumbie. For those
of you who like to shop till you drop, in the largest air-conditioned indoor
mall in the Caribbean, with plenty of parking and free shuttle service [audience
chuckles]. Are you willing to take a risk? Then visit the government's casino
central in the Caribbean, where you take your chances on the slot machines,
Chateau Prosser[5] will make your dreams come true [disco-ball-style lights fill
the stage]. And for those of you who like to party, party, party. Let's not forget
to keep our calendars updated and our dancing shoes polished for Sinbad's annual Memorial Day Soul Festival. Ladies and gentlemen, beyond the year 2000,
the miraculous, spectacular, and fabulous Virgin Islands is about to explode
[explosion sound with confetti] whether it be 1999 or the year 2000. I guaran-
tee that YOU will have the time of YOUR life.

The cheers from the audience followed Smith as she confidently left the ballroom.

Both Vanterpool and de Lagarde started talking again, this time directing
their comments less at the just-finished performance and noting only that it was
"powerful." They worked to calm the crowd sufficiently so that April Petrus could
enter and perform. Her cheering section erupted as the loudspeaker introduced
"the director of tourism, Mademoiselle April Petrus. Mademoiselle Petrus, welcome to France and the National Tourism Conference." Petrus walked down the
aisle in a business suit. As she approached the stage, an audience member sang,
"April showers bring me flowers," and the crowd erupted in a burst of good-na-
tured laughter. Petrus began with a litany of greetings in French, English, Spanish,
German, Japanese, and Danish before moving into the substance of her presentation: "This evening, I take you on a journey to America's paradise, the United
States Virgin Islands—St. Thomas, St. Croix, St. John, and Water Island. Why
choose one as your travel destination? Sun, fun, captivating sights, great shopping, and a truly cultural experience for you in paradise. Come with me to the
gems of the Caribbean. Our first stop is the Virgin Islands capital, St. Thomas."
She gestured toward the screen at stage left, and slides appeared. The audience
members mumbled and chuckled as they realize that Petrus had reproduced some
of what Smith did. "This emerald [island] with breathtaking views. From atop
lush green mountains, a [pause] view unfolds. The harbor with boats in ideal
waters. The town, Charlotte Amalie. Historic Danish architecture. Ready for
some boutique shopping? Let's take a stroll down Main Street for the best buys

in perfume, jewelry, souvenirs, liquor, and much more. Need a break? The crystal clear sapphire waters of Magen's Bay await you. It's time for liming [hanging out, socializing, relaxing]." Petrus then switched into a variety of different languages to offer tourists different foods and restaurants before returning to English. The crowd howled, and she continued: "Now that you've dined, you probably wish to burn a few calories. Then Emancipation Park or Fort Christian Museum are the places to visit. Tired? I bet you are. A relaxing evening in Water Island's magnificent hotel. Buenos dias." She rattled off a bit of Spanish, mentioning St. John before switching back to English once again. "Just twenty minutes from St. Thomas by ferry, the picture perfect treasure is the envy of the Caribbean. Unparalleled in beauty, St. John is a visitor's haven with white sand beaches and numerous nature trails. You will revel in paradise. Well, it's time to leave St. John." Petrus resumed her Spanish, announcing, "Vamonos a Santa Cruz [Let's go to St. Croix]."

> Welcome. St. Croix is a visitor's paradise. The towns of Christiansted and Frederiksted are true Caribbean meccas with buildings—for centuries. On our way downtown, let's discover the island, Fort Frederik and Fort Christianvern museum. We'll end our day on St. Croix with a cool refreshing sea bath.
>
> Our final destination is the most recent addition to the Virgin Islands, Water Island. Acquire a genuine appreciation for nature, and bask in the natural beauty of this unspoiled terrain. You have just experienced a taste of paradise. But you must return for carnival, when you will enjoy steel band music, calypso, parades, our friendly people, and have fun, fun, fun. St. Thomas, St. Croix, St. John, and Water Island, true gems of the Caribbean.

She again switched languages and spoke before finishing her presentation with the words, "Come to the United States Virgin Islands" and exiting down the aisle to the sounds of steel pans as the crowd shouted and screamed.

The crowd seemed genuinely enthusiastic about Petrus's presentation. Tentative at first and even a little chiding because of the similarity of the slide presentation to Smith's performance, the listeners warmed up to Petrus as she easily slipped from one language to the next in her imaginary appeal to European tourist officials.

ANALYSIS

These promotional performances are the stuff of modern-day queen shows, the presentation of self and of community. They require young women (and their team of coaches, consultants, and others) to identify and perform what it means to be from the Virgin Islands. The performances impress their audiences, demonstrating at least cursory knowledge of the territory's history, values, and physical attributes. Still, the presentations exist only here. They are performed only for the pageant audience, the organizers, coaches, and other contestants. Contestants/queens have scant opportunity to perform this presentation before any other audience or location. It is, therefore, a performance of imagination that requires a certain suspension of disbelief as the contestants collectively entertain and are entertained by their imaginary relationship with what makes them viable and valuable in the contemporary marketplace, the product of themselves and their resources, the commodification of their culture.[6]

These new manners of pageantry have relegated representation to the world of pageant contests and their imaginary relationship with the local tourist board or department. Although local queens have been more visible during some periods of recent history than others—for example, appearing in local commercials or gracing business advertisements—such occasions have, for the most part, been independent acts by particular businesses enamored of particular queens or the direct product of a queen's ingenuity and determination to be acknowledged. Such appearances have not resulted from a concerted effort by the territory's agencies to present the queen as the momentary poster girl for Virgin Islanders. Therefore, pageants and the resulting production of queens are virtually ignored by the larger governing bodies aside from the slick and formulaic letters by governing officials that grace the initial pages of carnival and program booklets. This situation has produced among pageant organizers some resentment and much tireless effort at change. The pageants function in an apparently liminal world, somewhere between the general public and the islands' government.

Pageants are nevertheless compelled to make the association with authority. Legitimacy requires that the pageants have an ultimate reason for existing. It is not simply the refinement of young women for the societal good, though civic duty remains a part of the equation. Pageants remain, as the Women's League demonstrated during the 1930s and 1940s, vehicles for the betterment of the local infrastructure. They are moneymakers. They support a web of franchises that work often invisibly, behind the scenes. Within this web of industry is a legitimized space for (primarily) gay male participation in the midst of the Caribbean, known to be a homophobic region. As handlers, advisers, and consultants, gays' participation in pageants carves a space of safety and acceptance in a performative form isolated from the wider (and largely homophobic) public. In addition to what they do for the islands' small gay presence, pageants function on the belief that women can improve their lives through these very choreographed steps. An association with authority legitimizes women, makes them purposeful, and not only assists in the construction of a more useful femininity but continues their historical role as civic participants. Pageants therefore carry on what the architects of tourism designed. With the support of a strong history of pageantry that speaks to tradition and gives the appearance of a cultural lineage none would want to disrupt, they market Virgin Islands culture via the shape of womanhood to the outside world. They give the greater public the appearance of being participants in a collective uplift of the territory, of the people, and of women. As a result, pageant topics remain consistent with tourism and its associations of consumption that the territory can sell and tourists can acquire.[7] As Smith clearly stated, pageants sell the Virgin Islands' "potential" to visionary developers. The islands are again packaged as the young women themselves are, a raw material waiting for refinement and societal or more specifically civic use.

Pageants have been refined to do a number of things: they demonstrate local modernity, civility, and an ability to compete in global arenas. They have use value for the women participating. They promote careers and therefore bestow class mobility for both contestants from state-supported housing, who can use the pageant to gain exposure to business and other communities, and those of higher economic standing, who use the contest as a means to cement their social position. At the same time, the queen is ostensibly serving the nation, becoming a worker for the territory, as is demonstrated clearly during the performative moment in the Miss U.S. Virgin Islands pageant, when the young women introduce themselves to their audience, describing who they believe they are, who they want the viewing public to believe they are, and why the crowd should support them as representatives of the territory.

INTRODUCTORY SPEECHES: SELLING THE NATIVE

Lynda Ortiz's introduction began with her vital statistics: Standing "at five foot three, weighing in at 110 pounds," Ortiz shadowboxed up to the microphone, following the theme and production number of the opening performance. The crowd quieted as she began to speak.

> Coming to you from the island of St. Croix, my name is Lynda. And I am here to let you know why I should represent you, my fellow Virgin Islanders, as Miss U.S. Virgin Islands. I was born and raised on St. Croix, and I am not only a Virgin Islander by birth but also at heart. Our distinct and innovative culture has been a part of me everywhere I've gone. When I lived in Japan, when the Japanese met me, they met the Virgin Islands. When I traveled to Mexico, when the Mexicans met me, they met the Virgin Islands. On my various trips to the States, when the Americans met me, they met a representative of their paradise islands. In case you're curious to know who Lynda is, let me give you

a glimpse before you see her at her best today. She is a Christian who loves and serves her Lord with all her heart and life [applause and cheering]. If you get to know her personally, you discover two things: she is extremely passionate and very sweet. Also, if you take her to the beach, give her a good Christian book, or even take her stargazing, she will be your friend for life. Above all, she loves God, and with that love she can also love you. So watch closely as today she captures your heart and convinces you that she should become the next Miss U.S. Virgin Islands.

Ortiz then playfully punched at the air, smiled, and found her way back to her place amid the other contestants on stage.

Analysis

Ortiz's speech was perhaps most indicative of the value pageant judges and audiences place on being a native Virgin Islander. While contest rules do not require contestants to be born in the islands, they must be legal residents in accordance with U.S. laws and the Immigration and Naturalization Service. Ortiz, a Crucian of Puerto Rican ethnicity, was clear about her role within the global network of communities and exposed this clarity in her opening speech. For her, representation traveled with her as she moved from nation to nation, irrespective of her potential role as queen. As a product of a tourist economy, Virgin Islands citizens always represent the Virgin Islands and encourage the industry, no matter how far across the globe. While Ortiz was clear about her status as a native Virgin Islander, she was less clear about what it might mean, painting a romantic, star- and beach-filled typical tourist playground. She reinforced the islands' colonial relationship with the United States when she stated, "On my various trips to the States, when the Americans met me, they met a representative of their paradise islands." The Virgin Islands' "belonging" to the United States formed part of her identification of herself and the islands in a larger global, geographic and national context. She is not alone in this ambiguity of nativeness and in the resulting anxiety that is produced by the category.

This anxiety exists locally around belonging and nativeness, is bound in rights, property, and wealth, and is predicated on a history that includes not only the islands' strategic military value to the United States during World War I but their role as an economic cash cow during and after World War II as a consequence of tax incentives offered to such major conglomerates as Hess Oil, Martin Marietta, and Harvey Alumina that relieved the companies of tax obligations to the Virgin Islands government for between ten and thirty years.[8] At the same time that these business and economic incentives lured companies to the islands, Virgin Islanders moved elsewhere in search of economic opportunity, creating a long-standing and acknowledged scarcity of native Virgin Islanders as other groups continually arrive and thrive. According to Klaus Albuquerque, "Native Virgin Islanders, and indeed, all black residents of the USVI, feel threatened not only demographically (in 1980, native born Virgin Islanders constituted only 47.2 per cent of the population), economically, and increasingly, politically, but also culturally. Confined to low-paying wage jobs, often denied beach access and traditional use of coastal resources, unable to afford land, housing, and the high cost of living, Virgin Islanders have become an embattled minority."[9]

In recent history, the tourism and real estate industries have joined the established business community, but few of these enterprises have directly and materially benefited locals. All of these industries have offered the rhetoric of support for locals through jobs since the inception of the government-assisted programs, but the reality is more closely a service of off-island, continental, or other interests. As de Albuquerque writes,

> In the 1960's the long awaited economic turn-around finally arrived because of a fortuitous combination of both external and internal factors. The former included the U.S. embargo of Cuba which diverted U.S. tourists and capital to the islands, the advent of jet aircraft which reduced travel time from the mainland, and an elastic low-cost labor supply from the nearby Leeward and Windward islands. The internal factors involved the "aggressive implementation of a broad array of growth policies by local officials," namely, the phase out of commercial sugar production, the creation of an industrial incentive program, and most importantly, aggressive lobbying in Washington. Realizing the USVI had significant tourism potential, Washington began to underwrite the massive infrastructure program that was necessary to support the large-scale modernization of the V.I. economy.[10]

The Virgin Islands economy soared during the late 1960s, slowed in the early to mid-1970s, and recuperated in the late 1970s and 1980s. While the industry showed "renewed vigor" and real estate values and rentals reached "dizzying heights," the "economic miracle" Albuquerque described also brought, as he says, social costs.[11] Most young locals were shut out of homeownership, signaling nonnative control of the economy or at least a shift in control from the "white and near white elite native class, to a new elite of white mainland entrepreneurs."[12] Catherine Sunshine assessed these "costs" in 1985:

> At least ten cruise liners dock daily at the duty-free port of Charlotte Amalie, St. Thomas, and Virgin Islanders must elbow their way through throngs of

American tourists on downtown streets. Many North Americans also live in the Virgin Islands, where they own land, businesses, luxury condominiums and retirement villas facing onto private beaches. . . . The Virgin Islands' economy is thoroughly controlled by U.S. corporations. The U.S. based Hess Oil Co. is the largest private employer, operating the western world's largest oil refinery on St. Croix. The relationship between Hess and the Virgin Islands administration has been tense, with Hess threatening to leave in response to demands for greater benefits for the islands. . . . Most small businesses are owned by non-blacks, including North Americans, Syrians, and Lebanese. The working class consists of Native Virgin Islanders and West Indian Immigrants from "down islands." . . . However, small business owners not infrequently hire transient white job seekers from the United States in preference to local blacks. . . . Not surprisingly the island air is often laden with tension. The continuous tourist invasion, the economic dominance of foreigners and the extreme congestion of the islands has fueled a suppressed hostility which occasionally breaks the surface.[13]

These pressures continue and have led to an overwhelming wariness among islanders, a persistent fear that outsiders will take advantage of locals. In response, birthright has become battleground, badge of pride, entrée, or, for nonnatives, cross. The pageant stage is a microcosm of these loaded issues. When Ortiz summoned the term *native*, she did so with the burden of history, economics, and race politics penetrating the contest. Her use of the word indicated a political position, not just a birthplace, that has been contested, embattled, and remains unstable. Virgin Islanders have persistently attempted to negotiate the perplexity of nativeness just as their queens have attempted year after year to define what it means to be who they are.

NATIVENESS DEFINED, NATIVENESS TESTED

In 1995, the carousel of race and power relations rotated again as the Virgin Islands legislature considered the ill-fated Casino and Resort Control Act, a bill introduced by controversial senator Adelbert Bryan. Among many provisos, the bill contained a number of "protective measures" for the island community, including a requirement that enterprises employ at least "90% . . . bonafide residents" and a proviso to set aside for native Virgin Islanders 51 percent ownership in two of six casino hotel licenses, for a total 17 percent native ownership of all the hotel and casino licenses being granted. The latter became the island public's most hotly debated issue of the time. The bill would have required a precise definition of a "native Virgin Islander." On February 21, 1996, a town meeting was held in Kingshill,

St. Croix. Guest speakers at the meeting included representatives of the Pequot Tribal Council (which runs Connecticut's Foxwoods Casino) and the National Indian Gaming Association as well as the Oneida tribe's director of legislative affairs. These speakers had been brought in to attest to the new law's good intentions and the benefits it would provide for native people.[14]

In local parlance, *native* most often signifies black persons or creoles or those of mixed-race (two terms rarely if ever used in the territory) whose ancestors resided on the islands for centuries. Because the majority of businesses are owned by nonblack residents, a measure to insert black presence and cut white residents out of any portion of the economic picture was not just offensive to the business majority but was seen as reprehensible. In response, opponents resorted to accusations of racism and divisive tactics. Most of these pronouncements were levied against Bryan, who had long made clear his problack position. Although *native* could have been avoided entirely by references to length of residence and cultural familiarity, the measure specifically invoked the term and would have created a written definition that would have made the term less fluid and made nativeness less negotiable, more fixed, more exclusionary, and forever more elusive for some.

Adelbert and his supporters produced a booklet containing "pivotal definitions" for the "native Virgin Islander": "any person born in the Virgin Islands prior to 1927; any person who is an offspring of parents born in the Virgin Islands prior to 1927; or any person born outside the Virgin Islands to Native Virgin Islands parent(s) while that parent(s) was studying abroad, or in any active military service."[15] Proponents chose 1927 because in that year, Virgin Islands citizens were granted the choice of remaining Danish subjects or becoming U.S. citizens, a choice that represented a critical determination of national identity. The Casino Gaming Bill distinguished between "Virgin Islanders" and "native Virgin Islanders," with the latter, "notwithstanding any law to the contrary . . . defined as any person born in the Virgin Islands." And a "bonafide resident" was defined as a "native Virgin Islander," a "Virgin Islander," or a person who had been domiciled in the Virgin Islands for at least five years or who had been born in the Virgin Islands.[16]

Panic exploded in the islands, primarily among the usually silent white business community, which has largely separated itself from the larger black community only to speak up when lucrative business and positions appear threatened. The Casino Gaming Act mobilized the white community, primarily through editorials in island newspapers and through the sole local television station. (Weekend radio programs are generally more egalitarian and representative of wider public opinion.) White residents and business owners threatened to move to more welcoming environments. In addition to loss of revenue, business leaders expressed concern that other, still more exclusionary measures would follow. The white community called on the "righteousness" of black business associates, lawmakers, and friends to fight a "bigoted and volatile" senator, depicting the dispute as involving prejudice and placing the bill's supporters on the defensive.

Although Native Americans had been brought in to demonstrate the sincerity of Bryan and other supporters of the Gaming Bill and to indicate the benefits that such laws had brought to the "people," *native* has significantly different meanings for Native Americans than for Crucians, St. Thomians, and St. Johnians—or for any Caribbeans other than Caribs, Arawaks, and Ciboneys. These indigenous peoples lived on the "continent of islands" before Europeans arrived. Virgin Islands "natives" represent the mélange of the New World—enslaved and imported West African labor; Danish, French, Spanish, English, Dutch, and Knights of Malta colonial influences; and other laborers from Asia and the South American continent. No indigenous people remain in the Virgin Islands. More recently, globalization has brought other nationalities and ethnicities—including people from China, India, and the Middle East as well as Europe, the United States, and Africa—to negotiate this terrain in the quest for better economic opportunity. The black majority that has risen from slavery to relative economic stability and in many cases affluence has drawn on African sensibilities to greater and lesser degrees, pride from movements within the territory, as well as the American civil rights, African American Black Power, and Jamaican Rastafari movements.

These combined elements have become the measure for cultural authenticity and savvy. Brazilian scholar Marta de Ulhoa Carvalho says that in her country, "national identity was constructed by an intellectual elite that created an ideal image of 'the people' and decided what kinds of traits were worth emphasizing and which ones were to be dismissed as decadent or unauthentic."[17] The Virgin Islands have undergone a similar process of identity making by the intellectuals who have designed an industry based in tourism as well as a cultural revitalization that feeds natives starving for identity markers. While the perceived Americanization of the territory threatens to remove all Caribbeanness, a grassroots contingent insists on its own requirements as the authentic machinery of nativeness in opposition to elite impositions. Can the pageant platform be an institution servicing both an interested elite and the grassroots? Can a beauty queen speak to both working-class islanders and the elite? Can this pageant performance serve both while articulating an identity that disrupts standardized notions of economic strata or the ways in which individuals transgress economic confines? The pageant does precisely this, negotiating the muddy territory of individual and group identities as its participants step cautiously from one economic and social position to the next, all the while articulating nativeness as they understand it.

Still, native culture absorbs and reworks practices that continue to come from both outside and within the Caribbean.[18] As the pageants demonstrate the American/Caribbean/creole mixture of aesthetics and social, economic, and political issues, Ortiz's use of *native* is as vague as the category itself. Never offering a definition of the term, Ortiz simply reminds the audience that whatever "native" is, she is it by nature of her birthplace. She represents for her country wherever she travels. Ironically, her most obvious "native" feature is her ambivalence, which does indeed make her a fitting example of a native woman.

Stuart Hall suggests that ambivalence is inserted into the center of the process of cultural identification, saying, too, that, "though they seem to invoke an origin in a historical past with which they continue to correspond, actually identities are about questions of using the resources of history, language, and culture in the process of becoming."[19] The project of tourism assists this process of becoming. Persistently attempting to attract visitors by becoming more product, more unique in their Caribbeanness, Virgin Islanders also seek to remain identifiably Caribbean so as not to be too American, more cultural so as not to lose their heritage, more hospitable, more economically viable, simply *more*. And Sherece Smith best demonstrates for Virgin Islanders what they might become more of.

SHERECE SMITH

Amid shouts and screams from the audience and swelling music, Vanterpool announced Smith, "standing five feet, seven inches tall and weighing in at 115 pounds." Then she introduced herself:

> The shimmering bays and beaches of St. John, the historical and architectural sights of St. Croix, the hospitality and personalities of St. Thomas, the [youth] and serenity of Water Island—the Virgin Islands are the essence of the Caribbean. Good afternoon and welcome, ladies, gentlemen, and judges. Representing the beautiful island of St. John, I am Sherece Smith. Standing before you at twenty-five years of age, five feet, seven inches tall and 115 pounds, I am truly indicative of the essence of the Caribbean and a grander vision for the new millennium. As a graduate of the Johnson and Wales University of Providence, Rhode Island, I was able to maintain dean's list status while attaining degrees in travel and tourism management and hospitality sales and meeting management, with future plans to further and complete my graduate education at the Johnson and Wales University, in Lausanne, Switzerland. My education has been a finishing for what has preceded a long list of ambassadorial duties for me—crowned St. John Princess in 1982, crowned Miss St. John in 1989, Ford Modeling Agency finalist 1991, member of the St. John Methodist Church, and member of the St. John Carnival Committee. As former information officer for the St. John Division of Tourism, I have worn many hats, of which include

advertising, showing, and promoting our beautiful island. I am currently employed at the Virgin Islands Water and Power Authority on St. John as customer service agent. My educational background, work experience, and pageant experiences have taken me around the world, including North America, South America, Central America, Europe, territories of Great Britain, and the entire Caribbean. Being well spoken and well traveled makes me no stranger to the public arena. Ladies and gentlemen, special thanks to my parents, my chaperone, my sponsors, and to the almighty God, from whom all blessings flow. Once again, I am Sherece Sharmaine Smith, your ambassador.

The rest of Smith's words were inaudible, drowned out by the noise of the crowd.

Analysis

The inclusiveness in Smith's presentation is evident in her regard of nativeness and its inevitable exclusions and her intentional inclusion of all the islands in the territory. Rivalry has always existed between the islands, based on the location of the islands' legislative and commercial headquarters in St. Thomas and that island's perceived unequal share of local and federal monies though St. Croix is larger and more populated. St. John, Smith's home, has an equally complicated relationship with St. Thomas. Most often treated as an appendage of the larger island, St. John is the silent sister, a small town and a tourist mecca. But Smith's presentation reasserted not only her position but that of her island in the territory, offering "a grander vision for the millennium," a decidedly forward-looking model rather than the customary backward "heritage" preservation–centered glance. Smith appealed to the territory's responsiveness to commercial ventures for the Virgin Islands and claimed her strategic place as its ambassador. In addition, she did not ignore the power of class and privilege, mentioning with pride her extensive travel experience and her refinement and education. These features accrue great respect in the territory and signal Smith's readiness as a savvy representative of the nation.

These introductory and promotional speeches, like the pageants in their entirety, express Virgin Islanders' personal and societal politics. The presentations betray values regarding bodies, regarding economic and social conditions within the territory. Women stand on these stages as models not only of the territory's ambivalence and ambiguities but also of the consistent straddling this and other island communities negotiate between models of western, capitalist, imperialist civility and Caribbean sensibilities and worldviews. Their growth and development have paralleled aesthetic and industrial movements, yet the territory retains the flavor, quality, and atmosphere of an island setting whose distinction from other Caribbean islands is perpetually in the making.

Part Three

I COME; YOU AH COME
(I HAVE ARRIVED; YOU WILL ARRIVE)

Chapter 6

THE BIG BUSINESS OF QUEENSHIP

A Competitive Edge?

The day after the Miss U.S. Virgin Islands 1999 contest, the islands were abuzz about the new queen. Sherece Sharmaine Smith was the first St. Johnian to win the crown since Elsa Hall in 1981. The airwaves were flooded with commentary on pageants' validity and usefulness; on the expenses to parents, businesses, and contestants; on the images pageants portray and whether the U.S. Virgin Islands contestants can really compete in global pageants.

St. Thomas's popular WSTA radio show, *Ideas and Issues*, a "roundtable for discussion on subject matters of concern to our community," featured perhaps the most in-depth conversation on the subject. With the theme from *Shaft* playing in the background, commentators "Caesar," Terrance Thomas, and Jean Forde opened the discussion by enumerating the contests of which they were aware: Miss U.S. Virgin Islands; Miss Big and Beautiful; Miss Carnival Queen, described as the "most coveted"; and other smaller contests. The commentators and their callers then moved on to one of the most potent complaints regarding the Miss U.S. Virgin Islands pageant: its scheduling makes it difficult for Virgin Islands representatives to compete effectively in the Miss Universe pageant. The Miss U.S. Virgin Islands competition, these critics argued, was held too close to the Miss Universe pageant, leaving the Virgin Island queen with too little time to prepare. The commentators asked, "Is it just a token thing that we send her to Miss Universe? Or are we serious about vying [for] and winning that competition?" They compared the territory's approach to that taken in Venezuela, which goes all out to support its representative.[1]

The comparison with Miss Venezuela was not accidental, as contestants from that country are surrounded by a slick and very public production apparatus.

Venezuela is notorious in the field of competitive pageantry, with professionals selecting, "preparing," and promoting women for the Miss Universe and Miss World
contests. That "preparation" includes advice for contestants about altering their
appearance in a myriad of ways, including plastic surgery.[2] Venezuela receives extensive attention because its contestants have recorded numerous victories in these
international contests. In spite of the emotional and physical costs to the country's
young women, the ends—including worldwide attention for the Caribbean and
South America as well as the individual payoffs for the young women involved—
often seem to justify the means.

The radio commentator's question about the purpose of Miss U.S. Virgin
Islands' participation thus struck at the heart of the contest's relevance for the
community at large and for the young women who participate. Ambiguity and
ambivalence particularly resonated here as members of the community weighed
for themselves and their listeners the material value of these pageants. In this chapter, I discuss one of the largest of the community's pageant-related issues: "Is the
pageant good for us?" I focus on preparation and training rituals as well as on the
people involved in the contestants' transformation and their stake in the industry.
I address the language used by the pageant and its organizers as they endeavor to
change a contestant into a new woman. This process repeats a movement from
raw to refined that the Caribbean has persistently negotiated since the beginning
of its colonial past. I use a narrative of the pageant's "chair treatment" to discuss
the function of criticism in the community and examine the effect of these manipulations on the bodies of black women in the territory as well as on their daily
behavior, sexuality, and appearance. Moreover, I examine what motivates women
of the community to participate in this machinery. Pageant participants in the
Virgin Islands offer an aesthetically diverse mixture of individuals and features
that results in the phenomenon that winning internationally is not necessarily a
goal. This internal focus and interplay sets the Virgin Islands apart in its aesthetics, values, and resultant political positions. In addition, the pageants are classed
events, run by individuals of a certain class who espouse the values of that class,
yet both class and shade can be irrelevant to the final outcome. Finally, despite its
profusion, pageantry is but one option that offers Caribbean women the kind of
visibility they have enjoyed since the end of colonialism.

IDEAS AND ISSUES

On February 25, 1999, Claire Roker, one of the architects of the modern queen
show in the Virgin Islands, flatly stated, "We do not choose women who can win
on the international stage." She elaborated, "If we see they are picking women

over five [feet], nine [inches tall]," then it does not make sense to "send some-one five [feet] three [inches]."[3] Roker suggested that pageant organizers observe the patterns of international winners and then find representatives who have the potential to triumph in those contests. Roker knows whereof she speaks, having clearly found a formula that works. Her Talented Teen Pageant has produced five international winners, but other Virgin Islands contests apparently have not taken this approach. As the outcomes indicate, winning internationally is clearly not the priority of local pageants. The community measures both local and international concerns, but local conceptions of success and womanhood outweigh interna-tional preferences.

The Virgin Islands' current lack of conformity with U.S. and European stan-dards is consistent with the contentions of those who declare that the territory has and abides consistently by its own values, whatever they may be. Local queens have always come from throughout the territory's broad, variable, and unclear range of notions of blackness and femininity, making each pageant a wide-open competition. Though time to prepare may remain a factor for some pageant orga-nizers and those wishing for outside recognition, winning internationally is more of an issue of aesthetic choices based on physical values. The conflict between local tastes and international success is palpable. The community is clearly aware of the winning attributes of international contestants but nevertheless makes choices that conflict with those attributes, illustrating the ways in which this island com-munity negotiates the conflict, often by sticking to its guns and celebrating its own values despite the international costs. The process of embracing the performances on local stages in spite of the standards of the day has been established too long for the community to return to any pretense of taking on white European images. This locally situated aesthetic adherence frees Virgin Island audiences and per-formers to create, perform, and enjoy locally crafted, hybridized performance in its many forms despite the dictates of international contests or schedules.

When Forde attempted to answer callers' questions regarding the prepara-tion of contestants, he added queries of his own: What impact does the pageant have on the community? What impact does it have on the contestants? Winners? Losers? And what demands does it place on families? Finally, Forde asked, "Is it good for the community?"[4] This issue persistently haunts many of the territory's pageants. The general consensus is yes, and organizers automatically answer in the affirmative, insisting in practiced language that pageants respond to a variety of needs, including the need for fund-raising for civic and social events.

One caller to *Ideas and Issues* expressed the belief that the Lions Club uses the event as a fund-raiser instead of as a platform to send a representative to Miss Universe. The club does not deny this accusation, which insinuates that the group's intentions are myopic and self-serving, seeking to provide mere entertainment rather than nation building. The caller described contestants from other countries (especially those in South America) as having their entire nations behind them, unlike the Virgin Islands. Lions Club officials called the radio show to defend themselves, arguing that the business community does not financially support the contestants, claiming lack of money. When Miss Virgin Islands travels to the Miss Universe competition, she lacks the entourage that accompanies most contestants and instead has only a skeleton crew. Another participant in the discussion wondered aloud whether the territory's plethora of contests contributes to the problem: Given the Virgin Islands' limited resources, how could the community possibly support all of the shows? In his view, small businesses receive a relentless stream of solicitors and "can't help everyone." Forde agreed, stating that every school and organization in the territory hosts a pageant.[5]

Other commentators on the show wondered about parental motivations for entering their daughters in pageants. The financial (and other) demands on parents are no doubt considerable: a Carnival Queen contestant can spend between five and eight thousand dollars on a dress. Forde suggested that the amount contestants are allowed to spend on clothing might be limited in the interest of alleviating economic hardship and leveling the playing field for those who cannot afford such expenditures.[6] But the realities of pageant competition in the Virgin Islands dictate a very different approach, one consistent with productions in sister islands and South America: all-out family and community excitement and involvement, whatever the financial costs. In this way, many communities embrace the spectacle of pageantry. Young women who cannot afford thousand-dollar dresses show initiative in garnering individual sponsorships as well as small-business support, a key determinant of their chances of winning. These individuals' presence and stories bring excitement to the shows and ratchet up the public's literal and figurative investment. Community support assists in building the audience, enthusiasm, and participation. Organizers play on this phenomenon when they insist that the community in general desires this kind of entertainment.

Forde also suggested that men support the contests because they offer an opportunity to view beautiful women.[7] This point of view demonstrates the strength of the heterosexual imperative in the Caribbean communities. However, multiple sexualities function within any given moment and enterprise, in the islands or anywhere, and sexual orientation is an important element of pageant production, not only among participants but also among advisers and audience.

Gay culture in the Caribbean is very controversial, with the presence of homosexuals often unacknowledged, and that community in many cases is fiercely underground.[8] Gay men are a troublesome presence in a region that touts its staunch heterosexuality, while the lesbian community is extremely submerged and functions with its own codes, as in many metropolitan areas. The orbit of pageantry in the islands includes an accepted and embraced place for homosexual men, however, meaning that Forde's comment does not truly reflect the pageant world. Although many straight men undoubtedly attend pageants with their partners, they are not the most influential presence. This sphere offers an unspoken acknowledgment and acceptance of the gay men who actively support this enterprise, providing a flair and splendor that the heterosexual world does not openly acknowledge. Thus, the gay male presence is expected and respected yet closeted. Not only are most participants (organizers, contestants, and their advisers) female, but most of those who attend are women. This is a community of women. As a result, the radio discussion seemed like an attack on the women who ran the pageant.

But the fact that the Miss U.S. Virgin Islands competition was held just a month before the Miss Universe contest was not solely the fault of pageant organizers. Several months earlier, two of the four contestants had backed out for personal reasons, requiring organizers to scurry to find new candidates or cancel the 1999 competition and allow the 1998 champion, Leah Webster, to reign for two years. But Webster would not have been eligible to compete in the 1999 Miss Universe pageant, which was being held in May in Trinidad, a location Virgin Islands organizers saw as offering a not-to-be-missed advantage for their candidate. According to Deborah Gottlieb, Lions Club pageant chair, club members decided to undertake an emergency recruitment effort.[9]

FROM RAW TO REFINED

After a few more false starts involving the withdrawal of contestants, the first rehearsal was scheduled for one o'clock on the afternoon of January 31 at Local Bodyz, a downtown St. Thomas health club. When I arrived, however, the place was locked, and no one was there. I called the Lions Club headquarters and learned that the meeting had been canceled because the pageant was again down to three contestants. Rehearsals were pushed back another week in hopes that another woman could be found. Pageant organizers, who had seemed willing to proceed with three contestants a few weeks earlier, had now decided that four were necessary to attract a substantial audience. The title of Miss U.S. Virgin Islands apparently no longer commanded significant power, or the level of scrutiny it required was chasing contestants to other pageants with fewer expectations and lower profiles. The Carnival Queen and Miss Big and Beautiful pageants, for example, may attract more entrants because they have fewer postcoronation expectations and do not require participation in subsequent international contests. According to Gottlieb, pageant organizers had lined up sponsors who had agreed to provide contestants with whatever was needed but still could not find four willing contestants from among the territory's population of more than one hundred thousand.[10] Gottlieb's statement contradicts the subsequent complaints offered on *Ideas and Issues* that financial backing for contestants was lacking.

In the following days, Lions Club members ventured to St. Croix and found Lynda Ortiz. Rehearsals finally began, enacting the restyling of womanhood. Island women move from raw to refined, or, as one highly visible coach said, the "mannish" behaviors of the "girls" get softened. Mannish or coarse behavior meant that these young women lacked training in "natural grace" in social settings. Their dealings with others, public speeches, or appearance would telegraph their class status. They might overtly express their sexuality in public, perhaps exposing more of their bodies than would be acceptable in middle- and upper-class environments. Alternatively, they might outfit themselves or move or behave in ways that betray something other than clearly identifiable heterosexual mannerisms, confirming their membership in "undesirable" groups.

REHEARSAL, FEBRUARY 6, 1999

The rehearsal was supposed to start at one o'clock but did not begin until about fifty minutes later. One contestant was missing. The contestants were informed that the show's theme would be "The Essence of the Caribbean." The choreographer suggested a boxing theme. The members of the organizing committee decided against a variety show and in favor of having one or two vocalists, thereby giving the audience "a chance to think."

After reviewing the schedule, Utha Williams, Miss U.S. Virgin Islands pageant consultant and trainer for many of the territory's young pageant contestants, lined the four women up to see what order would work best, taking into account the various women's heights and preferences. The committee determined the order, which would then remain unchanged. The contestants reviewed the basic standing position, with one foot at a forty-five-degree angle to the other. Williams claimed that this "position stance" gives the legs the advantage of looking "curvaceous and graceful," with "the front leg . . . framed by the back." She taught them how to change position and maintain position stance. She also suggested that the contestants lean their torsos backward after taking the pose and advised, "What direction you face is determined by focus—where it needs to be." Williams offered these tips from a little black book that she began keeping when she attended finishing school in New York and St. Thomas many years earlier. Conversation then turned to the Miss America pageant, held the night before. Following that example, the Virgin Islands contestants should look alert and be attentive, "stand like a lady and be graceful." The regal Williams urged the four Virgin Islanders to follow her example, using lift and carriage, and to take on stage personae, keeping their heads, eyes, and focus up: "Make eye contact around the audience. Look like a queen. Smile."[11]

The contestants took turns practicing walking, although Lynda Ortiz, the new-comber, looked on and did not participate. Carolyn Wattley was told to watch "her bounce"—the movement of her rear end. Sherece Smith received the same advice but with regard to her modeling affectations. The contestants received constant coaching: "Coming out of a turn, control, pivot, get heels up off the ground, make the walk look interesting." Again referring to the Miss America pageant, Williams asked, "How much modeling did you see last night?" She discouraged the inclination to flourish, advising against walking with hands on hips and suggesting instead that the women walk, pivot, and then place their hands on their hips. The women should "think poise at all times," a mantra that could simultaneously remind and convince. They should take small steps so that they did not end up stopped with their legs apart, and they should maintain "control at all times." The bouncy walk should be reserved for the swimsuit segment, but only the legs should move. The contestants should tone their bodies so that their flesh did not move as they walked. Williams also advised, "Don't be in such a hurry. Hold the pauses a little longer. Get control over those turns." She asked the women, "When you make your first appearance, how do you want the audience to see you? Full front? Or on an angle?" All moves should be planned, practiced, and under control. There was no room for the accident of just being. There was no such thing.[12]

That the pageant includes such training implies that the women's current state is insufficient both for them and for outsiders. Participation indicates a willingness to submit to the pageant's values and rigor and a general distaste for their prior state of being. The language of the training sessions betrays a disturbingly sexist outlook that resonates with earlier colonial portrayals of black women as unfeminine.

"Mannish" behaviors could indicate a contrary power relation that accords women a substantial amount of agency in a society whose values do not depend on Victorian notions of femininity. If black femininity depended less on woman as an attractive showpiece but rather was derived from her ability to maneuver through her material conditions and make a life for herself, might her characteristics be different? If her physicality were accepted as portraying the ways in which her life functioned rather than as denying her life's actualities, might her movement signal something else? In other words, if her body were muscular and taut because of the work she did, would she need to disguise it to appear soft? Is the alleged mannishness connected to labor and labor to class? Who has the privilege of hiring out their labor rather than doing it themselves? In a global culture where going to the gym and having a hard body is the desired physique and it is impossible to distinguish those who work out from those who work, is the hiding of the evidence of labor's effect on the body an antiquated and colonial position? Are the "mannish" behaviors ascribed to many black women associated with lower-class status? Heterosexuality? Homosexuality? What exactly is "mannishness"?

Why is a bouncing rear end a problem? Does an uncontrolled bounce indicate a freedom that is not appropriate for a woman, much less a black woman? In the post-1960s terrain, might an ass bounce—so revered during carnival and reviled elsewhere—be a defining yet controversial feature of a black femininity? In other words, is it all about the ass? In this context, are *poise* and *charm* synonyms for controlling that ass and that mouth? The power of the rear end is clearly visible in the body of the classic Caribbean female figure of a large-bottomed and dark-skinned woman in a straw hat who sells fruits and vegetables at market. The ass historically symbolizes health and fortitude. A woman with a healthy ass had an appetite and could clearly cook, a highly revered skill in Caribbean culture. Nowhere is the Caribbean mythology of the ass more noted than in the Jamaican Nanny of the Maroons figure, whose rear end was the focus of resistance against British troops in the 1700s.[13] Nanny's ass reportedly caught bullets aimed at the guerrillas of the Jamaican mountainside, protecting her people. She thus came to symbolize black resistance. This tale is believed to have been crafted by defeated and shamed British soldiers and was designed to humiliate the Jamaican public. However in true Caribbean/black style, the image of this woman was reappropriated from a shameful figure to one of power.[14]

While the mammy-like image of Nanny might not immediately capture the European-influenced imagination as a figure of desire, the ways in which hypocritical representations of this figure are at odds with history's record of the mammy's relations within the white household have been discussed at length.[15] She was clearly desirable and was often desired by the master of the house, who fathered many children by his black servants. She adhered to Caribbean values of health and solid bearing. Thus, while the image of the classic Caribbean woman may be a classed vision of black womanhood in the region, she also has become an iconic symbol. This woman of power and mystery, of earthiness and health, plays an important role in the community's basic needs and economics. She is a vital figure in Caribbean family life and its historic realities of commerce. And her sexuality becomes clear when local women chide one another about a "maaga" (meager or thin) woman's lack of desirability by claiming, "Only a 'daag' want bone" (only a dog wants a bone). A good heterosexual man wants a woman with some flesh to hold onto.

What does it mean in a Caribbean context to "have poise at all times?" Is poise the maintenance of composure in the face of the proverbial British troops? Is poise lifting one's skirt at the right moment to save the farm? Is poise the antidote to mannishness, knowing when and when not to let that ass bounce? In the same ambiguous fashion as identity politics, "poise" and "mannish" behavior become characteristics young women must adopt and avoid, respectively. They are the raw and the refined products of very complicated pasts. In perhaps less of a project of colonial regression and more one of reparation of a damaged image, these practice sessions may be training young Caribbean women to move and speak multilingually, to function on a number of levels as they advance within a global economy ill designed to accommodate their black bodies and tongues.

MOLDING AND SHAPING

The pageant advisers' lessons appear in the words and bodies of contestants after they move to the contest stage. Each of the contestants' introductory speeches contains a multitude of locally relevant issues. The contestants' language reflects the values instilled during the weeks of interfacing with the pageant's coordinators and etiquette advisers. Some of the women also hired or enlisted the help of image consultants or coaches, and they, too, played a part and developed a stake in the presentations. Hours before the show, those involved backstage learned to their astonishment that Sherece Smith and her team of coaches had rehearsed her promotional presentation more than a hundred times. This rumor caused both anticipation and fear among her competitors and created a sense of mystery and excitement about the upcoming performances. The transformation of the queen thus is no small feat. The trainers, coaches, and pageant organizers shine most when that transformation succeeds. When Carolyn Wattley took the stage on March 21, she symbolized the transformation from raw to refined. As the music swelled, the host introduced her, "standing at five feet four and a half inches tall, weighing in at 130 pounds," and she approached the microphone and launched into her speech:

> This crowd is obviously a TKO. Good afternoon, ladies and gentlemen, I stand here bright and sparkling, bearing one of our finest native fruits, island hospitality. On March 4, 1975, a very rare and beautiful gem was born on St. Thomas to Viola Wattley. She knew this gem must be forever cherished. Being exposed to our lovely tropical climate, this gem was smoothed by the force of rushing tides, burnished bright by our sun's rays, and cooled by trade winds. After twenty-four years of polishing, bursting with brilliance and beauty, I present myself to you today, an essence of the Caribbean. I am presently

studying business and psychology. Experience gained in these fields will allow me to fulfill my dream of opening an institute of hospitality and culture to help young Virgin Islanders recapture our proud heritage. At this time, I would like to thank my sponsors and my family: Leder Construction Company, Images in Paradise, Frank's Bakeshop, and Edie's Plumbing. Ladies and gentlemen, this proud Virgin Islands gem standing before you is contestant number 2, Carolyn Wattley.

According to Wattley, her refinement came from years of polishing by the natural forces of the Virgin Islands, not from the machinations of the legions of pageant professionals. She acknowledges a transformation but does not recognize the training of the Miss U.S. Virgin Islands pageant as the agent of that change.

The socializing process in which she has taken part appears in her self-identification for the audience. She locates her broader self with proof of her political savvy, gesturing toward the business of hospitality and its relation to tourism, both of which are inevitably connected to heritage. She discusses the need for Virgin Islanders to "recapture" their heritage, signaling the loss of history and cultural practice and taking up a familiar refrain in the Virgin Islands sociopolitical repertoire. Yet the specificity of the historical project of recuperation and retrieval remains unclear. For what moment in history do Virgin Islanders pine? A prevailing political positioning codes the encroachment of technology and the social conduct of contemporary youth as negative influences on Virgin Islands progress. Virgin Islanders are encouraged to move both forward and backward as they simultaneously embrace both the culture of their past, which seems to be disappearing with every technological advance, and the progress that promises fortune and global sophistication. The project of recuperation becomes a euphemism for black pride and a political positioning of the pro-native. At the same time, proponents of cultural recuperation acknowledge the need for a business approach to the territory's economic woes. Wattley's performance demonstrates the completion of her transformation from raw to polished and her accompanying intellect and cultural consciousness. She molds herself into her idea of the model contestant with the aid of her sponsors. These business connections provide the means through which contestants put together their performances, allowing them to enlist appropriate and often expensive coaching and the gear that adorns a winner.

April Petrus molded herself in the same manner as Wattley. Petrus, too, seeks to provide greater service to the community, and her introduction demonstrates these manipulations of language and peoples. Like the other contestants, Petrus was accompanied by a ring boy, and again the announcer opened with her vital statistics, declaring that she was "standing five feet, eight and a half inches tall, and weighing in at 140 pounds." After the crowd settled, Petrus began her piece:

From the American paradise and capital city of the United States Virgin Islands, Charlotte Amalie, St. Thomas, is the confident, gracious, diligent, and insightful future commissioner of education, Señorita April Petrus. As a Spanish instructor at the Ivanna Eudora Kean High School, I mold, I shape, I nurture, I advise, and I instruct tomorrow's leaders. In keeping with my philosophy of service before self, I function as an adviser for a myriad of clubs and activities on the Kean High campus. I am a member of the American Federation of Teachers and the Delta Sigma Theta Sorority Inc. As I anxiously await the fall, I will be completing a master of arts degree in administration and supervision. Special thanks to the Almighty; my parents, Raymond and Angela Petrus; my sponsors, Varlack Ventures and Hair for You; and all of my family, friends, and supporters. Ladies, gentlemen, and judges, the essence of the Caribbean is here with you today as I, April Petrus, contestant number 4, wish you a pleasant evening filled with five rounds of nonstop action. I thank you.

Petrus offered the shortest comments of all the contestants, but her words included "I mold" and "I shape." She reappropriated the language used in the contest and by pageant organizers as they discuss its virtues in the islands and elsewhere. This is the adopted language of insufficiency, of change. Petrus reproduced the language of the colonial relationship with the Caribbean, a relationship in which the region has historically been seen as a supplier of raw materials, as fodder for colonizers to refine, reimagine, and reshape in accordance with their desires. This colonial image of the islands was impressed on the native culture in the modular fashion described by Benedict Anderson and Partha Chatterjee. A critical function of imperialism is the creation of a crowded space that leaves no room for alternative imaginings.[16] This language indicates the transformation of women in this arena from unfinished to finished, unpolished to polished. It is perpetually used with regard to the shift of young island women from something indistinct, raw, or "mannish" to something refined and ladylike, portraying class, upbringing, and sophistication.[17] Petrus reproduced this language in the context of the minds and attitudes of the children in her care; they, like she, will be socialized to believe in the virtues of this kind of transformation. In keeping with her references to the importance of education and change, she demonstrates her worldliness and the territory's ethnic complexity as she adeptly uses Spanish, the language of neighboring Puerto Rico. Petrus thus acknowledged the important relationship between the Virgin Islands and its sister North American colony. Her use of Spanish also offered a nod toward the significant Puerto Rican community in St. Croix and the notable French presence in St. Thomas. Her language capabilities indicate the multifunctionality that Virgin Islanders previously had to invoke as they negotiated the many nations bumping up against one another in the territory. Both Wattley and Petrus not only practiced language for the pageant but were politicians in training, reaching out to their diverse constituencies. Although women generally do not choose to run in these pageants as a step on the road to a future political career, pageants nevertheless seem to provide women with an avenue into a political life. Rehearsing the presentation of their political selves, contestants demonstrate their grasp of the sound bite, the snippet of information that is intended to bind and win fans yet that reveals little.

Petrus's short introduction contains all of these expressions of change and class. Pageant language has tremendous power with regard to change and contestants' internalization of the values of "training" women of the territory to become more "ladylike." Organizers hope that the training manifests itself in contestants' every move throughout their lives, emphasizing not simply pageant training but life training. The watchful eye that Utha Williams asks the young women to employ—to criticize themselves before others can critique them—is a basic tenet of female-homosocial relations. Williams steps it up to institutional level. Her careful guidance underpins a new womanhood.

SEX, HAIR, AND THE QUEEN

Contestants receive directions that enable them to begin their journey toward refinement, toward the possibility of representing the Virgin Island woman. Why must they then be trained? Because pageants are statements not about who the Virgin Island woman is but about who she can be. These are contests about potential rather than expressions of any "natural" condition. Even the losers in the competition are transformed from raw material into polished women. Although pageant events do not explicitly use the word *common*, it can be used colloquially to refer to the everywoman or to imply a certain wanton sexuality or "low-class" behavior. I use the term to identify the everyday woman of the territory, although, in the Virgin Islands, sexual activity is something of an open secret.

Relations with the puritanical postures of the U.S. mainland are present yet are inconsistent with many local Virgin Islands behaviors. Virgin Islanders appear on the surface to have a relationship with sex and sexuality that is consistent with the prudery of its puritanical and colonial past, the truth is quite different. Islanders have sex, want sex, see sex, fight and sing about sex. It is an accepted and expected part of one's humanness and a privilege of adulthood. This attitude has led to a devastating situation in which the rate of HIV/AIDS infection is close to four times the U.S. average. The Virgin Islands have the fourth-highest rate of known HIV cases of all U.S. states and territories. The overall rate of HIV/AIDS in the Caribbean is second only to sub-Saharan Africa. In the Virgin Islands, the disease affects mostly middle-aged persons, because campaigns to encourage condom use and other preventive measures have been targeted primarily at youth rather than at older people, including those who are married or in other long-term relationships. Middle-aged citizens' behaviors, among them the rejection of condom use, clearly bear much of the blame for the disease's aggressive spread in the territory. The stigma of HIV perpetuates secrecy and denial about both homosexuality and heterosexual activity. Many Virgin Islanders deny the connection between HIV and heterosexual activity or HIV and drug use. Moreover, the disease affects disproportionate numbers of women and the poor in the Virgin Islands.[18]

In this way, the concern with who participates in what kinds of activities enters the pageant arena. In 1999, the pageant did not explicitly address sexual or drug-related activity. The presumption seemed to be that this group of women were not the type to participate in drug-related activity, a classed conclusion. However, the young women remained the targets of strict sexual monitoring, though the broader reality in the community may well have been much different. Although Virgin Islanders may have to contend with the harsh realities of HIV, it does not lie at the forefront of the collective consciousness. Traditional notions of suggestive performance are still at work. Sexy behavior is embraced, but only under specific conditions. Bodily behaviors such as dancing allow for the open demonstration of the possibilities for sexual activity. But the Virgin Islands is not a community like its neighbors to the south, where "fio dental" (thongs as thin as dental floss) pervade at beaches and the scantily clad are celebrated. A certain modesty of dress is expected, and opportunities for sexual expression are circumscribed. Dances such as calypso, dance hall, and "blues" (slow rhythm and blues tunes) set the stage for sensual or sexual expression,[19] yet pageant organizers attempt to deny that opportunity to contestants.

According to Petra Maximay, a contestant in St. Thomas's 1998 Big and Beautiful contest, one of the most infuriating restrictions to which she and other participants were subjected was the ban on their attendance at "boat rides," when the island residents, most of them black, sail out into the harbor on a ship and dance to calypso and blues music. Organizers deemed such activities "not a lady-like thing to do."[20] Contest organizers moralize behaviors and determine what quotidian cultural activities may be unfit events for potential queens. The drawing of such lines has always involved issues of class; for contestants from classes that embrace these behaviors, the pageant makes clear those distinctions. As a training ground for upward mobility, the contest imposes restrictions to which contestants must be willing to adhere.

These strictures eliminate the "rude gal," the carnival "mas dancer," and the "dance hall queen," women whose values or talents are explicitly based on their abilities publicly to demonstrate their sexual prowess. The pageant queen is the antithesis of this woman. She is not asexual but rather is, as Williams suggests, "in control." Upper-middle-class and elite women do not perform their sexuality in public. They indicate. Their dancing in public spaces offers a measure of sensuality. Where "wukkin up" or "goin' on bad" (explicit imitations of intercourse) might be the most obvious demonstrations of what a woman's hips and legs can do sexually, the "cultured" woman "wines," swaying her hips gently in a smooth figure eight or a circle. She gestures somewhat demurely toward sexual possibility, not allowing herself to get worked up, to *really* sweat. She remains cool, dignified, and controlled while demonstrating an obvious knowledge and valuing of calypso and its accompanying dancing. She is not trying to say that she is not a part of local culture but instead communicates that she knows it well and still can hint at the sexually knowledgeable woman who lies underneath her veneer, unleashed only under the most personal of circumstances.

Caribbean bodily practices constantly negotiate a multiplicity of meanings. The language of the pageant training seems to be saying that local womanhood, whatever its condition prior to the "official" handling, is somehow insufficient and that a refinement of the "raw material" is required to elevate young women's standing. Strong parallels exist between the production of a new and more serviceable womanhood and the treatment of other raw materials in the Caribbean for refinement and use by the U.S. mainland.[21]

Islanders offer very little resistance to this role and more often than not are grateful to play any part at all in the machinery of capitalism, thereby indicating their modernity and local participation in global matters. One of the few obvious examples of resistance is Rastafari's image of opposition to any form of colonial refinement. Rastafari embodies the raw—raw blackness, roots rock reggae, closeness to the earth, to the "authentic" nature of human existence, of origins and futures. According to eminent Caribbean novelist and historian George Lamming, "Rastafari has extended from a small and formerly undesirable cult into a dominant force which influences all levels of national life; and it has done so against formidable odds, political harassment and general condemnation. The Rastafari has dramatised the question that has always been uncomfortable in Caribbean history, and the question is where you stand in relation to your blackness."[22] As of 1999, no Rastafari woman had ever participated in the Miss U.S. Virgin Islands pageant. However, when asked about the participation of Rastawomen, pageant officials recalled one contestant who refused to relax her hair—black women's ultimate sign of resistance. For black women, hair has always been politicized. In Kobena Mercer's view, the handling of black women's hair has socialized it, "making it the medium of significant statements about self and society and the codes of value that bind them, or do not. In this way hair is merely a raw material, constantly processed by cultural practices which thus invest it with meanings and value."[23] This idea is consistent with the notion of the contestant herself as raw and invested with meaning once she is "processed" by the pageant proceedings. The manipulation of the hair, then, becomes a metaphor for the body of woman.

What a black woman does with her hair is emblematic of her political, spiritual, and personal choices. In the case of this contestant, organizers' proposed refinement of her raw material included the straightening of her hair. Although she successfully resisted, she also did not win the competition. I do not contend that her hairstyle or ideology, whatever her views regarding Rastafari or any other form of African-centered practice, prevented her from winning. However, this critique of the "raw" unrefined woman was embedded within my conversations with pageant officials. Contest personnel claimed that they did not disapprove of the look of her hair but that straightening it would make her tresses more "manageable," enabling her to change her routine, outfit, and look without the hassle of dealing with a bush of hair. Mercer reaffirms this position, noting that black women's hair functions as "a key ethnic signifier because, compared with bodily shape or facial features, it can be changed more easily by cultural practices such as straightening. Caught on the cusp between self and society, nature and culture, the malleability of hair makes it a sensitive area of expression."[24] Pageant organizers saw themselves as attempting to convince this young woman to become more "flexible," insisting that relaxing her hair would permit her the *freedom* to change her appearance. Simply put, her rawness was inconvenient. For her, in contrast, her hair served as her arena of expression and was nonnegotiable. As Deborah Grayson writes, "The choices black women make about hairstyle or body appearance often mean the difference between acceptance or rejection by groups and individuals."[25] In the pageant setting, the underlying aesthetic does not support hair that appears to be natural. Although Mercer contends that all hair endures a measure of artifice (meaning the manipulation of human hands), some forms of that artifice are not appreciated in the pageant context. And much to the chagrin of that contestant, the pageant's judges apparently agreed with the organizers that the winner needed to have the appearance of an entire body under control; an Afro, or hair that refused to be tamed in the conventional sense, did not meet the requirements for a queen.

Rastafari has its own queens, operating within the codes of another type of artifice. Rastafari queens, however, might relate to the pageant queens in the double coding of images and in the negotiation of their sexuality—that is, with visibility or the lack thereof and in terms of a specific kind of representation. According to Rastawoman Maureen Rowe, the Rastafari queen achieves her position by "occupying a pedestal which precludes sexuality. She is separated from her sexual nature and becomes almost a religious icon and cultural role model. This makes it possible for the Rastaman to have at least two women, one fulfilling bodily sexual needs and the other cultural/spiritual. The rigid dress code prescribed for Queen contrasts radically with the flexibility allowed the Other woman; for example loose skirts that conceal the body versus fashionable tight jeans that reveal all."[26] Rowe exposes Rastafari's internal ambiguities, its persistent conditions of gender bias and double standards. Yet Rastafari's inconsistencies are no less complicated than any other group's, particularly in relationship to women's responsibilities and representations. As Rastawoman becomes "empress" or queen, she takes on the position of cultural role model, a role that is often at odds with a vibrant and visible sexuality. Both in the Rastafari community and on the pageant stage, the elevation of woman to the pedestal of queen *contains* her potential power. Despite the differences in expression, both communities suppress woman's power. The double coding of madonna/whore disallows woman's fullness as a sexual being while holding her up as the emblem of powerful femininity and keeper of culture. As Maximay discovered with regard to the boat rides, a woman cannot be both a queen contestant and a commoner. She cannot express her sexuality yet simultaneously be upheld as a model for the territory. Why not? Woman is separated from her sexual (threatening) nature. The beauty pageant requires that only married women have sexuality. Only under such circumstances can the sexually active woman be held up as an exemplar of righteousness and respectability. But by the time she achieves the coveted title of Mrs., her sexual potency is less of an issue. The salvaging of her virginal appearance is unnecessary. Women in the Mrs. Virgin Islands pageant are, for the most part, participating to prove their continuing sexual vitality, a stark contrast from the motives of the younger set.

Standard queen shows require contestants to be between the ages of sixteen and twenty-one. They must never have been married and have no children, and they must be "presentable" and "easy to train" and "mold." In the words of one pageant official, they go in raw and come out, "well, something else."[27] There is the guise of the virginal, the pure, and of course the heterosexual. The foregrounding of these positions demonstrates the operation of these systems of monitoring and influencing women's behaviors. Women in this community usually bear children relatively early in life, with the process of becoming a mother historically and culturally serving as the initiation process that accords the title of "woman" or adult. This may be one of the cultural reasons why condom use is less favored than health professionals recommend. While class differences play some role, the culture as a whole still encourages young women to bear children. Therefore, finding childless contestants has always posed a challenge. Rejecting traditional practices that originated in a once solidly agricultural community, contests require young women to embrace another model, promising that that model offers the greatest chances for material and social success. Island communities that embrace pageants apparently have adopted the puritan American attitude—in some regard, at least publicly—toward the unions between men and women. Nevertheless, with these issues of rawness and sexuality versus refinement and chastity at the center of the values of the queen pageant machinery, those who choose to enter the contest arena and those who see themselves outside it are affected by similar regulating systems, though in very different ways. This phenomenon offers a measure of business at work—that is, the business of (re)shaping female behavior—that takes teams of individuals and organizations persistently pursuing and policing one another in the interest of a good show. Local women respond by adopting or refuting "beautiful," "acceptable," "womanly" behavior, receiving and transmitting these messages both implicitly and explicitly. Women are encouraged to make their hair (and thus themselves) more manageable. Women are admonished for dancing in the streets. Women are told to bleach their elbows and knees to remove evidence of hard work. Women are drilled in the ways of walking, sitting, standing, and discussing themselves and other relevant issues in ways that simultaneously say something and very little. "Poise," that quality pursued by the pageant and its contestants as offering access to social and economic mobility, becomes a symbol of superficiality, of form without content. For a people who have historically been judged superficially, "poise" becomes an idea evacuated of substance. What, then, are they rehearsing? The answer is *control*.

SITTING PRETTY

Fascinated Europeans of the Victorian era viewed the African body as lascivious in its abandon, promiscuous in its articulation of hips, and in desperate need of control. The measures to do so were and often still are implemented by the church, legislative bodies, and internalized attitudes of sectors of the populace that seek to appear "civilized" and cultured and thus adopt and adhere to these limited perceptions of their behaviors. As these biased interpretations of the movement of the black body have been internalized, the perceived need for control has manifested itself in a variety of public settings, including the pageant. Control is the central issue that pageant organizers impart to contestants and that women are required to incorporate into their behaviors and values. Control of the unruly black female body begins within the rehearsal process, when many contestants receive what is benignly called the chair treatment. Each contestant sits in a chair facing her competitors, who critique her appearance. According to Utha Williams, this stage of training helps contestants realize how they appear to others and thus aids them in determining what they need to take care of before they leave home. In Williams's words, "Once people know you are a contestant, they will look to find fault," holding women to a higher standard. There is an expectation of difference. And, she argues, "You need to look at yourself with a critical eye before others do."²⁸

Open criticism and commentary based on appearance is a common practice in the Virgin Islands, a national pastime. It forms part of the regulatory system designed to check members of the community and thereby avoid a collapse of the social contract. The practice is learned from the early stages of childhood and serves both defensive and offensive purposes. Skill in deflecting or responding to outward criticism is a community value in the Virgin Islands. Such criticism is seen as sharpening the mind, even though feelings can be hurt in the process, and as creating a defensive system that is particularly visible in women's postures and attitudes. Nowhere are backs as stiff or gazes held as high as in the Caribbean, where stature might well deflect the barrage of appearance-related comments. The queen shows heighten this feature of local culture to magnificent proportions. In this context, Williams believes, her approach represents the only sensible strategy, teaching the contestants to evaluate themselves before others do so and find flaws. Williams calls this chair treatment "constructive criticism." Others call it something else.²⁹

Sherece Smith, for example, called it the "firing squad," reflecting her apprehension regarding the institutionalized version of a familiar practice, although the pageant version of this practice was relatively benign. One contestant was told that she had dark knees and that she should use bleaching cream to make them the same color as the rest of her legs. Other grooming issues that came under scrutiny included clothing, facial skin, the need for manicures and pedicures, eyebrows, and makeup. This segment made the contestants nervous, and they rushed to criticize themselves before others could do so. They tentatively offered mild commentary to one another. Smith told Ortiz to smile more when she speaks and to be less timid. Williams suggested that the women "start to match your maturity like a big young woman, not like a teenager." She accused them of holding back their smiles and urged them, "Let it out."³⁰

Other coaching involved the correct ways of approaching and occupying a chair. Each woman should use her peripheral vision, turn so that her back leg touches the edge of the chair, and then sit on the edge and slide gently back. Her feet should remain in the position stance, crossed at the ankle, or side by side, but legs should not be crossed—that position is too casual. Wattley was told that her feet were crossed but her legs were wide open, and she responded that her thighs were large. No one had an answer for her—she had to figure out a solution on her own. The women were also advised to think in terms that would assist them on the stage, to say to themselves, "I am gliding across the stage with as much grace and poise as I can." They should conceive of themselves as selling not what they are wearing but who they are, their personality. The women were also directed to walk lightly, to avoid letting mistakes show on their faces, to break behavioral practices, to think about how they want others to see them and then to behave accordingly. They learned how to "work the microphone," to practice speaking with assurance and maintain eye contact with the audience and judges.[31]

They were also advised to keep up with current events, both national and regional, by reading newspapers so that they could answer questions in sound bites with some meat. Finally, advised Williams, they should think about commercials: "Sell the VI to someone who does not know about us. And the last thing before you leave the stage, smile."[32]

Many of these suggestions involve training the women in a European aesthetic, in a kind of gentility. At the same time, Williams and other pageant officials also worked to instill one of the critical qualities of a black aesthetic, what Robert Farris Thompson has dubbed the aesthetic of the cool. They are guided to move without impact ("so you cannot be heard"), to prevent mistakes from showing on their faces, to think and answer quickly and intelligently. Moreover, the contestants should practice these behaviors so that they become second nature. If a mishap occurs onstage, the training will carry them through. While this aspect of the training can be interpreted as another controlling device meant to contain the power of the feminine, to harness the black body, and to suppress current (presumably flawed) behavior, it also physically enacts the creole condition. It mixes a minimum of two worlds, the African and the European. It demonstrates habits, customs, and values reflecting multiple origins and manifests in that laboratory of synthesis, the Caribbean.

Williams's words resonated when the Miss U.S. Virgin Islands contestants were invited to present themselves before St. Thomian audiences at the Miss Big and Beautiful pageant.[33] The show itself was quite disorderly but offered the four Miss U.S. Virgin Islands participants an opportunity to get a sense of what they were up against. Before a capacity crowd at the Reichold Center for the Arts, Miss Big and Beautiful presented the low end of contest spectacle. Despite its billing as an avenue for the appreciation of large-sized women, the contest attracted an audience that appeared more interested in seeing big women make missteps and toyed with the audience's voyeuristic curiosity. Audience members responded with expressions of pleasure and intrigue when a contestant slipped up, lost a shoe, forgot a line, or made any other kind of mistake. Contest organizers' decision to have the women appear not only in the standard swimwear but also in "loungewear/lingerie" played to the audience's voyeuristic tendencies. No other contest provides this kind of exposure in so many categories. Under the guise of "appreciation," the Big and Beautiful contest repeatedly offered the audience opportunities to ridicule contestants. The Miss U.S. Virgin Islands contestants learned that the public would show them no mercy in the event that they made mistakes and that every word of Williams's advice had been intended to protect them. Their first public appearance helped them to understand fully, perhaps for the first time, what they needed to do to become serious competitors before the island public.

Smith and Petrus did well at Miss Big and Beautiful, appearing smooth and sharp and demonstrating that they would be the real contenders for the title of Miss U.S. Virgin Islands. Wattley, however, faltered, grimaced, and looked around behind herself—precisely the mistakes on which she had been corrected during rehearsals. Ortiz was nondescript.

DEVELOPING AN IMAGE

Despite Ortiz's lack of a statement at Miss Big and Beautiful, Rachel Riddle, a confident and large female presence in any room, believed that Ortiz might be a sleeper. The night before the Miss U.S. Virgin Islands show, Riddle described "St. Croix," as she called Ortiz, as exuding personality, an attribute the other three contestants lacked. Ortiz had the least technical support among the contestants, and Lions Club organizers were running around town to take care of her. Riddle believed that despite Petrus's popularity, her only real asset was her smarts. Although she had previously been chosen Carnival Queen, Riddle thought that honor would be irrelevant in this setting because the two pageants look for different things. The judges who select the Carnival Queen look for voluptuousness and talent, she said; "You can study a dance for weeks and perform it at Carnival Queen pageant and win. It is not a sustained something. It is about flash and pizzazz, a one-shot explosion. This is different." In Riddle's view, Smith had what the Miss U.S. Virgin Islands judges were looking for—she had been well trained and her ease and personality *seemed* natural—but lacked what Ortiz had naturally.[34]

Smith's history demonstrates the importance of training in the polishing process. By the time of the 1999 competition, Smith was a veteran pageant entrant and winner, selected as Miss St. John Princess in 1982 and Miss St. John in 1989 and a contestant for Miss American Virgin Islands (the franchise that takes its contestants to Miss World)—in short, a recipient of numerous periods of training. To a much greater extent than any of the other 1999 Miss U.S. Virgin Islands contestants, she had had a career in pageants. The winner of the 1998 Miss U.S. Virgin Islands competition, Leah Webster, had a similar résumé. Both women not only had the benefit of a succession of pageants in which to refine their approaches but also had winning teams of support personnel, using professional image consultants to help them reach their ultimate goal. A friendly coach to make dress and talent recommendations is no longer enough, given the high stakes of pageantry, its enormous costs, and the once-in-a-lifetime opportunities it offers.

Two of the 1999 Miss U.S. Virgin Islands contestants, Smith and Wattley, enlisted high-powered consultants, while Ortiz was probably the least prepared. A teenage friend—knowledgeable but by no means a seasoned adviser—came from St. Croix to assist with her makeup. Petrus had the casual help of family and a few friends, but she too lacked hired help. Smith and Wattley, in contrast, pulled out the big guns. Wattley obtained the help of the flamboyant William "Champagne" Chandler, holder of numerous Carnival King of the Band titles and a successful pageant contestant on his own. In 1996, Chandler was selected Mr. Virgin Islands (taking home the Mr. Popularity and Mr. Photogenic awards at the competition) and was a semifinalist for Mr. USA. During rehearsals, Chandler and his mostly gay male entourage freely shouted suggestions to Wattley and comments about other contestants, offering advice on all facets of her attire and presentation.

Smith went even further, employing two professional advisers. The first, Riddle, was also overseeing the participation of another young woman in the Carnival Queen competition; with the end of the Miss U.S. Virgin Islands pageant, she would devote her full attention to that contest. Riddle had already managed the successful candidacies of numerous women in other contests in the territory. Coaching a series of pageant winners becomes a badge of honor for coaches and image consultants, the stuff of which reputations are made. Many coaches do not charge fees for their services, so the reputation is often the payoff. Riddle served as Smith's mover and shaper, attending all rehearsals and helping Smith rehearse her presentation seventy-one times between midnight and four o'clock in the morning on the night before the contest. According to Riddle, Smith learned to behave as though every practiced move were hers naturally. "Natural" became a studied condition, one in which the coach was expert. The artifice of Smith's presentation—what Mercer terms the "agency of human hands"[35]—created an illusion of natural countenance.

Smith's second adviser, Lorna Webster, a self-described image consultant and the mother of Leah Webster, is a dress designer who also has a reputation for crafting pageant winners. Lorna Webster is selective about the clients she takes on; she designed Smith's dress and accessories but was otherwise invisible. According to Webster, she follows a simple formula: When young women approach her, she determines whether they are "trainable"—that is, whether they have the attitude of a winner. Webster's day job is as the director of corporate registry in the Virgin Islands, and she also owns a clothing store and is a wedding planner. She became involved in the pageant world in the early 1980s as a consequence of her daughters' desire to participate. She sees her image consulting work as a public service, similar to her talks to children about careers, personal hygiene, and the benefits of "being positive." She believes that such efforts build and reveal character and encourages her charges to follow this path. Webster's daughters assist her pageant work, serving as speechwriters for her contestants.[36]

Webster has at times become so involved in the process of grooming contestants that she arranges to have them live with her and her family. There, the young women become immersed in the culture of the elite, living the role they are learning to play. This tactic works toward the goal of making a contestant's "naturalness" the kind of behavior consistent with an upper-middle-class aesthetic. The contestant becomes an intern in her own progress toward upward mobility. Webster insists that this process helps build self-esteem and character, and when contestants cannot find the necessary environment at home, she will provide it, making her home into a training ground.[37] While her tactics may be more extreme than those used by other image consultants, the basic premise is not.

Like Webster and Riddle, Chandler has coached numerous pageant winners. The director of a modeling agency, Roses and Champagne, he argues that the involvement of specific coaches, chaperones, and image consultants enhances the drama and draws audiences to contests, providing an admixture of "excitement," "entertainment," and "enjoyment—you know all of that is going to be in there."[38] Chandler thus exposes the multiple levels of the competition, which go far beyond the young women in front of the curtain to include those behind the scenes, whose reputations are at stake and who are competing as well.

Chandler is one of the few consultants who admits to receiving a fee for his advice. He often does not request a specific amount but instead asks his client to select a sum. Fees range between five hundred and a thousand dollars, sometimes more, depending on the importance of the contest and on his personal relationship with the contestant. Chandler at times has coached as many as three contestants at once, but high-level competitions such as Miss U.S. Virgin Islands require private training. As demand increases, so do the fees. Chandler is motivated by the transformation he witnesses in the contestants he coaches, who go from girls in school uniforms to women "dressed up like dolls" onstage.[39] Chandler is fascinated by the trappings of queenship and its supplemental benefits, including celebrity status.

WHY DO THEY RUN?

Claire Roker seconds the importance of celebrity to the pageant equation in the Virgin Islands, declaring her belief that many girls and women are motivated to participate by the attention they receive "from parents and friends [and] even the wider public that they don't get elsewhere and perhaps crave."[40] However, the question of why women participate in pageants also generates many other answers, none of them quite satisfactory and all seemingly rote. Among the reasons cited by coordinators and general hangers-on are pageants' role in building self-esteem, decreasing shyness, and offering young ladies a debutante-like service. For example, one woman from Thomasville, an economically depressed area of St. Thomas, explained the participation of her obese fourteen-year-old daughter in a small pageant as a way not only to overcome her shyness but also to "gain self-esteem" and alter her relationship with others. According to the mother, other children had relentlessly teased the girl until she entered the local contest. Despite the family's poverty and the significant amount of money expended on the girl's participation in the pageant, her mother believed the experience to have been worth every cent.[41]

While such answers come easily and repeatedly from those in the pageant orbit, Roker's assessment might be most accurate. Beginning with the long-ago selection of carnival's calypso kings and queens, Virgin Islanders have been in love with royalty, willing to endure amplified scrutiny to gain amplified attention. And few conditions outside of pageants and political office offer women the opportunity to receive special attention or notice.

Celebrity and its accompanying visibility may serve as a veneer for submerged issues of empowerment or the lack thereof. Pageants assert a woman's presence within the communal space/communal imaginary in glamorous, glorious ways not present in the everyday conditions of island life. The purveyors of Virgin Islands pageant culture have always been women from sororities and social and civic organizations—in short, relatively powerful groups. Despite their fairly privileged status, they possess significant enough feelings of invisibility within the culture to motivate them to produce spectacles that place young women at the forefront of the collective consciousness.

This invisibility within the culture is peculiar because numerous Caribbean women have achieved high social and political positions of power, becoming artists, activists, philosophers, medical professionals, and politicians as well as excelling in other fields. Even before the advent of universal suffrage in the Greater Antilles in the 1940s, women were politically active in their communities, as chapters 1 and 2 discuss.[42] And in the 1960s and 1970s, women played significant roles in the independence movements of many Caribbean nations. Yet although women have been a fixture in Caribbean politics and history, contemporary Caribbean gender imbalances are also renowned.

Women in the region have come to expect an amount of constant male attention that in other locales might well be construed as harassment. Women's daily demeanors become steeled against this attention, as they employ the body language and the protective stance Williams proffered as the first line of defense against the criticism that assaults women daily, an embodiment of the "tuffness" Gina Ulysse describes in Jamaican culture. According to Ulysse, the face must register "an impenetrable sneer or no expression at all. Chin is held up high. Shoulders are hoisted slightly and pushed back. Chest is forward. The walk is languid yet always with a sense of purpose. It is an attitude equivalent to a mask reinforced by a suit of steel."[43] This mask most often comes into use in the public sphere, where poor or working-class women must conduct their business. Middle- and upper-class women also use this mask as a defense against sexual attention, criticism, and/or ridicule in public settings, as protection against assault. It is part and parcel of the training Williams offers her contestants. While she uses the smile as a component of the mask, it nonetheless remains a mask, designed to offset the attentions that are part of being a highly visible figure.

If a mask is a necessary accoutrement in defending against a certain kind of visibility, what attention do contestants seek? Is it serious professional consideration? If so, why do Virgin Islands women use spectacle to exact additional exposure and acknowledgment? Are they playing into Peggy Phelan's "visibility trap"? In Phelan's view, visibility "summons surveillance and the law; it provokes voyeurism, fetishism, the colonial/imperial appetite for possession."[44] Voyeurism and fetishism were clearly issues in the Big and Beautiful pageant, where large women willingly presented themselves to multiple gazes, serving as objects of desire while satisfying the voyeuristic tendencies of an audience all too willing to participate in the contestants' unveiling. Women engage in contradictory stances by participating in these and other performative events that are hinged on sexuality/femininity and that expose those involved to voyeuristic gazes while touting an acknowledgment of power and beauty. This contradiction exists in all pageant performances, from toddler events to senior contests.

But why do women perpetuate such practices for audiences that primarily comprise other women? The answer seems to lie in the need for public performance and for a performance space that is for the most part theirs. This performance space does not deny or determine the exposing nature of pageants that has always made them controversial. Pageants generate this controversy because they expose competing bodies, reinforce classed aesthetic and moral values, and complicate the relationships between political and economic power and sexual and performative presences.

As pageants provide a sense of power and importance in society, they have real impact despite their status as a carnival event, outside the reality of everyday existence. In the Virgin Islands, the middle class remains suspicious of the idea of visual or performance art as a life's work, preferring traditional nine-to-five office work or dawn-to-dusk agricultural labor; queen shows, however, allow women to indulge their creative interests without incurring the stigma of being an "artist." Women can exist within more conservative local positions, dabbling in a "talent" in service of a tangible goal. These events have a defined beginning, middle, and end, unlike the instability of a career in the arts. Pageants give performance and art obvious practical functions and take limited amounts of time (at least for those satisfied with the realm of amateur performance). Thus, queen shows retain a certain political and practical appeal despite their seeming disconnection from reality. These practicalities—some of them purely personal and psychological— bear little connection to the benefits of pageants generally cited by organizers, consultants, and participants.

The mother of the obese girl had entered her in their local pageant for practical reasons, seeking to relieve her daughter's social stigma. And indeed, her participation had practical benefits, although it is not clear whether they were the benefits the mother had intended. For this family, visibility offered what Phelan proposes is one part of a complicated equation whereby "it is assumed that disenfranchised communities who see their members within the representational field will feel greater pride in being part of such a community."[45] Even though her daughter's participation did not assert any real power outside of the confines of her own small world, the girl's involvement gave this woman a feeling of connection to the island's larger pageant continuum, a sense that she was adhering to the values of those she deemed exemplary.

Critics might argue that larger pageants, too, relegate women to demi-worlds that have little or no greater social, spiritual, or political impact. By engaging themselves in this "pretend" world, women may divert themselves from efforts that could change material conditions. Visibility here might serve as a smoke screen for what is real, that elite and virtually untouchable world of which women such as the mother will likely never be a part. In this view, invisibility could have the potential for power in ways that visibility does not. This is not to say that existing under the radar is a powerful position or that women should be satisfied with less. Rather, in this instance, the visible is a manifestation of what is not. In Phelan's words, "What is not visibly available to the eye constitutes and defines what is—in the same way as the unconscious frames ongoing conscious events. Just as we understand that things in the past determine how we experience the present, so too can it be said that the visible is defined by the invisible. Or, as Marianne Moore puts it, 'The power of the visible / is the invisible.'"[46]

Power often operates invisibly. As Phelan points out, "If representational visibility equals power, then almost-naked young white women should be running Western culture."[47] Therefore, it follows, straight men of the Virgin Islands do not need pageants—they have power and thus do not need visibility. But this is not precisely true. The territory's historically established family and business relations have given women an independence that goes largely unrecognized. Their influence is subtle, however, less evident, at least on the surface, than that of their male counterparts. For this reason, the standard feminist critique of Caribbean female power is insufficient. The subtleties of women's performance of femininity and power must be examined through a more acute and culturally specific lens.

Many contestants and their families fiercely believe in the benefits of visibility. Pageant organizers warn potential contestants that they cannot turn back after entering this arena. Forever after, the community will judge these women as potential queens, holding them to higher standards than those used for common women. Moreover, the selection of Virgin Islands queens who do not fit the preferred model for international contest winners resists the model of visual representation dictated by European-influenced white dominance. Globally, therefore, the presence of Virgin Islands queens at competitions such as Miss Universe disrupts the white European norm. And locally, the pageants provide a reification not only of who the individual queen is but also of who the women of the territory are—a celebration of a local norm. Thus, while the pageant's training and refinement of young women may appear to undermine the notion of a norm embraced by the local community, the physical differences between Virgin Islands queens and those from other regions disrupt the conventions of European- and U.S.-dominated pageants. Refinement and an alteration of the common woman may be at work, and a level of "polish" is certainly associated with the middle- and upper-class performance produced by the Miss U.S. Virgin Islands contest, but the type of women involved and their acknowledgment (to whatever degree) of the culture are critical. The pageant's practicalities, functions, and relation to visibility serve as both a cure and a curiosity for many women in the community. Some women unquestioningly accept queen shows, while others resist or completely ignore them. Many women are ambivalent. Still others have entered that arena to investigate its mythical properties and have arrived at conflicted conclusions.

Chapter 7

AUDIENCE, APPETITES, AND DRAMA

The Mystery of Pageantry

Marise James was born and reared on St. Croix, the daughter of local celebrity Randall "Doc" James. After receiving her primary and secondary education at Catholic schools on the island—St. Mary's Elementary and St. Joseph's High School—she traveled to the United States and attended George Washington University in Washington, D.C. She initially intended to follow her father into the field of medicine but instead earned a bachelor of arts degree in zoology and then returned to St. Croix in 1979 to teach physical science, first at Elena Christian Junior High, then at Central High School and night school. In 1981, she decided to run for Miss U.S. Virgin Islands. After winning the competition, she parlayed her position as queen of the territory into a job in the Department of Tourism, one of the few pageant winners to do so. In 1986, she became a real estate attorney, and in 1999, when I interviewed her, she was forty-one years old and the owner of a school for paralegals. James had clearly done something right. Had her queenship assisted in her success? Why had she chosen pageant competition as part of her path? What had her contest experiences been, and what did she think of the enterprise in hindsight?[1]

My conversation with James provides a map for the terrain of this chapter as I explore why young women participate in pageants, why local audiences flock to these events, and what role drama (often provided by the judging) and scandal play in this formulation. Pageant audiences are fascinated by failure and the ever-present threat of a contestant's dramatic public downfall. Local communities' attachment and commitment to contests does not truly involve "beauty" but rather involves the pursuit of modernity and participation in a practice that keeps the territory both in internal dialogue and in conversation with other global societies.

Keeping up with economic and social currents represents an underlying theme of business machinations in the territory. Like many small nations, the Virgin Islands desires to be contemporary without losing itself. The changing interests of the pageant sphere have provided a vehicle for examining systems of power, economics, and social relations that impact the lives of Virgin Islanders of both sexes and both within and outside pageant doors.

The chapter opens by detailing two women's experiences with the Miss U.S. Virgin Islands pageant. I then move on to examine the value and location of contests in the collective imaginary, how such competitions provide participants at all levels with a form of women's theater, amateur performance, national sovereignty, and cultural pride.

GROWING UP WITH QUEENS

Queen shows are an indelible part of the Virgin Islands cultural landscape. James was first impressed by the Miss Talented Teen contest, attending from the time she was fourteen until she left for college, although she lost interest shortly after returning to the island. She watched as participating friends moved from these teenage contests to the Miss St. Croix pageant. Members of her family had never participated in the shows or been fans. When James decided to throw her hat in the ring, the members of her immediate family were not particularly supportive. They believed strongly in her intellect and objected to her placing herself in the position of beauty contestant. But she was tall—five feet, ten inches—and had always had an interest in modeling, and she had grown up with American magazines such as *Glamour* and *Seventeen*.

James made the move from avid watcher to participant after an aunt who owned a beauty shop suggested that she and a cousin try out a contest. She had played basketball in college and enjoyed the competition, and she consulted one of her friends, who agreed that she should try. James believes that she enjoyed the Miss U.S. Virgin Islands experience contest more than any of the other contestants because she never thought about winning but instead just wondered "What's this all about?" The other competitors, in contrast, "*had* to win. It was a life-and-death thing."

> Everything was riding on them winning. And they were competitive, very competitive. Now, I am competitive, but . . . I always felt, my winning this contest is based on somebody else's subjective view of me. . . . I always wanted to know why would somebody participate in a contest that I thought was really out of your control? Because it's subjective, very subjective. Unlike playing basketball,

where I put the ball in the hoop, and, you know, to a certain extent the referee has control. But not really. Because if you're playing according to the rules, you should win, and if you're more talented, more skilled. [In a track competition, if] you run across the line first, you're the winner. But with judges and beauty, how do you know what they want?

Subjectivity of judging is the beauty contest wild card, the X factor. On WSTA's *Ideas and Issues* radio show, commentator Terry Thomas noted, "There are a lot of hidden rules in a lot of pageants that people know exist."[2] Contest judging in the Virgin Islands has generated much debate, as power is wielded and futures are determined by a select group that enforces the image and aesthetic chosen by contest organizers.

JUDGING MISS U.S. VIRGIN ISLANDS

Marise James's point about judging is fundamental to pageant outcomes. The lack of an objective standard of judgment is the reason for audience excitement. Veteran consultant Lorna Webster believes "that pageants select judges to get the results they want. It's as simple as that. Yes, [the outcome] can be fixed, [but] a lot of times it doesn't always work out the way that [organizers] want it to."[3] The idea of impartial judges is espoused publicly but clearly is eschewed privately. Those involved in the contests generally believe that organizers "attempt" to be fair but also feel that countless factors—for example, class, skin shade, and family influence—affect the selection of a winner. Most participants, both onstage and behind the scenes, and audience members believe that pageants are inherently susceptible to corruption and are surprised and pleased when the outcome appears to be fair.

Pageant organizers' criteria for selecting judges may very well result in biases toward particular participants. Nevertheless, as Webster pointed out, the judges at times make unexpected choices. Judging is a complicated and contested endeavor both in the Virgin Islands and elsewhere, and numerous judging-related scandals have arisen. In Jamaica, judging controversies have reflected the island's long and troubled history of colonial race relations. According to Natasha Barnes, black women have been and remain marginalized in Jamaican pageants, suffering from judging biases that privilege European notions of beauty and that reflect general power dynamics in the society as a whole. In the 1940s and 1950s, Jamaican "beauty contests gave prizes to contestants judged as possessing the 'best eyes,' prizes that would never be awarded to anyone with brown or black eyes. Prize trips for winning queens habitually included destinations like Miami, Florida, a city that was vehemently Jim Crow at the time. Judges were often members of the island's political and business elites and were closely associated with the sponsors of the competition as well as with the contestants themselves."[4] And similar practices have persisted. In 1999, critics charged that one Jamaican pageant offered little chance for contestants with "an Afro appearance to win." Moreover, "class attitudes also prevail. Most of the contestants—and winners—are from the middle and upper class. Some are not even residents of the country."[5] Color and class status clearly undergird judging and contest outcomes Jamaica. The Virgin Islands case is much more nuanced.

Accusations of class bias among judges have been persistent among disappointed contestants, especially when poor but talented women do not win. According to Webster, when residents of state-subsidized housing for members of the working or lower classes choose to compete, they are hard to beat because they generally have the overwhelming support of their community.[6] This statement indicates the idea that popular will can affect outcome and illustrates some of the contradictions and complexities of pageant performance that engage the public. But the popular choice does not always win. So what exactly are judges judging?

Leslie Prosterman has studied county fairs in the U.S. Midwest and found that "the judging process involves a process of responsiveness, accountability, and location of self in community."[7] In the best of circumstances, therefore, judging approximates community consensus. But what is the community in question? The Virgin Islands includes multiple communities. Barnes and others have accused the contests of adhering to certain middle- and upper-class values and judges of expressing a community consensus that is true to the values only of that particular group. Non-group-members who participate in the game agree (perhaps unknowingly) to play by that group's rules. However, they do receive instruction in those rules during rehearsals, when contestants are directed in the codes and conduct of the relevant class.

Despite the variety of community codes, some criteria for judging appear to be universal—confidence, fairness, and understanding of the event's values and a conveying of knowledge. Prosterman argues that judges must know the field, examine the skills and results in each section for which they are responsible, and be versatile. A judge who adheres to these criteria not only "displays the cultural rules (the plan, the requirements) but tacitly agrees to execute or complete them."[8] Whether Virgin Islands pageant judges meet these qualifications is unclear. Audience members' sole chance to acquaint themselves with judges occurs on the night of the show. Miss U.S. Virgin Islands competitors also encounter, assess, and are assessed by the judges the preceding evening. The people selected as judges often have relatively high standing in the community, possessing considerable visibility and/or talent. Those selected as judges frequently include business leaders, sometimes politicians, and on occasion artists. Organizers entrust the judges with protecting pageant values.

Judges' standards and ideals come from a variety of sources, not simply from directives provided by pageant organizers, although, Webster, for one, believes that organizers should provide clear instructions: "When you are selecting judges for a pageant, you should give them a crash course in your judging criteria step by step."[9] Such exterior sources include but are not limited to the media, prior education, and exposure to multiple cultures and their values through personal experience. All of these interactive moments create the standards by which judges determine who is representative.

One of Webster's keys for success in the pageant arena is to learn the judging criteria so that she can prepare her clients in accordance with the rules by which they are playing. With this background, Webster believes, it becomes difficult for her contestants to lose.[10] She and James agree about the importance of knowing the rules of the game, but James is less certain that simply doing so can ensure a win. Contestants who believed that they were playing by the rules but nevertheless lost would certainly agree with James's point of view.

Learning the rules and their associated middle-class values is an integral part of the rehearsal and polishing process. Any contestant who misses those lessons is out of luck when she takes the stage to be judged. Pageant hosts reiterate the contestants' powerlessness at that point by repeating, as fashion commentator Vernelle S. de Lagarde did at the 1999 Miss U.S. Virgin Islands pageant, "The judges' decision is final." In truth, however, the judges' decision is not always final, particularly when it is clear to members of the audience, organizers, and even the judges that something is amiss and scores must be recalculated. These instances provide drama for the audience as well as the contestants, offering moments of reckoning for judges who had believed that they had the power to swim against the tide and determine who would be queen. At such moments, the people reign.

THE DRAMA

In the summer of 1971, Utha Williams won the Miss U.S. Virgin Islands contest, held in St. Thomas. Competitions had been staged off and on since 1961, most recently in 1967, when Gail Garrison was crowned.[11] The 1971 pageant included nine contestants from St. Thomas, St. Croix, and St. John—"a big thing" for the territory, according to Williams. Pageant events were held on each of the three islands, and the final was televised live across the island, something that had never happened before and has not been repeated.[12] Williams's selection on live television may have increased the sting of later developments, as much of the Virgin

Islands community watched firsthand as a statuesque, dark-skinned woman was declared queen of the territory. Williams was crowned while wearing her swimsuit, a beauty pageant faux pas—pageant organizers did not realize that the contestants should have been in their evening gowns. Other indications of organizers' naïveté soon became apparent as well.

Williams was employed as a secretary in the legal council's office of the legislature. She had received pageant training and experience on the mainland. In 1967, she took a beauty consulting training course at New York City's Afro Miss America Models, qualifying her to teach modeling and various aspects of pageant preparation. As a kind of community service, Williams put her training to use preparing contestants for the Carnival Queen competition from the late 1960s through the mid-1970s. She also worked as a volunteer trainer at the Pan American Finishing School and Career College, which sponsored the 1971 Miss Virgin Islands pageant. The head of the charm school, Sam King, had purchased the franchise from Miss Universe, and he asked Williams to become a contestant. She protested, arguing that she was training young women for other contests and that at twenty-seven, she was too old. King persisted, obtaining a set of guidelines from Miss Universe that would become the criteria for the local competition that year and into the future. According to the guidelines, contestants had to be between the ages of seventeen and twenty-eight. Williams agreed to run and stopped her work at the charm school.

King and a team of volunteers, including Patricia Francis, Mimi Richards, and a host of others, began working to shape the contest late in January or early in February. The pageant was to be held in June, with Miss Universe the following month. In March, Williams turned twenty-eight, but King assured her that her age clearly did not violate pageant rules. According to Williams, she entered the pageant late, long after other competitors had been recruited.

Organizers took the pageant to unprecedented heights, and competition clearly was stiff. The contestants made high-profile appearances at a variety of locations across the community—for example, they participated in the "Poise and Personality Review" at St. Thomas's Limetree Hotel dressed in their formal attire. For the two-dollar admission price, members of the community could watch the contestants present essays before the judges and then could participate in a dance with music provided by a live band. However, contestants never knew who the judges were or when they would be judged—surveillance could be taking place at any time. After the contest ended, Williams discovered that one backstage attendant who helped with makeup was a judge, charged with informing the other judges about goings-on behind the scenes.

Governor Melvin H. Evans and his wife attended the televised final, as did John L. Maduro, the president of the Virgin Islands legislature, indicating the pageant's importance. When Williams was declared the winner, the governor placed the crown on her head. The contestants then changed into their evening gowns and attended the official Coronation Ball. Williams was ecstatic. She had the entire community's adoration. But her reign and euphoria lasted a mere four or five days.

She spent her first "crazy, wonderful day" as queen answering congratulatory telephone calls and receiving well-wishers. The following day, she met with King and his entourage to gather photographs and personal information, which would immediately be sent via express service to Miss Universe officials in Miami. After receiving the package, however, Miss Universe representatives immediately sent King a telegram declaring that Williams exceeded Miss Universe's age limitation and could not participate in the international pageant. According to Miss Universe officials, the regulations' requirement that contestants be *between* seventeen and twenty-eight excluded women who were not yet eighteen or who were older than twenty-seven. King, however, had interpreted the rules as permitting seventeen- and twenty-eight-year-olds to compete. (Miss Universe officials have subsequently rewritten the guidelines to avoid this confusion.)

The problem almost immediately became known to the Virgin Islands public, and according to Williams, "Lord, it was *confusion!*" Within a day of receiving the telegram and without telling Williams, King called two meetings, one with the judges and another with the other contestants, to see how members of those groups wanted to proceed. Contest rules dictated that if the queen could not serve, the first runner-up would take over. But King apparently was not sure that this situation met the criteria for a queen who was unable to serve and was ignorant of the formal procedure for declaring a new queen. He contacted first runner-up Cherri Creque, unlike Williams a member of a prominent and wealthy Virgin Islands family. The Creque camp decided that she would represent the Virgin Islands at the Miss Universe pageant only if Williams was formally disqualified and Creque declared the true winner. Although Miss Universe would have accepted a runner-up as a representative, the Creques refused that option.

King acceded to the Creques' demands and stripped Williams of her crown, contradicting the community's wishes. Williams believes that her "grassroots background" and relative lack of social position led King to take away her crown in the face of the Creque family's political and social power. Creque went on to compete for the Miss Universe title, becoming the Virgin Islands' first and only semifinalist and finishing in the top twelve. She received a royal welcome when she returned to the territory.

Williams lost official acknowledgment of her title (pageant documents listing past queens do not include her name), but sponsors and the community have continued to recognized her accomplishments. She retained all her awards except for one trophy. She offered to turn her prizes, including an all-expense-paid trip to Europe—over to Creque, but sponsors said no. However, Williams refused to return her crown, scepter, and sash, which she believed she had earned. King suffered a backlash from his unpopular decision, as community opinion of him dropped dramatically. Local television personality Addey Ottley accused him of being spineless and bowing to "big family" pressure. Newspaper editorials lambasted King and heralded Williams's graciousness and "lady-like" behavior during the fiasco. Even years later, when new pageants revive the subject, Williams is remembered approvingly.[13] Williams's experiences represent both the best and the worst of the contest world. Her poise under difficult circumstances has demonstrated the resilience and capacity for endurance that has been a part of queenship since the slave era.

The 1971 contest signaled the advent of a new era of expanded, technologically modern, and glorified competition. Members of the community became excited as they developed a sense of involvement with and ownership of the event and of kinship with these women who could represent them and this new era to the outside world. The downside hit hard. Community members discovered their own and Williams's powerlessness to affect the outcome. Audiences discovered precisely which groups wielded power and the ways in which that power could be used, particularly when class and culture collided. Williams was deprived of agency and a voice in the decision over her immediate future. Community members were disempowered in the decision-making process, and although the judges were not at the forefront of the debacle, the public developed a distrust of judges and the nascent belief that behind-the-scenes dealings could corrupt the process. The Virgin Islands public also discovered that along with his franchise, King had purchased a U.S.-dictated value system that would persistently clash with Virgin Islands pageants. Moreover, Creque's caramel-colored complexion may have been a more acceptable fit in the colonial imaginary than Williams's darker skin, leading to Creque's unmatched success internationally (though I do not mean to slight her professional capabilities in the least). Creque's adherence to U.S. shade preferences did not reflect the Virgin Islands. Williams was selected in the Virgin Islands, and King's misunderstanding of the rules prevented her from representing stateside. Although the 1970s were a time of unprecedented black consciousness and empowerment, these ideas had not yet necessarily penetrated the Miss Universe pageant.[14]

Despite the controversy, Williams represented the best of what pageantry offered the Virgin Islands, a chance to honor accomplished young women and to celebrate blackness and culture and an outlet for mass gathering, mass imagining, and communal experience. Though events might not have unfolded as organizers had intended, the audience got more than its money's worth of drama. In what has become a platform for voyeurism and drama, Virgin Island audiences are compelled by those elements.

Over the next ten years, pageants in the Virgin Islands took place with minimal grumbling and no scandal. By 1981, when Marise James ran for queen, the Lions Club (through its women's auxiliary, the Lioness Club) had taken over the Miss U.S. Virgin Islands franchise, and King was no longer involved, although the reasons for his departure are unclear. That year's contest included six women, three from St. Croix, one from St. John, and two from St. Thomas. James was the underdog, both because of her status as a Crucian and because she was an unknown on the pageant circuit. Because she was not favored to win, James believes that she felt a freedom, a lighthearted attitude of wonder and experimentation, that the other contestants lacked. During the show, James followed Evadney "Peaches" Rodgers, the crowd favorite, in the contestant lineup, which "was hard. When she came out, the clap was just tremendous, and then I came out and I got a warm welcome. But being that I am competitive, I said, 'I can change these people's minds.' . . . Maybe not the judges, but the audience." James believes that her attitude had a lot to do with her acceptance and reception by the crowd. She confidently introduced herself to the audience, and the crowd realized there might be someone else on the program to consider. When she emerged for her second appearance, in her evening gown, she could feel the public's curiosity. During the swimsuit segment, her athletic figure allowed her to "prance about" confidently, she recalled. For her "cultural costume," she dressed as a palm tree and moved a lot, and she felt that the crowd was beginning to sway in her favor. The oral presentation at the show's end secured James's win.

James had extensive experience in oratory contests and debates and was a relaxed and smooth public speaker. She decided to go against the grain, eschewing the discussions of lighthearted issues favored by other contestants in favor of a speech about women in the Virgin Islands—"how we play a significant role in politics, economics, raising families . . . that we're strong women in our communities, and that basically if a man was threatened by us, that was his problem. And I ended with this statement I found in a magazine: 'A man of quality is not threatened by a woman for equality.' And the crowd went OFF!" With this forceful and passionate message, James highlighted the local culture's persistent chauvinism and "tremendous amount of sexism." By the time of the question-and-answer segment, James knew she had won the crowd's affection. The final question was a an old standby—how to improve tourism and the islands' economy. James talked about training people and explained tourism's value to the economy.

When the winners were announced, James received the Miss Congeniality and Miss Intellect prizes. She believed that the latter was a particular honor because "every single woman in that contest was very smart." But then Rodgers was declared second runner-up, a result James found surprising because she believed Rodgers had done well throughout: "That threw me off. I said, 'Oh, this is one of those contests where you have no idea who is going to win.' If anybody had won, I expected her to be the winner." The audience seemed shocked, and many people walked out. The contestants knew something was amiss. James took first runner-up. When Fidelis Bell was announced as the winner, only her close friends clapped. Members of the Lioness Club came to the front of the stage and tried to figure out what had gone wrong. The club president asked James when she was scheduled to go back to St. Croix and told her not to leave. Even the judges expressed dismay. Despite the confusion, the coronation party went on as usual, although spirits were low.

The following day, the Lioness Club asked Rodgers, Bell, and James to meet individually with the judges. Bell came out of her meeting in tears, and James entered the room in which the judges were waiting. Again serving as a judge, Ottley informed James that another judge, John Jowers, who headed the Virgin islands Council on the Arts, had given James all zeros to ensure that she would lose and that Bell, whom he favored, would win. The judges decided to throw out all of Jowers's scores, making James the queen, Rodgers first runner-up, and Bell second runner-up. James went on to represent the Virgin Islands in the Miss Universe pageant, but her moment had been stolen. She had been deprived of the honor and excitement of being crowned in front of a cheering crowd. Bell, who was never accused of having cheated, handled the matter with grace and professionalism.[15]

The incident stunned James and cemented her awareness not only of the subjectivity of judging but also of the possibility of cheating. She came to believe that future contests would likely involve further duplicity. Her subsequent experiences as a Miss U.S. Virgin Islands judge and organizer of the Miss St. Croix contest have increased her wariness. During the Miss Virgin Islands pageant, James worked hard to make sure that she did nothing that could have been construed as giving the Crucian contestant an advantage. And during one Miss St. Croix competition, a judge deliberately gave the popular choice low scores in an attempt to aid one competitor. James conferred with attorney Jada Finch Sheen, the other contest organizer, and, unbeknownst to the judges, the audience, or the contestants, eliminated that judge's assessments for all participants.

Contest judging reflects the larger political and social rivalries among the islands. Many Crucian women have long declined to participate in territory-wide events because of the bias (real or perceived) that forms an inherent part of the contests. Increased opportunities for women outside of the pageant setting may also have contributed to the decline in the number of contestants, but doubts about the fairness of these competitions have developed and will be difficult to eradicate.

In February 1995, the Miss U.S. Virgin Islands pageant included six contestants, three of them from St. Croix. One of the Crucian contestants, Karima Gordon, was particularly strong, but she finished as first runner-up to Kim Boschulte of St. Thomas. The incident enhanced misgivings about the levelness of the playing field. According to James, "Crucians were turned off by" the 1995 events. "The girl they sent [to Miss Universe] was fat. . . . People were like, 'Are they crazy?!' [Boschulte] may have been good that night. I don't know. She may have been better than the other girls in speech, in presentation, in maybe her evening gown, but that swimsuit picture turned everybody off. And the girl from here, I understand she was tall and beautiful and well spoken. Crucians have never really participated like they did before." According to Deborah Gottlieb, who served as the Lions Club pageant president during 1999, Boschulte won in accordance with the rules of the game. Whatever popular opinion held, the five-foot, four-inch, 125-pound Boschulte met the criteria that had been supplied to the judges, and so her victory was fair.[16]

Boschulte heard about the undercurrent of discontent when she won but points out that the public is unaware of the judging that occurs outside of the general public's view: "What people need to realize is that it's not necessarily what you see onstage, but it's the points and what they're being judged on. The criteria actually determines who is the queen."[17] This situation may well contribute to the audience's distrust of the process. But the 1995 contest clocked in at 5.5 hours, meaning that further segments are unlikely to be added to what the public sees on the stage. Boschulte had a budget of ten thousand dollars and worked with a team of designers, personal assistants, and image consultants from both St. Thomas and Puerto Rico so that she excelled at the contest's stated criteria.

The exemplar of the privileged pageant contestant, Boschulte clearly used to her full advantage her class and community standing and her access to Puerto Rican and local expertise. Puerto Rican and by extension South American aesthetics and contest savvy come into play in the Virgin Islands when local contestants are fortunate enough to tap into that experience. South American influence in Puerto Rican pageants is legendary, and Miss Puerto Rico has gained significant notice in the global pageant arena. And while contests in South America and Puerto Rico are also riddled with issues of race and class bias, those countries have been visible participants in the global articulation of "beauty" in the pageant industry.[18] Boschulte did not place at Miss Universe, perhaps because her features—most notably, her relatively short stature—are not typical of the women who do well internationally.[19] However, her class and her light skin may have given her an advantage internationally, although these characteristics have not been calculable assets in the local pageant arena, and this time they did not work in the international arena.

Lorna Webster was one of Boschulte's consultants, and in this case, at the local level at least, Webster's approach of acquiring criteria and molding her charges accordingly worked. But Virgin Islanders, who have historically perceived pageants as the domain of popular determination, a concept held over from the days when the tickets a contestant sold assured her win, the idea of a select group determining the representative for the masses does not go down easily. Nevertheless, Boschulte's win did not cause a popular uproar and was not perceived as some sort of gross miscalculation requiring redress. Moreover, her victory clearly illustrates that there is no one set of physical characteristics required of Virgin Islands queens.

BEING IN THE GAME

Virgin Islanders' apparent never-ending love of beauty contests and ability to support them financially and psychologically are only rarely discussed. The March 23, 1999, *Ideas and Issues* show, then, is notable as one of the few public forums that has examined the troubling questions regarding the appearance of Virgin Islands pageant queens. Jean Forde offered some provocative comments on that show:

> Pageants instill self-esteem, etc., but they also paint a fake picture of what beauty actually is. You will never find a thick lipped, a big-nose individual with short hair who has a natural look about them . . . but you always want that the best-looking one have to be the one with the finer features, the one closest to the Caucasian features. Okay? And that end up becoming a problem and end up sending the wrong message. Secondly, you have those that send the message that everybody ought to be anorexia [*sic*]. Is this the message that you're sending to your child? That you only look good if you have these other people's features? That you only look good if you "bag-a-bones" and you "maaga" [thin] and you skinny?
>
> Then, too, there is the other side of the argument, and I'm going to give you all of it on the table. You take Miss Big and Beautiful—what is the message here? Here you have a bunch of individuals parading again in swimsuits showing cellulite, etc. [who] certainly are overweight. And you have—I mean the argument, it goes against every single thing your doctor and nutritionist have told you. I mean, is that the image you are sending to your child? That it is all right to be unhealthy? There are arguments that come from all angles, you know? So, I mean, do we need beauty pageants? Can't we just say we are all beautiful people? Why do we need pageants to say we are beautiful?[20]

The idea that a simple declaration of collective beauty would eliminate the community's desire for pageants is reductive. Forde's rant on the ills of local health is displaced. Virgin Islanders face the same problems with weight, food choices, and food preparation that plague residents of many other countries. The Miss Big and Beautiful pageant does not bear responsibility for any of those problems.

Pageants had an important role in African American social and political history. One of the slogans of the Black Power movement was "black is beautiful." The pageant participation of black contestants indicated their acknowledgment, acceptance, and competence in a game that powerful global forces had established.[21] Thus, other than positing black women as beauties in their own right and establishing the existence of multiple standards of beauty, beauty was really not the concern at all.

The dominant pageant culture has worked to maintain European and white American political economic and aesthetic dominance over alien cultures, undermining other people's sense of self and creating a desire to be that which they are not. According to Naomi Wolf, "Beauty is a currency system like the gold standard. Like any economy, it is determined by politics, and in the modern age in the West it is the last, best belief system that keeps male dominance intact." In reality, what she terms the "beauty myth" seeks to prescribe behavior rather than appearance.[22] Thus, her argument supports my assertion that the preoccupation with the components of beauty—who has it, what it is—sidetracks us from real conversations about power and influence. Island nations are influenced by beauty and its accompanying businesses only in their desire to be contemporary, to be players in the game. This desire keeps postcolonial countries and territories beholden to outside groups and creates the markets and mentalities that maintain these locales' lack of power. Island nations contribute to their own subordination by supporting these enterprises.

Forde's comments thus betray his biases about blackness and beauty, while pageant results in the Virgin Islands counter those biases. Virgin Islanders have chosen representatives from throughout the spectrum of black figures, and therefore it cannot be said that Virgin Islanders do not believe in their own beauty. They do not need pageants to prove their beauty to others or themselves. Virgin Islands pageants resist more than they adhere to dominant notions of beauty, as a look at the women who have been chosen as queen proves. Queens have not been limited to those with light skin.[23] No racial or other aesthetic preference dominates. Pageants in the Virgin Islands do not appear to have perpetuated the gross injustices that have weighed down Jamaican pageants.[24] Virgin Islands contests have evidenced no dominance of narrow European features over broad African appearances, no dominance of mixed-race women over those with jet-black skin. Virgin Islands queens have been short, tall, thin, chubby, elegant, dowdy, svelte, and buxom. In Lorna Webster's words, "You can be short and [have a] nappy head and win. Shade doesn't matter, because we are on different turf here. This is the only place where you can be fat and win. You can be short and win. You can be tall and win. You can be ugly—what the masses consider ugly—and win. You can be anything and win here because we have a different form of acceptance."[25] Virgin Islands assessments of beauty differ from those proffered and influenced by the United States, despite the tense relations between these local and international standards. The persistent discord between these aesthetics keeps local winners and audiences both condemned to the outside of international pageant arenas and proud of sticking to their own guns. Virgin Islands communities remain resistant in their appreciation and celebration of bodies that differ from dominant examples of beautiful. However, this appreciation of difference represents more than resistance; it also indicates a consistency with Africanist and multinational roots: "In Dakar [in the twentieth century], the generation gap has blurred the standards of beauty to accommodate different age groups. While a slim girl of sixteen—nicknamed "disquette"—may be an object of desire and will go out with her midriff exposed (*djamar out*), larger women called *diongoma* are still respected and appreciated. They also have their beauty contests where measurements (44-36-56 in.) are highly praised. . . . While the ideal of the thin Western model has spread to urban societies, the *diongoma* still has her place."[26] These African models offer opportunity for many ideals to coexist. Islanders, too, follow this aesthetic, which Webster terms being "satisfied with what we are."[27] And despite their appreciation and clear awareness that their aesthetics differ from American/European-influenced ideals, Virgin Islanders insist on competing and representing on global stages. Populated not only by women who fit the cookie-cutter American beauty ideal, pageants in the Virgin Islands have room for both the long-legged and thin Sherece Smith and the shorter, more rounded Carolyn Wattley.

Despite the local respect that accrues to women who possess Smith's build, a conflicting local aesthetic can be seen in the image of the iconic Caribbean woman, the ubiquitous buxom black woman with a wide hat and a wide bottom. She has become synonymous with Caribbeanness, native womanhood, and history and is associated with culinary expertise of the "typical" (black and native) island woman. Her appearance, from Caliban's mother, Sycorax, in Shakespeare's *The Tempest* to Nanny of the Maroons to the contemporary Weed Woman responsible for the care of her extended island family, is a cipher in all things Caribbean. The thin, svelte, figure that commands attention in a more global fashion and the Nanny figure mark the visible extremities of a diverse penumbra, sometimes troubled, debated, berated, or celebrated.

AUDIENCE

For audiences, excitement is heightened and interest is piqued by this area of contestation between what is acceptable and what is not in an island representative. The relatively small size of the Virgin Islands community means that everyone has some tie to one of the contestants or her family. But why do such ties translate into attendance? According to James, people come just for the entertainment. Webster concurs: "Contests appeal because we don't have much to do here. . . . We are a people slowly losing our culture."[28] If contests are one of the culprits in this loss of culture (and the definition of "loss of culture" is unclear in a community with so many cultures), then how are the image consultants and organizers who perpetuate pageants complicit? Webster chimes in with the popular refrain of cultural recuperation rather than the notion of a progressive creole existence that persistently mixes old with new. By participating in and embracing pageants, as they have since the sixteenth century, Virgin Islanders enable contests to remain contemporary. By refashioning them—not necessarily to suit the demands of the larger franchises but rather in keeping with local aesthetic preferences, performances, and references—island citizens perpetuate creole practice. Wittingly or unwittingly, Virgin Islanders advance the form by being who they are and doing what they do, even as they mimic offshore preferences. Therefore, if locals think of pageantry in terms of abundance rather than loss, they participate not in the disappearance of culture but in its production and are at the forefront of modernity, not chasing its rear. For that reason, audience participation—the witnessing of this production—has value.

In Webster's view, because islanders live in such a little melting pot, they are always in danger of losing culture. On the "small island" of St. Thomas, she notes, "we have the French, Spanish, Haitians, Eastern Caribbeans, Jews, and others that celebrate their culture. There is no exclusive culture on this island, not even the culture of the land. And [all of these cultures] do not mix—not well. The cultural loss is happening because we don't see a need to be interested in other people's culture. If we are interested in others' culture, they become interested in ours." She cites the example of black moko jumbies, lead by Hugo Moolenaar, who shared with (white) others on the island: "Now we see white kids performing. Others took that culture and started making a profit from it, cut him out of the deal, and he was no longer needed." Similarly, she contended, "Native organizations can [no longer] afford to hire people to" learn the craft of steel pans. "If you don't have money, you don't have access." According to Webster, an Eastern Caribbean woman, something is wrong with the fact that native performances can no longer be viewed in the Virgin Islands.[29]

The Virgin Islands community has been subject to great destabilization since the 1950s. The islands are now home to a complicated balance of existences. While Webster's accusations contain a measure of truth, "native performances" are also happening all the time. The idea of "native" or "cultural" performance as something historic, frozen in time, holds less appeal for local audiences than for tourists. Local audiences are interested in contemporary performances. These productions may incorporate traditional materials, but locals are increasingly interested in witnessing the islands' modernity and ability to compete with the wider world. Pageants incorporate contemporary issues, styles of dress, ways of speaking, values, and technology. Queen shows keep their participants and their audiences up to date and perhaps ahead of the curve.

AUDIENCE, CIVIC PRIDE, AND THE COMPELLING NATURE OF FAILURE

Virgin Islanders are fascinated by the ferocity of competition and the possibility of failure. Island audiences routinely cheer and revel when a contestant makes an onstage blunder. According to Webster, "As an audience, we're brutal," a phenomenon she blames on the fact that "we are not educated enough to realize it doesn't pay to pit contestant against contestant."[30] But such enjoyment of others' misfortunes is part of the game, and women who decide to compete on island stages know the stakes. Colleen Ballerino Cohen, Richard Wilk, and Beverly Stoeltje contend that beauty contests worldwide "are almost always . . . driven by scandal, discord, and dispute. There is always a division between frontstage and backstage, a rupture between the objective selection of a winner in the main event, and all the other interests that both contestants and viewers know are influencing the outcome, the class-based, the personal, the political. It is the 'something more' going on in beauty contests that is at the root of their enduring attraction for both their audiences and their ethnographers."[31] For audiences, this area of division between the two worlds creates an elevated tension and forms the basis of contestation. Audiences want to be there when the "something more" takes place. Islanders have a penchant for the dramatic, and pageants present excellent circumstances for combustion. According to Sarah Banet-Weiser, "A typical Miss America pageant is a blend of components borrowed from other traditional public events: the talent competition is in the grand tradition of carnivals, and pageants clearly resonate with parades through both the array of women on stage and the actual parading of bodies. They are also reminiscent of sporting events, because competition is always their focal point."[32] The fever of the competition, heightened by the carnival atmosphere, also draws audiences. Because the possibility of failure is always a part of the competitive game, island audiences pack competitions, waiting for a slip, a fall, a blunder to crack a contestant's perpetual smile. Research on contests and their voracious appeal for American audiences has led journalist Neil Steinberg to conclude that our collective unquenchable desire to witness failure is a product of our educational system, which "has created the terrifying image of failure that dwells in our inner souls, the dread, paralyzing demon to be avoided at all costs, the burning red F, the stigma, the shame." Public failure renders the individual more human, closer to the spectator. The performance, Steinberg continues, "assumes the emotional impact of failures within our own lives." By his estimation, the world seems more genuine, more human, more funny, through the screen of failure.[33] Lorna Webster believes that the downside of contests is that the element of failure is particularly crushing because "we do not prepare young girls for failure." With winning as the expectation, contestants find losing especially painful and handle it poorly.[34]

Still, audiences also flock to Virgin Islands pageants for other, more communal reasons, including elements of civic ritual and pride.[35] Pageants have become a sort of national pastime, a vital element of local culture despite the changes they have undergone. Pageants are not imposed by the outside but rather are embraced from within and re-created in accordance with local aesthetics and style. According to Cohen, Wilk, and Stoeltje, "Beauty pageants are *typical*, as elements of mass consumer culture, of a kind of entertainment that subtly influences the ways we see ourselves and our communities. On a global scale, pageants and contests are representative of a kind of television-mediated linkage that ties larger and larger segments of the world population together into a single audience; they are part of a global 'civic' culture of sports, world music, and entertainment. They make us all part of something larger, at the same time they assure us of our own distinctiveness."[36] Pageants undoubtedly have all of these effects in the Virgin Islands. Audiences there are convinced of their distinctiveness within the form. They experience feelings of connectedness to a grander scheme. Attendance demonstrates participation in national cultural production, albeit imagined (what Dennis Kennedy has dubbed a "phantom national identity"), and ritual.[37]

For women in the audience, beauty competitions serve another purpose. According to Banet-Weiser, the Miss America pageant is the civic ritual of the United States, "a vital source of knowledge for many young women about the disciplinary practices of femininity."[38] While contests can be seen as a disciplinary practice for the women involved (for example, via rehearsals), some women use pageants as a standard by which to model or measure personal femininity. The contest thus serves not simply as entertainment and as training for contestants; it also provides a larger circle of women with an education in a very gendered and classed behavior.

Mikhail Bakhtin celebrated the earthly, vulgar, obscene pleasures associated with the medieval communal celebration of carnival for their ability to degrade status distinctions.[39] But although carnival degraded the status quo for some people, the bourgeoisie increasingly construed its activities "as disgusting, as abject, as the antithesis of civility and decorum." Contests endeavor to disassociate themselves from these behaviors despite their reliance on the festivities of carnival to generate attendance. According to Dennis A. Hemphill, carnival became in part the festival of the Other. At such events, "the subordinate classes became the object of a gaze conceptualizing itself as respectable and superior by substituting observation for participation."[40] The substitution of observation by participation required a policing of behavior whereby the lower classes had to prove their sophistication and worldliness. Codes of behavior for spectatorship are established and reasserted in a myriad of ways—the pricing of tickets, the expected attire for attendance, the way in which the audience is continuously instructed on how to behave during the show. The entire event serves as what both Kennedy and Allen Guttman call "class education."[41] Pageants inform audiences about changes in manners and expectations in various sectors of the community. Fans participate in this educating experience and accept or reject the dictates issued from the stage as well as the rules of the viewing audience space.

PAGEANT AS THEATER/CONTEST AS SPORT

Audiences generally disregard the preferred etiquette only when they perceive an outcome as unfair or when they strongly support what they perceive as fair—for example, Sherece Smith's 1999 victory, when audience members rushed the stage and disrupted the planned pomp and circumstance. This exuberance brought to mind crowd behavior at sporting events, when excitement moves people to indulge in various behaviors that under other circumstances would be considered inappropriate for members of the middle and upper classes. According to Kennedy, at sporting events, "openly emotional behavior is sanctioned as the level of excitement gathers force."[42] Connecting fan behavior to gender, Kennedy further suggests that sporting environments are male spaces; pageants may be seen as the reverse, a female space that frees mostly women and homosexual men to act up in the same way that straight men do at sporting events. Women can "go on" (behave) at pageants in ways that are not permissible under many other conditions outside of carnival.

Beauty contests are indeed akin to sporting events, but comparisons to straight theater are less exact but nevertheless appropriate. Contests have the valuable and elusive element of live theater, and they are the most frequent venue in which the community sees women perform. The experience has an irreproducible nature, and there is no way to re-create the monumental moments of drama. For anyone not in attendance, what happens is merely hearsay.[43] Pageant audiences participate in "world-making," elaborate cogs in the machinations of "a way of ordering that is not 'out there.'"[44] Pageants are their own demi-worlds, fostering "a sense of exciting significance."[45] As sports become social theater, producing spectator arousal through competition, they are mimetic, gesturing toward something warlike through "make-believe" settings.[46] Queen shows become mimetic by gesturing toward women's relationships to governance, to economic power, to the realities of femininity in the daily production of culture. Contestants pretend to wield power. Audiences collectively agree to suspend disbelief and participate in world-making, in celebrating women's power, real or imagined, in bearing witness to drama, bravery, talent, intelligence, ingenuity, and the display of the best and sometimes the worst of what the islands have to offer one another on a stage that honors the amateur and floats somewhere between theater and street performance.

Smith's talent presentation exemplified a performance of imagination. Her direction of Virgin Islands tourism into the twenty-first century carved a place for her vision and perceived capacities as a young woman interested in the hospitality industry. She impressed the audience members and took them along with her in her world making, thereby altering the pageant's relationship with agents of change. One of these created worlds enabled the island to shed its colonial identity and participate as a sovereign nation, thereby generating regional pride. This process resembles what Arlene Davila describes in her discussion of Puerto Rican sports and contests.[47] Smith's creative inclusion of the Virgin Islands in the global economy offered the members of the pageant audience a slick national identity, pride, and the evidence they needed to situate themselves squarely in a modern moment.

CONCLUSION

Re-Situating the Caribbean with Womanhood Front and Center

According to Cynthia Enloe, "There are at least two sorts of feminized beauty . . . the revealed and the hidden."[1] I have identified a multiplicity of feminized beauties—that is, behaviors and characteristics associated with the participation of women of the U.S. Virgin Islands in beauty contests. These identifications do not confine black womanhood to a circumscribed area or set of individuals but indicate the breadth of Virgin Islands women's experience and the performance of deeply rooted historical connections. That women of the region can perform the roles of the raw and the polished, the commercial and the traditional, the upper class and the common, and everything in between indicates the ways in which these neat categories are persistently in dialogue with and dependent on one another. In queen shows, the rituals of preparation, the informal intracontest communications and competitions, and the more formalized onstage presentations dictate the weight of Virgin Islands productions. Here, the revealed and the hidden aspects of Virgin Islands and all Caribbean women's lives function in tandem and resist any attempts at fixity. These shows are a messy business. Their fluidity betrays mixtures of identities and sensibilities. They display aesthetic, performative, and quotidian resistances to specific boundaries of race, shade, and class that would make this study a tidy picture and would relegate it to the more commonly depicted pictures of Caribbean and subaltern pageant performances. Instead, the Virgin Islands demonstrate their unique position by resisting these conventional assertions.

From slavery to modernity, island women have needed dualism (at a minimum) to survive. In the Virgin Islands, slave women who became queens to their black public maintained this duality, remaining within their caste yet pushing its boundaries to inform, protect, and entertain their people. As the social and political conditions of black people shifted and autonomy and power slowly grew, the queens' roles altered. They became workers for the nation and a civic symbol, and the stage became the place where the ideal nation was at times imagined, performed, and contested. Onstage, the ambiguities of Caribbean identifications momentarily solidified and gained approval or harsh criticism from an island public that acknowledged shared experiences and suspended disbelief. At this moment of performance, the community accepts (sometimes begrudgingly) this model, this queen, whomever she is at a given historical moment, as the symbol of a unified Virgin Islands in tune with a greater Caribbean and world culture. Audiences suspend the "real" in favor of imagining themselves as a unified nation, imagining their relation to the greater Caribbean and the United States, imagining their participation in the global economy, and imagining what ideal island women look like and what they are capable of. Virgin Islanders thrust themselves into the collective mix, even if that mix and their participation in it are imaginary. Their participation also forces a disruption of others' imaginations, requiring them to expand or at least consider alternatives.

Colleen Ballerino Cohen, Richard Wilk, and Beverly Stoeltje describe the beauty pageant as the place or space where culture, power, and global economies collide on stage, not simply as a meat market. As universal and diverse as pageants may be, all demonstrate a group's values, sense of self, morality, and gender relations. Pageants also fight to maintain their own identities, which are just as important as the identities that might be absorbed in the global pageant process.[2] Beauty competitions display Virgin Islands national values and materials. Young women perform cultural dexterity as they move easily between tradition and innovation, between ideas and practices of the past and those of a technological and highly fluid global culture. With this fluidity, young women have come to identify pageants as roads to a specific kind of opportunity. Pageants have become a path women can follow to achieve their desires. Sometimes, what they seek is fame; other contestants want an opportunity otherwise beyond their reach or a voice where they have otherwise felt silent. Often, participants are interested in something else entirely. In queen shows, "becoming" is most significant. And more than just the becoming of the contestants is at stake; multiple identity constructions (and maintenance) take place, and the machinery that supports these events is also shaped as organizers, consultants, hangers-on, and anyone else with some connection is invested in their own becoming. Consultants become local demicelebrities as their contestants garner success, as their clothing adorns winner after winner, as the polished women they turn out solidify their creators' importance in the process and thus the health and well-being of the community.

For the women involved, material success (or at least the absence of failure) offers evidence of the pageant's effectiveness and serves as an argument for its continuation. In 1987, journalist Venetia Harvey offered readers of *Probe* (the magazine of the *St. Croix Avis*) a report on some past queens. Most of the women had gone on to lead unremarkable but respectable lives. Some continued to work as models and actors, while others were turned off by the pageant experience and drastically shifted their foci, raising families or starting businesses in the territory or elsewhere. A few former queens have established themselves in distinguished careers.[3] Nevertheless, all of the women Harvey contacted—even those who insisted that they would not participate today because of "the audiences and controversies"—said that their involvement in the queen show had been a memorable experience for one reason or another.[4] Participating in the pageant had been a rite of passage, an initiation of sorts into a class of movers and shakers if not into a different economic class.

In the Virgin Islands, where most young women have been touched by pageantry in one way or another, resistance to queen shows can be exhibited merely by refusing to participate in this national pastime. People who have resisted have not been studied as a group to determine their comparative "progress." But plenty of the territory's women have succeeded as scholars, as artists, as senators, as businesspersons, as health professionals, as real estate moguls, or in other fields and have done so outside the pageant arena. Thus, pageants by no means offer the region's women their only avenue to success. Pageants are merely one very visible avenue that provides a grand spectrum of the ways in which notions of class, sex, race, gender, power, history, and performance function within a small and very vibrant community. Pageants of all types, from Miss Big and Beautiful to Miss Virgin Islands Senior to Carnival Queen, certainly resist and submit to a variety of regulatory models of women's bodies and behaviors. At many levels, Virgin Islands women, both pageant participants and nonparticipants, have functioned within or subverted definitions of femininity dictated by queen shows and their supporters.

Pageant performance is important in a place where the everyday triumphs of women are seldom recognized or celebrated and the queen show offers a moment in the national spotlight, an opportunity to be acknowledged broadly and publicly. As one teenage pageant participant in North America told Hillary Carlip, "I entered the pageant because I wanted to be special, I wanted to be noticed. I thought that by being successful people would look at me the way they look at my friends. I wanted people to admire me."[5] These sentiments are consistent with those of women in the Caribbean, where, as Natasha Barnes writes, women never get representational status as national heroes: "The idolatry that surrounds winning Caribbean beauty queens is dramatic, unique," and significant in reflecting on the history of race and class relations and on the ongoing struggle regarding the ways in which blackness and black women are powerful and of course beautiful.[6]

Just as *beauty* is clearly a code word for a larger set of concerns, pageants have also been a means for the working out of "natural" cultural production and modernity. Pageants incorporate local and international standards, global notions of beauty, commercial products, contemporary ideas, and advertising concepts, and contestants reflect global as well as local attitudes and values. Regardless of Virgin Islands' political dependency on the United States or its ongoing negotiation of economic marginalization, pageants persist.

Pageant rituals of preparation and performance contribute to a communal feeling for contestants and audiences. The pageants exist on the grassroots level and as such offer a style of performance not often seen on "professional" stages. Pageant content is eminently suited to local tastes. The shows persist because they are historically adept at answering to the needs, desires, preferences, and appetites of Virgin Islanders. Like the cariso women and tea meeting queens of yesteryear, pageants are in tune with the population, constantly delivering and adapting to their audiences' changing appetites and preferences regarding cultural performance.

Pageants always reflect the weight of history. As black, female bodies arrive on stage, attempting to package themselves for their and others' convenience, to prove or disprove their civilization or commonness, they do not and cannot succeed in their own containment. Their presence exceeds customary expectations. Their regard as representatives of "the Virgins" is itself a radical concept.

NOTES

INTRODUCTION

1. Utha Williams, interview by author, St. Thomas, February 6, 1999; Miss U.S. Virgin Islands Pageant booklet (St. Thomas: privately printed, 1999).
2. David Edgecombe, interview by author, St. Thomas, January 1999.
3. Though there have been instances of controversial male and drag shows that fell under the similar titles, the common presentation of "queen shows" remains a women's event.
4. See Barnes, "Face of the Nation"; Ulysse, "Conquering Duppies in Kingston"; Thomas, *Modern Blackness*; Maxine Leeds Craig, *Ain't I a Beauty Queen?*; Banet-Weiser, *Most Beautiful Girl*; Cohen, Wilk, and Stoeltje, *Beauty Queens*.
5. See Barnes, "Face of the Nation"; Davila, "El Kiosko Budweiser"; King-O'Riain, *Pure Beauty*; Thomas, *Modern Blackness*; Ulysse, "Conquering Duppies in Kingston"; Yano, *Crowning the Nice Girl*.
6. Watson and Martin, "Miss America Pageant," 117.
7. Mintz, *Caribbean Contours*; Trouillot, *Peasants and Capital*; Sheller, *Consuming the Caribbean*, 5.
8. Stuart Hall, "Negotiating Caribbean Identities," 24–39.
9. The United States purchased more than one hundred islands from Denmark in 1917. As a territory, the Virgin Islands are in a colonial relationship with the United States: citizens cannot vote or run for the presidency and have no possibility of consideration for statehood unless existing laws are amended.
10. See Boyer, *America's Virgin Islands*; Williams, *From Columbus to Castro*.
11. See Boyer, *America's Virgin Islands*.
12. Willocks, *Umbilical Cord*, 374. See also Gerard, "Social Configuration and Some Problems," 157.
13. Nancy Cole, "Territory's Hispanics See Power in Numbers: Latest U.S. Census Figures Mark Minority Group as Country's Largest," *Virgin Islands Daily News*, July 11, 2003, available online at http://www.virginislandsdailynews.com/index.pl/article_archive?id=222072 (accessed August 7, 2007).
14. Maurer, *Recharting the Caribbean*, 67.
15. Sunshine, *Caribbean*, 176.
16. Chatterjee, *Nation and Its Fragments*, 6.
17. Davila, *Sponsored Identities*, 18–22.
18. Du Bois, *Souls of Black Folk*; Jackson, *Real Black*.
19. Benitez-Rojo, *Repeating Island*, 18.

20. Davila, *Sponsored Identities*; Stuart Hall and DuGay, *Questions of Cultural Identity*.
21. Curtin, *Atlantic Slave Trade*.
22. Hartman, *Scenes of Subjection*, 12; Shepherd, Brereton, and Bailey, *Engendering History*; Beckles, *Centering Woman*.
23. Shepherd, Brereton, and Bailey, *Engendering History*; Beckles and Shepherd, *Caribbean Freedom*; Beckles, *Natural Rebels*.

CHAPTER 1

1. Williams, *From Columbus to Castro*.
2. Boyer, *America's Virgin Islands*, 14.
3. Curtin, *Atlantic Slave Trade*, 21.
4. Ibid.
5. Thomas, *Modern Blackness*, 33.
6. Foucault, *History of Sexuality*; Sekula, "Body and the Archive." Beckles, a Caribbeanist and historian, discusses the historiography of women in the colonies of the eighteenth century in "Sex and Gender," 125–40.
7. Foucault, *History of Sexuality*, 4–5.
8. Gilman, "Black Bodies, White Bodies," 209.
9. Ibid., 212–19. Through the examination, dissection, and dismemberment of individuals such as Sarah Bartmann as a symbol of black femininity, the exaggeration of sexual features in the white imaginary then served as "proof" of black sexual excess.
10. Catherine Hall, *Civilising Subjects*, 17.
11. Ibid.
12. Beckles, "Sex and Gender," 137.
13. Beckles, *Natural Rebels*.
14. Paiewonsky, *Eyewitness Accounts*.
15. Ibid., 152.
16. Courlander, *Treasury*, 94, quoting Virgin Islands scholar Antonio Jarvis
17. The chica is described as similar to the calenda, a dance where the hips and lower portion of the body move vigorously while the torso remains statuesque. The chica, calenda, and bamboula all have similar descriptions in a variety of historical accounts (Emery, *Black Dance*, 21–26).
18. Ibid., 21. Emery believes that nuns would not likely practice numerous African dances, and she therefore assumes that the bamboula was indeed the chica.
19. Lewisohn, *St. Croix under Seven Flags*, 136.
20. Oliver, "St. Croix Dancing," 44.
21. Emanuel, *Bamboola Dance*, 1.
22. Ibid.
23. Oliver, "St. Croix Dancing," 44.
24. Willocks, *Umbilical Cord*, 222.
25. Lewisohn, *St. Croix under Seven Flags*, 205.
26. Lekis, *Dancing Gods*, 36.
27. Ibid., 182, 181; Oliver, "St. Croix Dancing," 69.
28. Neville A. T. Hall, *Slave Society*, 116.
29. Oliver, "St. Croix Dancing," 71–72; Lewisohn, *St. Croix under Seven Flags*, 244–45.
30. Weed quoted in Lewisohn, *St. Croix under Seven Flags*, 245.
31. Oliver, "St. Croix Dancing," 73.

32. Weed quoted in Neville A. T. Hall, *Slave Society*, 119.
33. Williams, *From Columbus to Castro*, 250–51; Knight, "Haitian Revolution."
34. Neville A. T. Hall, *Slave Society*, 227; Oliver, "St. Croix Dancing," 83.
35. Oliver, "St. Croix Dancing," 83.
36. Lewis, *Virgin Islands*, 30.
37. Boyer, *America's Virgin Islands*, 96.
38. Ibid., 70.
39. Cadaval, "Folklife," 236.
40. Willocks, *Umbilical Cord*, 212. The mythology behind these figures had established for many years that there were only three queens (Richardson, *Seven Streets*, 124, 140). In August 2004, historian Wayne James discovered additional details that pointed to a fourth queen, Mathilda, who had been subsumed by the character of Bottom Belly ("Life of Queen Mathilda," *St. Croix Avis*, September 30–October 1, 2007).
41. Willocks, *Umbilical Cord*, 212.
42. Thora Visby-Petersen quoted in Nicholls, *Old-Time Masquerading*, 11.
43. Cadaval, "Folklife," 16.
44. Lewisohn, *St. Croix under Seven Flags*, 284.
45. Rivera, *Growing Up*, 55–56.
46. Lekis, *Dancing Gods*, 85.
47. Du Bois, *Souls of Black Folk*, 16–17.

CHAPTER 2

1. Peiss, *Hope in a Jar*, 86.
2. Ibid., 33.
3. Ibid., 34.
4. Rooks, *Hair Raising*, 40.
5. "Local," *St. Croix Avis*, December 27, 1938, 2.
6. Nicholls, *Old-Time Masquerading*, 47.
7. Ibid., 4.
8. "Christmas Carnival—F'sted Junior High School," *St. Croix Avis*, December 16, 1938, 1.
9. Boyer, *America's Virgin Islands*, 138.
10. Ibid., 139.
11. Commonwealth status has also denied Puerto Ricans and Guamanians voting rights in U.S. elections (Maga, "Citizen Movement").
12. Boyer, *America's Virgin Islands*, 139–72.
13. Willocks, *Umbilical Cord*, 265.
14. Boyer, *America's Virgin Islands*, 143.
15. Lewis, *Virgin Islands*, 85.
16. Dookhan, *History*, 270.
17. Boyer, *America's Virgin Islands*, 148.
18. Ibid., 164.
19. Boyer, *America's Virgin Islands*, 164.
20. Kelley, *Race Rebels*, 17.
21. Leary, "Taking Bearings," 92.
22. Kelley, *Race Rebels*, 20. See also Scott, *Moral Economy*.
23. Boyer, *America's Virgin Islands*, 165.
24. Lewis, *Virgin Islands*, 59.

25. Boyer, *America's Virgin Islands*, 57.
26. Ibid., 146.
27. Ibid., 159.
28. According to Lewis, "The average Virgin Islands Negro, the same as the Senate committee pointed out, was highly literate (most of the miniscule 4 per cent classified as 'illiterate' were adult immigrants from Puerto Rico and the British Islands), a steady patron of the public libraries, an avid reader of a number of small newspapers that were widely discussed in the three towns, a member of labor unions (one whose remarkable feature was the membership of men and women on an equal footing, equal wages), an extremely law-abiding citizen, rarely given to alcoholism, a zealous churchgoer, and possessed of habits of natural courtesy and loyalty that made him and his like renowned as superior house servant throughout the West Indies—a general picture startlingly different from the image that the average white American entertained of the Negro in the world as he knew it" (*Virgin Islands*, 85–86). Lewis nonetheless is discussing a "servant." That a servant would be the image of the average Negro in the West Indies illustrates the chasm between the classes and races; education and the ensuing class mobility remains highly valuable for working-class Virgin Islanders.
29. Ibid., 107.
30. Boyer, *America's Virgin Islands*, 176–77.
31. Ibid., 169–70.
32. Ibid., 169.
33. Ibid., 168.
34. Lewis, *Virgin Islands*, 240.
35. Ibid.
36. "Miss Helen Francis Named 'Miss Virgin Islands of 1947,'" *St. Croix Avis*, February 24, 1947, 1.
37. Whether this society was a dues-paying private society or one open to all willing participants is unclear, as, therefore, is the class standing of its participants.
38. "Beauty and Talent at Pageant," *Virgin Islands Daily News*, October 8, 1948, 1.
39. Clarence "Cherra" Heyleger, interview by author, St. Croix, June 30, 1993.
40. Moran, "Carrying the Queen," 147.
41. Ibid., 148.
42. Anderson, *Imagined Communities*, 6–7.
43. Chatterjee, *Nation and Its Fragments*, 6.
44. Boyer, *America's Virgin Islands*, 183.
45. Anderson, *Imagined Communities*, 4. In offering an interpretation for the "'anomaly' of nationalism," Anderson writes, "My point of departure is that nationality, or, as one might prefer to put it in view of that word's multiple significations, nation-ness, as well as nationalism, are cultural artifacts of a particular time."
46. Bhabha, *Nation and Narration*, 1. Bhabha comments on the establishment and content of nations: "Nations, like narratives, lose their origins in the myths of time and only fully realize their horizons in the mind's eye. Such an image of the nation—or narration—might seem impossibly romantic and excessively metaphorical, but it is from those traditions of political thought and literary language that the nation emerges as a powerful historical idea in the west. An idea whose cultural compulsion lies in the impossible unity of the nation as a symbolic force. This is not to deny the attempt by nationalist discourses persistently to produce the idea of the nation as a continuous narrative of national progress, the narcissism of self-generation, the primeval present of the *Volk*."

47. Scarry, *On Beauty*, 3. According to Scarry, "Beauty brings copies of itself into being. It makes us draw it, take photographs of it, or describe it to other people. Sometimes it gives rise to exact replication and other times to resemblances and still other times to things whose connection to the original site of inspiration is unrecognizable."

48. *Women's League Tenth Anniversary Souvenir Booklet, 1946–1956* (Charlotte Amalie, St. Thomas: n.p., 1956), 3.

49. Ibid.

50. Ibid., 4; "Women's League of St. Croix to Be Formed Tomorrow Night," *St. Croix Avis*, May 14, 1947, 1.

51. *Women's League Tenth Anniversary Souvenir Booklet*, 5.

52. Ibid.

53. Ibid.

54. Ibid., 4.

55. Ibid.; "Carnival, Fair Planned for Freedom Year Celebration," *Virgin Islands Daily News*, March 12, 1948, 1; *Souvenir Booklet, Freedom Centennial Celebrations, 1848–1948, Saint Croix, Virgin Islands, U.S.A.* (n.d., n.p.), 4. These rituals of letters from elected officials continue to this day as evidence of a pageant's importance.

56. "Centennial Ball to Be Gala Event: Crowning of Queen; Special Feature," *St. Croix Avis*, July 1, 1948, 1.

57. "All Votes for Centennial Queen Are 5 Cents," *St. Croix Avis*, June 19, 1948, 4; "Three More Chosen for Cen. Queen," *St. Croix Avis*, June 14, 1948, 1; "Cen. Queen Comm. Discusses Costumes," *St. Croix Avis*, June 9, 1948, 1.

58. "Centennial Ball to Be Gala Event: Crowning of Queen; Special Feature," *St. Croix Avis*, July 1, 1948, 1.

59. Maxine Leeds Craig, *Ain't I a Beauty Queen?*

60. "High School Contest for Miss CHS Closes 8 Tonite," *St. Croix Avis*, October 29, 1947, 1; "Rita De Chabert Wins Title of Miss CHS," *St. Croix Avis*, October 30, 1947, 1; "Large Audience Sees Miss CHS Crowned," *St. Croix Avis*, November 3, 1947, 1, 4.

61. "Fashion Show Well Attended," *Virgin Islands Daily News*, April 3, 1952, 1.

62. "Plans Complete for Girl Scout May Festival: Mrs. DeCastro to Pick Girl Scout Queens," *Virgin Islands Daily News*, May 29, 1952, 1; Willocks, *Umbilical Cord*, 376–77. According to Willocks, Puerto Rican immigrants and their descendants "created a sub-culture within the" larger Virgin Islands culture, although that subcultural activity is concentrated on St. Croix, which has the territory's largest Puerto Rican community.

63. Cohen, Wilk, and Stoeltje, *Beauty Queens*, 6–7.

64. "The Women's League to Send Cables to Washington," *Virgin Islands Daily News*, May 12, 1954, 1. As James Bough and Roy C. Macridis write, that the Revised Organic Act kept the Virgin Islands as an "unincorporated territory" was important because it followed "the established patterns of relationship between the United States and its possessions and [satisfied] opponents of statehood in the Congress that the Virgin Islands, not being even an 'incorporated' territory, was more than one step away from that cherished constitutional status of 'statehood'" (Bough and Macridis, *Virgin Islands*, 123).

65. Bough and Macridis, *Virgin Islands*, 132. In 1966, Resolution 346 increased the number of seats from eleven to fifteen, with seven senators each from St. Thomas and St. Croix and one St. John resident elected by residents of all three islands.

66. At the time, the Virgin Islands had no airfield that could accommodate larger planes, restricting tourism to a dribble of visitors from Puerto Rico and the few who traveled from New York or Miami directly to St. Croix. See Creque and Goeggel, *Study*.

CHAPTER 3

1. "Tourist Board of St. Thomas Hold Organization Meeting," *St. Croix Avis*, May 1947, 1.
2. "Henle Here: Will Meet with Tourist Board," *Virgin Islands Daily News*, November 9, 1948, 1.
3. "Tourist Board Buys 1000 Virgin Islands Magazines," *Virgin Islands Daily News*, November 22, 1948, 1; *Virgin Island Magazine*, 1956–57, St. Croix Landmarks Society.
4. *Virgin Islands View*, September 1967, St. Croix Landmarks Society.
5. "Tourist Board Holds Quarterly Meeting," *Virgin Islands Daily News*, June 9, 1952, 1.
6. "Head of Antigua Tourist Board Visits Here," *Virgin Islands Daily News*, May 29, 1952, 1; "King and Queen of Carnival Proclaimed," *Virgin Islands Daily News*, August 26, 1952, 1.
7. "V.I. Carnival a Huge Success," *Virgin Islands Daily News*, September 3, 1952, 1; "V.I. Carnival Featured in New York Times," *Virgin Islands Daily News*, August 25, 1952, 1.
8. See Hobsbawm and Ranger, *Invention of Tradition*.
9. de Albuquerque, "'Is We Carnival,'" 52.
10. Ibid.
11. "Old Fashioned Christmas Festival Biggest Seen Here," *St. Croix Avis*, December 27, 1952, 1; "History of the Festival," *St. Croix Mas Festival '56* booklet, 1–2, St. Croix Landmarks Society.
12. "Old Time Festival Furnish Bulk of Entertainment," *St. Croix Avis*, December 29, 1953, 1.
13. Neville A. T. Hall, *Slave Society*, 208.
14. "Troupes, Clowns, Whip Dancers, Steel Bands Expected," *St. Croix Avis*, December 11, 1953, 1.
15. "Hell's Gate Steel Band Thrills St. Croix at Christmas Festival," *St. Croix Avis*, December 30, 1953, 1.
16. "Festival Committee Meets; Might Become Annual Event," *St. Croix Avis*, January 10, 1953, 1.
17. Richardson, *Seven Streets*, 147.
18. Schrader, *Maufe, Quelbe, and T'ing*, 52.
19. "Harry Edward, Miss Tutein, Winners in Festival Contest," *St. Croix Avis*, December 20, 1954, 1.
20. Jessica Tutein, interview by author, St. Croix, March 4, 1999. The St. Croix Christmas Festival did not have another king until 2004, when a king's competition was added to the lineup of events.
21. Ibid.
22. Ibid.
23. Sheryl Petersen, who often performed with Butcher Brown, was legendary for her skill and performance of these skits, which feature double entendres, class blunders, and raw Crucian language that demonstrates national pride and stirs audiences.
24. Clarence "Cherra" Heyleger, interview by author, June 30, 1993.
25. Ibid.
26. Banner, *American Beauty*, 288.
27. Ibid., 289.
28. Ibid.
29. Clarence "Cherra" Heyleger, interview by author, St. Croix, June 30, 1993.
30. Claire Roker, interview by author, St. Croix, February 25, 1999.
31. Ibid.
32. Ibid.

33. Ibid.
34. Miss U.S. Virgin Islands contestants are expected to compete in the international contest and enter the regional contest with this goal. For a time, the Miss American Virgin Islands contest competed with the Miss U.S. Virgin Islands pageant and sent contestants to Miss World. However, internal discord relegated Miss American Virgin Islands to the virtual property of one prominent St. Thomian who owned the franchise for a few years and selected representatives without the "burden" of an actual contest. The competition has currently disappeared, although some people are attempting to resurrect it and give Miss U.S. Virgin Islands a literal run for the money.
35. Venetia Harvey, "Focus on Former Queens," *Probe* (*Avis* newsmagazine), September 20–21, 1987, 1, 7.
36. Carnival booklet (St. Thomas: privately published, 1996), 63; Utha Williams, interview by author, St. Thomas, April 12, 1999.

CHAPTER 4

1. Unless otherwise noted, all quotations and information regarding the pageant come from the author's observations and from the author's audio recording of the Miss U.S. Virgin Islands pageant performance, St. Thomas, March 21, 1999.
2. Carolyn Jenkins, interview by author, St. Thomas, February 6, 1999.
3. Utha Williams, interview by author, St. Thomas, March 21, 1999.
4. *Essence of the Caribbean: Miss U.S. Virgin Islands Pageant* (booklet), March 21, 1999, in possession of the author.
5. Ibid., 5.
6. Stuart Hall, "Introduction," 4.
7. See Kaplan, Alarcon, and Moallem, *Between Woman and Nation*; Parker et al., *Nationalisms and Sexualities*.
8. Stuart Hall, "Introduction," 4.
9. Abrahams, *Man of Words*.

CHAPTER 5

1. Claire Roker, interview by author, St. Croix, February 25, 1999.
2. Borland, "India Bonita," 75.
3. Claire Roker, interview by author, St. Croix, February 25, 1999.
4. While the Carnival Queen pageant in St. Thomas is the most popular pageant, often with more than ten contestants per year, it has no formal franchise. Thus, winners begin and end their reign on the island, with no promise of further mobility or visibility.
5. Jeffrey Prosser, a Nebraskan, owns the *Virgin Islands Daily News*, two local cable television firms, a bank, and the telephone and wireless services company on all three islands. See Michael Allen and Mitchell Pacelle, "Island Empire: A Guy from Nebraska Hits It Big in St. Croix but Triggers a Backlash," *Wall Street Journal*, February 1, 2000, A1.
6. Chambers, "Thailand's Tourism Paradox," 103.
7. See Sheller, *Consuming the Caribbean*.
8. Boyer, *America's Virgin Islands*, 351–55.
9. de Albuquerque, "'Is We Carnival,'" 56.
10. Ibid., 51.
11. Ibid.

12. Ibid.
13. Sunshine, *Caribbean*, 176.
14. Adelbert Bryan, *Casino Gaming and Destination Resort Roundtable* (St. Thomas: Virgin Islands Legislature, 1996), 10.
15. Ibid., 13.
16. Ibid.
17. Carvalho, "Tupi or Not Tupi MPB," 163.
18. Cadaval, "Folklife," 13.
19. Stuart Hall, "Introduction," 5.

CHAPTER 6

1. *Ideas and Issues*, WSTA radio, audio recording, St. Thomas, March 23, 1999.
2. ABC News, *Primetime Live*, Segment 2, video recording, November 27, 1996.
3. Claire Roker, interview by author, St. Croix, February 25, 1999.
4. *Ideas and Issues*, WSTA Radio, audio recording, St. Thomas, March 23, 1999.
5. Ibid.
6. Ibid.
7. Ibid.
8. See Bengelsdorf, "[Re]Considering Cuban Women," 229–55. See also Atluri, *When the Closet Is a Region*; Alexander, "Erotic Autonomy," 63–100.
9. Deborah Gottlieb, interview by author, St. Thomas, January 24, 1999.
10. Ibid.
11. Miss U.S. Virgin Islands rehearsal, St. Thomas, February 6, 1999.
12. Ibid.
13. See Cooper, *Noises in the Blood*, 49; Shepherd, *Women in Caribbean History*, 61.
14. Kamau Brathwaite, lectures, New York University, 1993–95. See also Beckles, *Centering Woman*; Cooper, *Noises in the Blood*; Mathurin, *Rebel Woman*.
15. Beckles, *Centering Woman*; Bush, *Slave Women*; Shepherd, Brereton, and Bailey, *Engendering History*; Gaspar and Hine, *More Than Chattel*; Gilman, "Black Bodies, White Bodies"; Neville A. T. Hall, "Anna Heegaard."
16. Anderson, *Imagined Communities*, 81; Chatterjee, *Nation and Its Fragments*, 5.
17. The distinction Ulysse describes between *lady* and *woman* in Jamaica ("Uptown Ladies and Downtown Women," 148) does not function in the U.S. Virgin Islands. In this context, *woman* is a figure of value that reads across class. Both *lady* and *woman* can be used in this community to similar effect. Here they indicate age and familiarity more than anything else.
18. Matt Gove, "AIDS and HIV Cases in the V.I. Could Reach 4 Times the National Average," *Virgin Islands Daily News*, n.d., available online at http://www.virginislandsdailynews. com/index.pl/article_archive?id=327233 (accessed July 2007); Marty Schladen, "After Two Decades, AIDS Still Fueled by Stigma and Discrimination," *Virgin Islands Daily News*, December 2, 2002, available online at http://www.virginislandsdailynews.com/in-dex.pl/article_archive?id=257323 (accessed July 2007); Joy Blackburn, "V.I.'s 2002 AIDS Rate among Worst in U.S.," *Virgin Islands Daily News*, January 16, 2004, available online at http://www.virginislandsdailynews.com/index.pl/article_archive?id=288474 (accessed July 2007). Because the Virgin Islands is a U.S. territory, it is excluded from membership in the Caribbean Epidemiology Centre, which provides resources for member countries and conducts studies of the AIDS/HIV problem. Thus, as Blackburn states, the Virgin Islands is

stuck in a sort of "limbo" in this public health crisis, much as it is in its status as a Caribbean nation.

19. This is a controversial and loaded comment on my part, and I am clear about its implications. Islanders have historically been deemed an oversexed people, and the sexualization of dances has been part of a centuries-long racist and destructive assault on them. I am not saying that this is some kind of debased behavior that has been asserted by historical travel accounts but that the attitudes about sex and how sex relates to activities such as dancing are regarded differently and therefore occupy a very important and particular role in the society. Through dancing and other social activities, Virgin Islanders shape and rehearse their more intimate relations with one another.

20. Petra Maximay, interview by author, St. Thomas, January 26, 1999.

21. See Sheller, *Consuming the Caribbean*.

22. Horace Campbell, *Rasta and Resistance*, 1.

23. Mercer, "Black Hair/Style Politics," 100.

24. Ibid., 103.

25. Grayson, "Is It Fake?," 13.

26. Rowe quoted in Cooper, *Noises in the Blood*, 10.

27. Clarence "Cherra" Heyleger, interview by author, St. Croix, June 30, 1993.

28. Miss U.S. Virgin Islands rehearsal, St. Thomas, February 6, 1999.

29. Ibid.

30. Ibid.

31. Ibid.

32. Ibid.

33. Contests do not normally have public associations with one another. While it may be understood that contestants in different pageants informally communicate style preferences and ideas, secrecy is de rigueur, and surprise constitutes an important element of each contestant's performance. In this instance, an appearance unrelated to the content of the Miss U.S. Virgin Islands pageant could do no harm.

34. Rachel Riddle, Miss U.S. Virgin Islands rehearsal, St. Thomas, March 20, 1999.

35. Mercer, "Black Hair/Style Politics," 111.

36. Lorna Webster, interview by author, St. Thomas, February 4, 1999.

37. Ibid.

38. William Chandler, interview by author, St. Thomas, February 2, 1999.

39. Ibid.

40. Claire Roker, interview by author, St. Croix, February 25, 1999.

41. Anonymous, telephone interview by author, St. Thomas, January 21, 1999.

42. See also Shepherd, *Women in Caribbean History*, 154–86.

43. Ulysse, "Conquering Duppies in Kingston," 18.

44. Phelan, *Unmarked*, 6.

45. Ibid., 7.

46. Ibid., 14.

47. Ibid., 10.

CHAPTER 7

1. All information regarding and quotations from Marise James are taken from Marise James, interview by author, St. Croix, March 3, 1999.

2. *Ideas and Issues*, WSTA radio, audio recording, St. Thomas, March 23, 1999.

3. Lorna Webster, interview by author, St. Thomas, February 4, 1999.

4. Barnes, "Face of the Nation," 288.

5. Howard Campbell, "Jamaican Beauty Contest under Fire for Selecting 'Brown' Winner," *New York Amsterdam News*, October 14–20, 1999, 2. See also Ulysse, "Uptown Ladies and Downtown Women," 152.

6. Lorna Webster, interview by author, St. Thomas, February 4, 1999.

7. Prosterman, *Ordinary Life, Festival Days*, 106.

8. Ibid., 110, 111–12, 125.

9. Ibid., 141; Utha Williams, interview by author, St. Thomas, February 3, 1999; Lorna Webster, interview by author, St. Thomas, February 4, 1999.

10. Lorna Webster, interview by author, St. Thomas, February 4, 1999.

11. *Probe (Avis* newsmagazine), September 20–21, 1987, 2.

12. Unless otherwise noted, all information regarding Williams and the 1971 pageant and quotations from Utha Williams are taken from Utha Williams, interview by author, St. Thomas, February 3, April 12, 1999.

13. "An Analysis; Utha Williams Forfeits Title of Miss V.I.," n.d., "Beauty Queen Disqualified as Over Age," *St. Thomas Home Journal*, July 12, 1971, Letter to the Editor, *St. Thomas Home Journal*, July 12, 1971, "No Crown but a True Queen," *Virgin Islands Daily News*, January 2, 1995, all in Utha Williams scrapbook.

14. Maxine Leeds Craig, *Ain't I a Beauty Queen?*

15. "New Miss VI Named; Judge Disqualified," *Virgin Islands Daily News*, May 12, 1981, 1; "Dethroned Queen Wants to Crown New Miss VI," *Virgin Islands Daily News*, May 15, 1981, 3.

16. Deborah Gottlieb, interview by author, St. Thomas, January 24, 1999.

17. Kim Boschulte, interview by author, St. Thomas, February 4, 1999.

18. See Davila, *Sponsored Identities*.

19. Like the callers to the March 1999 *Ideas and Issues* program, Boschulte blamed the Lions Club and the lack of time between events for her lack of success at Miss Universe (Kim Boschulte, interview by author, St. Thomas, February 4, 1999).

20. *Ideas and Issues*, WSTA radio, audio recording, St. Thomas, March 23, 1999.

21. Maxine Leeds Craig, *Ain't I a Beauty Queen?*

22. Wolf, *Beauty Myth*, 12, 14.

23. See past booklets; Venetia Harvey, "Focus on Former Queens," *Probe (Avis* newsmagazine), September 20–21, 1987.

24. Ulysse, "Conquering Duppies in Kingston"; Barnes, "Face of the Nation," 285–306.

25. Lorna Webster, interview by author, St. Thomas, February 4, 1999.

26. Vormese, "Ethnic Beauty," 246.

27. Lorna Webster, interview by author, St. Thomas, February 4, 1999.

28. Ibid.

29. Ibid.

30. Ibid.

31. Cohen, Wilk, and Stoeltje, *Beauty Queens*, 7.

32. Banet-Weiser, *Most Beautiful Girl*, 57.

33. Steinberg, *Complete and Utter Failure*, 85, 15.

34. Lorna Webster, interview by author, St. Thomas, February 4, 1999.

35. Banet-Weiser, *Most Beautiful Girl*, 57; Kennedy, "Sport Shows," 277.

36. Cohen, Wilk, and Stoeltje, *Beauty Queens*, 10–11.

37. Kennedy, "Sport Shows," 277.

38. Banet-Weiser, *Most Beautiful Girl*, 57.
39. Hemphill, "Revisioning Sport Spectatorism," 49.
40. Ibid.
41. Guttman, *Sports Spectators*, 121; Kennedy, "Sport Shows," 281.
42. Kennedy, "Sport Shows," 279.
43. Ibid., 280; Hemphill, "Revisioning Sport Spectatorism," 54.
44. Hemphill, "Revisioning Sport Spectatorism," 54.
45. Atkinson, "Fifty Million Viewers," 53.
46. Ibid., 49.
47. Davila, *Sponsored Identities*, 148.

CONCLUSION

1. Enloe, *Bananas, Beaches, and Bases*, 9.
2. Cohen, Wilk, and Stoeltje, *Beauty Queens*, 2.
3. Venetia Harvey, "Focus on Former Queens," *Probe* (*Avis* newsmagazine), September 20–21, 1987, 1–7.
4. Ibid., 7.
5. Carlip, *Girl Power*, 320.
6. Barnes, "Face of the Nation," 302.

BIBLIOGRAPHY

Abrahams, Roger. *The Man of Words in the West Indies: Performance and the Emergence of Creole Culture*. Baltimore: Johns Hopkins University Press, 1983.

Ahmed-Ghosh, Huma. "Writing the Nation on the Beauty Queen's Body: Implications for a 'Hindu' Nation." *Meridians: Feminism, Race, Transnationalism* 4, no. 1. (2003): 205–27.

Alexander, M. Jacqui. "Erotic Autonomy as a Politics of Decolonization: An Anatomy of Feminist State Practice in the Bahamas Tourist Economy." In *Feminist Genealogies, Colonial Legacies, Democratic Futures*, ed. M. Jacqui Alexander and Chandra Talpade Mohanty. New York: Routledge, 1997.

Alexander, M. Jacqui, and Chandra Talpade Mohanty, eds. *Feminist Genealogies, Colonial Legacies, Democratic Futures*. New York: Routledge, 1997.

Anderson, Benedict. *Imagined Communities*. London: Verso, 1983.

Anzaldúa, Gloria, ed. *Making Face, Making Soul/Haciendo Caras: Creative and Critical Perspectives by Feminists of Color*. San Francisco: Aunt Lute, 1990.

Ashcroft, Bill, Gareth Griffiths, and Helen Tiffin, eds. *The Empire Writes Back: Theory and Practice in Post-Colonial Literatures*. London: Routledge, 1989.

———. *The Post-Colonial Studies Reader*. London: Routledge, 1995.

Atkinson, Michael. "Fifty Million Viewers Can't Be Wrong: Professional Wrestling, Sports-Entertainment, and Mimesis." *Sociology of Sport Journal* 19, no. 1 (2002): 47–66.

Atluri, Tara L. *When the Closet Is a Region: Homophobia, Heterosexism, and Nationalism in the Commonwealth Caribbean*. Working Paper 5. Bridgetown, Barbados: Centre for Gender and Development Studies, University of West Indies, 2001.

Baker, Houston, Manthia Diawara, and Ruth Lindeborg, eds. *Black British Cultural Studies: A Reader*. Chicago: University of Chicago Press, 1996.

Bakhtin, Mikhail. *Rabelais and His World*. Trans. Helene Iswolsky. Bloomington: Indiana University Press, 1984.

Banet-Weiser, Sarah. *The Most Beautiful Girl in the World: Beauty Pageants and National Identity*. Berkeley: University of California Press, 1999.

Banner, Lois W. *American Beauty*. Chicago: University of Chicago Press, 1983.

Barnes, Natasha B. "Face of the Nation: Race, Nationalisms, and Identities in Jamaican Beauty Pageants." In *Daughters of Caliban: Caribbean Women in the Twentieth Century*, ed. Consuelo López Springfield. Bloomington: Indiana University Press, 1997.

Barriteau, Violet Eudine. "Constructing a Conceptual Framework for Developing Women's Transformational Leadership in the Caribbean." *Social and Economic Studies* 52, no. 4 (2003): 5–49.

Barry, Tom, Beth Wood, and Deb Preusch. *The Other Side of Paradise: Foreign Control in the Caribbean*. New York: Grove, 1984.

Beckles, Hilary McD. *Centering Woman: Gender Discourses in Caribbean Slave Society*. Kingston, Jamaica: Randle, 1999.

———. *Natural Rebels: A Social History of Enslaved Black Women in Barbados*. New Brunswick, N.J.: Rutgers University Press, 1989.

———. "Sex and Gender in the Historiography of Caribbean Slavery." In *Engendering History: Caribbean Women in Historical Perspective*, ed. Verene Shepherd, Bridget Brereton, and Barbara Bailey. New York: St. Martin's, 1995.

Beckles, Hilary McD., and Verene Shepherd, eds. *Caribbean Freedom: Economy and Society from Emancipation to the Present: A Student Reader*. Kingston, Jamaica: Randle, 1996.

Bengelsdorf, Carollee. "[Re]Considering Cuban Women in a Time of Troubles." In *Daughters of Caliban: Caribbean Women in the Twentieth Century*, ed. Consuelo López Springfield. Bloomington: Indiana University Press, 1997.

Benitez-Rojo, Antonio. *The Repeating Island: The Caribbean and the Postmodern Perspective*. Durham, N.C.: Duke University Press, 1992.

Bhabha, Homi K., *The Location of Culture*. London: Routledge, 1994.

———, ed. *Nation and Narration*. London: Routledge, 1990.

Black, Jan Knippers. "Responsibility without Authority: The Growing Burden for Women in the Caribbean. *Review of Social Economy* 55, no. 2 (1997): 235–42.

Borland, Katherine. "The India Bonita of Monimbo." In *Beauty Queens on the Global Stage: Gender, Contests, and Power*, ed. Colleen Ballerino Cohen, Richard Wilk, and Beverly Stoeltje. New York: Routledge, 1996.

Bough, James, and Roy C. Macridis, eds. *Virgin Islands, America's Caribbean Outpost: The Evolution of Self Government*. Wakefield, Mass.: Williams, 1970.

Boyer, William. *America's Virgin Islands: A History of Human Rights and Wrongs*. Durham, N.C.: Carolina Academic, 1983.

Brand, Peg Zeglin, ed. *Beauty Matters*. Bloomington: Indiana University Press, 2000.

Brathwaite, Edward. *The Development of Creole Society in Jamaica, 1770–1820*. Oxford: Clarendon, 1971.

Browne, Katherine. "Work Style and Network Management: Gendered Patterns and Economic Consequences in Martinique." *Gender and Society* 14, no. 3 (2000): 435–56.

Bundles, A'Lelia. *On Her Own Ground: The Life and Times of Madam C. J. Walker*. New York: Scribner, 2001.

Bush, Barbara. *Slave Women in Caribbean Society, 1650–1838*. Bloomington: Indiana University Press, 1990.

Butler, Judith. *Bodies That Matter*. London: Routledge, 1993.

———. *Gender Trouble: Feminism and the Subversion of Identity*. New York: Routledge, 1990.

Cadaval, Olivia. "Folklife of the U.S. Virgin Islands: Persistence and Creativity." In *Festival of American Folklife*. Washington, D.C.: Smithsonian Institution/National Park Service, 1990.

Campbell, Horace. *Rasta and Resistance: From Marcus Garvey to Walter Rodney*. Trenton, N.J.: Africa World, 1987.

Canclini, Nestor G. *Hybrid Cultures: Strategies for Entering and Leaving Modernity*. Minneapolis: University of Minnesota Press, 1995.

Caraway, Nancie. "Gender, Tyranny: Coded Bodies, Femininity, and Black Womanhood." In *Segregated Sisterhood: Racism and the Politics of American Feminism*. Knoxville: University of Tennessee Press, 1991.

Carvalho, Marta de Ulhoa. "Tupi or Not Tupi MPB: Popular Music and Identity in Brazil." In *The Brazilian Puzzle: Culture on the Borderlands of the Western World*, ed. David J. Hess and Roberto A. DaMatta. New York: Columbia University Press, 1995.

Carlip, Hillary. *Girl Power: Young Women Speak Out! Personal Writings from Teenage Girls*. New York: Warner, 1995.

Case, Sue Ellen. *Feminism and Theatre*. New York: Routledge, 1988.

———, ed. *Performing Feminisms*. Baltimore: Johns Hopkins University Press, 1990.

Chambers, Erve. "Thailand's Tourism Paradox: Identity and Nationalism as Factors in Tourist Development." In *Conserving Culture: A New Discourse on Heritage*, ed. Mary Hufford. Urbana: University of Illinois Press, 1994.

Chatterjee, Partha. *The Nation and Its Fragments: Colonial and Postcolonial Histories*. Princeton: Princeton University Press, 1993.

Cohen, Colleen B., Richard Wilk, and Beverly Stoeltje, eds. *Beauty Queens on the Global Stage: Gender, Contests, and Power*. New York: Routledge, 1996.

Collins, Patricia Hill. *Black Feminist Thought: Knowledge, Consciousness, and the Politics of Empowerment*. New York: Routledge, 1990.

Cooper, Carolyn. *Noises in the Blood: Orality, Gender, and the "Vulgar" Body of Jamaican Popular Culture*. Durham, N.C.: Duke University Press, 1995.

Courlander, Harold. *A Treasury of Afro-American Folklore*. New York: Crown, 1976.

Cowley, John. *Carnival, Canbouley, and Calypso: Traditions in the Making*. New York: Cambridge University Press, 1996.

Craig, Ian Wallace. "Actions Speak Louder: Women in the Caribbean Documentaries of Everyday Life." *Journal of International Women's Studies* 3, no. 1 (2001): 65–73.

Craig, Maxine Leeds. *Ain't I a Beauty Queen? Black Women, Beauty, and the Politics of Race*. Oxford: Oxford University Press. 2002.

Creque, Darwin, and Harry Goeggel. *A Study of the Tourist Industry in the Virgin Islands*. St. Thomas, Virgin Islands: Division of Trade and Industry, 1964.

Crew, Spencer R., and James E. Sims. "Locating Authenticity: Fragments of a Dialogue." In *Exhibiting Cultures: The Poetics and Politics of Museum Display*, ed. Ivan Karp and Steven D. Levine. Washington: Smithsonian Institution Press, 1991.

Curtin, Philip D. *The Atlantic Slave Trade: A Census*. Madison: University of Wisconsin Press, 1969.

Davies, Carole Boyce. *Out of the KUMBLA: Caribbean Women and Literature*. Trenton, N.J.: Africa World, 1990.

Davila, Arlene. "El Kiosko Budweiser: The Making of a 'National' Television Show in Puerto Rico." *American Ethnologist* 25, no. 3. (1998): 452–70.

————. *Latinos, Inc: The Marketing and Making of a People*. Berkeley: University of California Press, 2001.

————. *Sponsored Identities: Cultural Politics in Puerto Rico*. Philadelphia: Temple University Press, 1997.

Davis, Kathy. *Reshaping the Female Body: The Dilemma of Cosmetic Surgery*. New York: Routledge, 1995.

Dayan, Daniel, and Elihu Katz. *Media Events: The Live Broadcasting of History*. Cambridge: Harvard University Press, 1992.

de Albuquerque, Klaus. "'Is We Carnival': Cultural Traditions under Stress in the U.S. Virgin Islands." In *Caribbean Popular Culture*, ed. John A. Lent. Bowling Green, Ohio: Bowling Green State University Popular Press, 1990.

DeBooy, Theodor, and John T. Farris. *The Virgin Islands, Our New Possessions*. Philadelphia: Lippincott, 1918.

Dent, Gina. *Black Popular Culture*. Seattle: Bay, 1992.

Desmond, Jane. "Invoking the 'Native': Body Politics in Contemporary Hawaiian Tourist Shows." *Drama Review* 41, no. 4 (1997): 83–109.

Dookhan, Isaac. *A History of the Virgin Islands of the United States*. Epping, Eng.: Caribbean Universities Press for the College of the Virgin Islands, 1974.

Du Bois, W. E. B. *The Souls of Black Folk*. New York: Fawcett, 1961.

Emanuel, Charles H., Sr. *The Bamboola Dance*. N.p., n.d.

Emery, Lynn Fauley. *Black Dance: From 1619 to Today*. Princeton: Princeton Book, 1972.

Enloe, Cynthia. *Bananas, Beaches, and Bases: Making Feminist Sense of International Politics*. Berkeley: University of California Press, 1989.

Foucault, Michel. *The History of Sexuality: An Introduction*. Vol. 1. Trans. Robert Hurley. New York: Vintage, 1978.

Freeman, Carla. *High Tech and High Heels in the Global Economy: Women, Work, and Pink-Collar Identities in the Caribbean*. Durham, N.C.: Duke University Press, 2000.

Gaspar, David Barry, and Darlene Clark Hine, eds. *More Than Chattel: Black Women and Slavery in the Americas*. Bloomington: Indiana University Press, 1996.

Gerard, Philip A. "Social Configuration and Some Problems." In *Virgin Islands, America's Caribbean Outpost: The Evolution of Self Government*, ed. James A. Bough and Roy C. Macridis. Wakefield, Mass.: Williams, 1970.

Getz, Donald. *Festivals, Special Events, and Tourism*. New York: Van Nostrand Reinhold, 1991.

Gilman, Sander. "Black Bodies, White Bodies: Toward an Iconography of Female Sexuality in Late Nineteenth-Century Art, Medicine, and Literature." *Critical Inquiry* 12, no. 1 (1985): 204–42.

Glissant, Edouard. *Caribbean Discourse: Selected Essays*. Charlottesville: University Press of Virginia, 1989.

Gottschild, Brenda Dixon. *The Black Dancing Body: A Geography from Coon to Cool*. New York: Palgrave Macmillan, 2003.

Grayson, Deborah R. "Is It Fake? Black Women's Hair as Spectacle and Spec(tac)ular." *Camera Obscura: Feminism, Culture, and Media Studies* 36 (1995): 13–30.

Guttman, Allen. *Sports Spectators*. New York: Columbia University Press, 1986.

Hall, Catherine. *Civilising Subjects: Colony and Metropole in the English Imagination, 1830–1867*. Chicago: University of Chicago Press, 2002.

Hall, Neville A. T. "Anna Heegaard: Enigma." *Caribbean Quarterly* 22, nos. 2–3 (1976): 62–73.

———. *Slave Society in the Danish West Indies*. Mona, Jamaica: University of the West Indies Press, 1992.

———. "Slaves Use of Their 'Free' Time in the Danish Virgin Islands in the Later Eighteenth and Early Nineteenth Century." *Journal of Caribbean History* 13 (1980): 21–43.

Hall, Stuart. "Introduction: Who Needs Identity?" In *Questions of Cultural Identity*, ed. Stuart Hall and Paul du Gay. London: Sage, 1996.

———. "Negotiating Caribbean Identities." In *New Caribbean Thought: A Reader*, ed. Brian Meeks and Folke Lindahl. Kingston, Jamaica: University of the West Indies Press, 2001.

Hall, Stuart, and Paul du Gay, eds. *Questions of Cultural Identity*. London: Sage, 1996.

Hartman, Saidiya. *Scenes of Subjection: Terror, Slavery, and Self-Making in Nineteenth-Century America*. New York: Oxford University Press, 1997.

Hemphill, Dennis A. "Revisioning Sports Spectatorism." *Journal of the Philosophy of Sport* 22 (1995): 48–60.

Hill, Donald R. *Calypso Callaloo: Early Carnival Music in Trinidad*. Gainesville: University Press of Florida, 1993.

Hobsbawm, Eric, and Terence Ranger, eds. *The Invention of Tradition*. Cambridge: Cambridge University Press, 1983.

hooks, bell. *Ain't I a Woman: Black Women and Feminism*. Boston: South End, 1981.

———. *Feminist Theory: From Margin to Center*. Boston: South End, 1984.

Jackson, John, Jr. *Real Black: Adventures in Racial Sincerity*. Chicago: University of Chicago Press, 2005.

James, Stanlie M., and Abena P. A. Busia, eds. *Theorizing Black Feminisms: The Visionary Pragmatism of Black Women*. New York: Routledge, 1993.

Jensen, Peter Hoxcer. *From Serfdom to Fireburn and Strike: The History of Black Labor in the Danish West Indies, 1848–1916*. Christiansted, St. Croix: Antilles, 1998.

Joseph, May. "Diaspora, New Hybrid Identities, and the Performance of Citizenship." *Women and Performance* 7–8, no. 1–2 (1995): 3–13.

———. *Nomadic Identities: The Performance of Citizenship*. Minneapolis: University of Minnesota Press. 1999.

Kaplan, Caren, Norma Alarcon, and Minoo Moallem, eds. *Between Woman and Nation: Transnational Feminisms and the State*. Durham, N.C.: Duke University Press, 1999.

Kelley, Robin D. G. *Race Rebels: Culture, Politics, and the Black Working Class*. New York: Free Press, 1996.

Kennedy, Dennis. "Sport Shows: Spectators in Contemporary Culture." *Theatre Research International*, 26, no. 3 (2001): 277–84.

Khalideen, Rosetta, and Nadira Khalideen. "Caribbean Women in Globalization and Economic Restructuring." *Canadian Woman Studies* 21, no. 4 (2002): 108–13.

King-O'Riain, Rebecca Chiyoko. *Pure Beauty: Judging Race in Japanese American Beauty Pageants*. Minneapolis: University of Minnesota Press, 2006.

Kirshenblatt-Gimblett, Barbara. "Authenticity and Authority in the Representation of Culture: The Poetics and Politics of Tourist Production." *Kulturkontakt Kulturkonflikt* 26 (1987): 59–69.

Knight, Franklin W. *The Caribbean: The Genesis of a Fragmented Nationalism.* New York: Oxford University Press, 1990.

———. The Haitian Revolution. *American Historical Review* 105, no. 1 (2000); available online at http://www.historycooperative.org/journals/ahr/105.1/ah000103.html (accessed 25 July 2007).

Kozol, Wendy. "Miss Indian America: Regulatory Gazes and the Politics of Affiliation." *Feminist Studies* 31, no. 1 (2005): 64–95.

Lazarus-Black, Mindie. "Bastardy, Gender Hierarchy, and the State: The Politics of Family Law Reform in Antigua and Barbuda." *Law and Society Review* 26, no. 4 (1992): 863–900.

Leary, Paul. "Taking Bearings: The United States Virgin Islands, 1917–1987." Lecture sponsored by the St. Thomas Friends of Denmark and the Virgin Islands Humanities Council, 1988.

Lekis, Lisa. *Dancing Gods.* New York: Scarecrow, 1960.

Lent, John A., ed. *Caribbean Popular Culture.* Bowling Green, Ohio: Bowling Green State University Popular Press, 1990.

Lewis, Gordon K. "An Introductory Note to the Study of the Virgin Islands." *Caribbean Studies* 8, no. 2 (1968): 5–21.

———. *The Virgin Islands: A Caribbean Lilliput.* Evanston, Ill.: Northwestern University Press, 1972.

Lewisohn, Florence. *St. Croix under Seven Flags.* Hollywood, Fla.: Dukane, 1970.

Lieu, Nhi T. "Remembering 'the Nation' through Pageantry: Femininity and the Politics of Vietnamese Womanhood in the Hoa Hau Ao Dia Contest." *Frontiers* 21, no. 1–2 (2000): 127–51.

López, Rick A. "The India Bonita Contest of 1921 and the Ethnicization of Mexican National Culture." *Hispanic American Historical Review* 82, no. 2 (2002): 291–328.

Maga, Timothy P. "The Citizen Movement in Guam, 1946–1950." *Pacific Historical Review* 53, no. 1 (1984): 59–77.

Mani, Bakirathi. "Beauty Queens: Gender, Ethnicity, and Transnational Modernities at the Miss India USA Pageant." *Positions* 14, no. 3 (2006): 717–47.

Mathurin, Lucille. *The Rebel Woman in the British West Indies during Slavery.* Kingston: Institute of Jamaica for the African-Caribbean Institute of Jamaica, 1975.

Maurer, Bill. *Recharting the Caribbean: Land Law and Citizenship in the British Virgin Islands.* Ann Arbor: University of Michigan Press, 2000.

McAfee, Kathy. *Storm Signals: Structural Adjustment and Development Alternatives in the Caribbean.* Boston: South End, 1991.

Meeks, Brian, and Folke Lindahl, eds. *New Caribbean Thought: A Reader.* Kingston, Jamaica: University of the West Indies Press, 2001.

Mercer, Kobena. "Black Hair/Style Politics." In *Welcome to the Jungle: New Positions in Black Cultural Studies.* New York: Routledge, 1994.

Minh-ha, Trinh T. *Woman, Native, Other: Writing Postcoloniality and Feminism.* Bloomington: Indiana University Press, 1989.

Mintz, Sidney W. *Caribbean Contours*. Baltimore: Johns Hopkins University Press, 1985.

Momsen, Janet H. *Women and Change in the Caribbean*. Bloomington: Indiana University Press, 1993.

Moran, Mary H. "Carrying the Queen: Identity and Nationalism in a Liberian Queen Rally." In *Beauty Queens on the Global Stage: Gender, Contests, and Power*, ed. Colleen Ballerino Cohen, Richard Wilk, and Beverly Stoeltje. New York: Routledge, 1996.

Neimark, Jill. "Why We Need Miss America: The Miss America Pageant Demonstrates Important Truths about the Country and Its People." *Psychology Today*, September–October 1998, 40–46.

Nicholls, Robert W. *Old-Time Masquerading in the U.S. Virgin Islands*. St. Thomas: Virgin Islands Humanities Council, 1998.

Nugent, Maria. *Lady Nugent's Journal of Her Residence in Jamaica from 1801 to 1805*. Ed. P. Wright. Kingston, Jamaica: Institute of Jamaica, 1966.

Oliver, Cynthia. "St. Croix Dancing: The Contemporary and Historical Path of Dance on the U.S. Virgin Island of St. Croix." Master's thesis, New York University, 1995.

Olwig, Karen Fog. *Global Culture, Island Identity: Continuity and Change in the Afro-Caribbean Community of Nevis*. Switzerland: Harwood Academic, 1993.

Ong, Aihwa. *Flexible Citizenship: The Cultural Logics of Transnationality*. Durham, N.C.: Duke University Press, 1999.

Oza, Rupal. "Showcasing India: Gender, Geography, and Globalization." *Signs: The Journal of Women in Culture and Society* 26, no. 4 (2001): 1067–95.

Paiewonsky, Isidor. *Eyewitness Accounts of Slavery in the Danish West Indies*. New York: Fordham University Press, 1989.

Parker, Andrew, Mary Russo, Doris Sommer, and Patricia Yaeger, eds. *Nationalisms and Sexualities*. New York: Routledge, 1992.

Peiss, Kathy. *Hope in a Jar: The Making of America's Beauty Culture*. New York: Metropolitan, 1998.

Phelan, Peggy. *Unmarked: The Politics of Performance*. New York: Routledge, 1993.

Plato. *Philosophies of Beauty*. Ed. Albert Hofstadter and Richard Kuhns. Chicago: University of Chicago Press, 1976.

Plaza, Dwaine. "Transnational Grannies: The Changing Family Responsibilities of Elderly African Caribbean-Born Women Resident in Britain." *Social Indicators Research* 51, no. 1 (2000): 75–89.

Prince, Mary. *The History of Mary Prince: A West Indian Slave*. Ed. Moira Ferguson. Ann Arbor: University of Michigan Press, 1993.

Prosterman, Leslie Mina. *Ordinary Life, Festival Days: Aesthetics in the Midwestern County Fair*. Washington, D.C.: Smithsonian Institution Press, 1995.

Rahier, Jean Muteba. "Body Politics in Black and White: *Señoras, Mujeres, Blanqueamiento* and Miss Esmeraldas 1997–1998, Ecuador." *Women in Performance: A Journal of Feminist Theory* 11, no. 21 (1999): 103–19.

Richardson, Evelyn. *Seven Streets by Seven Streets*. New York: Blyden, 1984.

Rivera, Eulalie. *Growing Up on St. Croix: Recollections of a Crucian Girlhood*. Christiansted, St. Croix: Antilles Graphic Arts, 1987.

———. "Tea Meeting." In *Festival of American Folklife*. Washington, D.C.: Smithsonian Institution/National Park Service, 1990.

Roach, Joseph. *Cities of the Dead: Circum-Atlantic Performance*. New York: Columbia University Press, 1996.

Rogozinski, Jan. *A Brief History of the Caribbean: From the Arawak and Carib to the Present*. New York: Plume, 2000.

Rohlehr, Gordon. "Articulating a Caribbean Aesthetic: The Revolution of Self-Perception." *Caribe: Retrospective, 1976–1982* 6, no. 1 (1982): 16–21.

Rooks, Nowile M. *Hair Raising: Beauty Culture and African-American Women*. New Brunswick, N.J.: Rutgers University Press, 1996.

Rowe, W., and V. Schelling. *Memory and Modernity: Popular Culture in Latin America*. New York: Verso, 1991.

Scarry, Elaine. *On Beauty and Being Just*. Princeton: Princeton University Press, 1999.

Schiach, Morag. "A History of Changing Definitions of 'the Popular.'" In *Discourse on Popular Culture: Class, Gender, and History in Cultural Analysis, 1730 to the Present*. London: Polity and Blackwell, 1989.

Schrader, Richard. *Maufe, Quelbe, and T'ing: A Calabash of Stories*. Christiansted, St. Croix: Antilles Graphic Arts, 1994.

Scott, James. *The Moral Economy of the Peasant: Subsistence and Rebellion in Southeast Asia*. New Haven: Yale University Press, 1976.

Scranton, Philip, ed. *Beauty and Business: Commerce, Gender, and Culture in Modern America*. New York: Routledge, 2001.

Seguino, Stephanie. "Why Are Women in the Caribbean So Much More Likely Than Men to Be Unemployed?" *Social and Economic Studies* 52, no. 4 (2003): 83–120.

Sekula, Allan. "The Body and the Archive." *October* 39 (1986): 3–64.

Senior, Oliver. *Working Miracles: Women's Lives in the English-Speaking Caribbean*. Bloomington: Indiana University Press, 1991.

Sheller, Mimi. *Consuming the Caribbean: From Arawaks to Zombies*. London: Routledge, 2003

Shepherd, Verene A., ed. *Women in Caribbean History: The British and Colonised Territories*. Kingston, Jamaica: Randle, 1999.

Shepherd, Verene A., Bridget Brereton, and Barbara Bailey, eds. *Engendering History: Caribbean Women in Historical Perspective*. New York: St. Martin's, 1995.

Smith, Honor Ford. *Lionheart Gal: Lifestories of Jamaican Women*. London: Women's Press, 1986.

Sprauve, Gilbert A. "About Man Betta Man, Fission and Fusion, and Creole, Calypso and Cultural Survival in the Virgin Islands." In *Festival of American Folklife*. Washington, D.C.: Smithsonian Institution/National Park Service, 1990.

Springer, Pearl Eintou. *The New Aesthetic and the Meaning of Culture in the Caribbean*. Port of Spain, Trinidad: National Carnival Commission Carifesta VI Secretariat, 1992.

Springfield, Consuelo López, ed. *Daughters of Caliban: Caribbean Women in the Twentieth Century*. Bloomington: Indiana University Press, 1997.

Steinberg, Neil. *Complete and Utter Failure: A Celebration of Also-Rans, Runners-Up, Never-Weres, and Total Flops*. New York: Doubleday, 1994.

Stewart, Charles, and Rosalind Shaw, eds. *Syncretism/Anti-Syncretism: The Politics of Religious Synthesis*. London: Routledge, 1994.

Sunshine, Catherine A. *The Caribbean: Survival, Struggle, and Sovereignty*. Boston: South End, 1980.

Surowiecki, James. *The Wisdom of Crowds: Why the Many Are Smarter Than the Few and How Collective Wisdom Shapes Business, Economies, Societies, and Nations*. New York: Doubleday, 2004.

Thomas, Deborah A. *Modern Blackness: Nationalism, Globalization, and the Politics of Culture in Jamaica*. Durham, N.C.: Duke University Press. 2004.

Trouillot, Michel-Rolph. *Peasants and Capital: Dominica in the World Economy* Baltimore: Johns Hopkins University Press, 1988.

Ulysse, Gina. "Conquering Duppies in Kingston: Miss Tiny and Me, Fieldwork Conflicts, and Being Loved and Rescued." *Anthropology and Humanism* 27, no. 1 (2002): 10–26.

———. "Uptown Ladies and Downtown Women." In *Representations of Blackness and the Performance of Identities*, ed. Jean Muteba Rahier. Westport, Conn.: Bergin and Garvey, 1999.

Vormese, Francine. "Ethnic Beauty." In *Beauty, the Twentieth Century*. New York: Universe, 2000.

Warner, Keith. *Kaiso! The Trinidad Calypso: A Study of the Calypso as Oral Literature*. Washington, D.C.: Three Continents, 1982.

Watson, Elwood, and Darcy Martin. "The Miss America Pageant: Pluralism, Femininity, and Cinderella All in One." *Journal of Popular Culture* 34, no. 1 (2000): 105–26.

———, eds. *There She Is, Miss America: The Politics of Sex, Beauty, and Race in America's Most Famous Pageant*. New York: Palgrave Macmillan, 2004.

Westergaard, Waldemar. *The Danish West Indies (1671–1754)*. New York: Macmillan, 1917.

Williams, Eric. *From Columbus to Castro: The History of the Caribbean, 1492–1969*. New York: Vintage, 1970.

Willocks, Harold W. L. *The Umbilical Cord: The History of the United States Virgin Islands from Pre-Columbian Era to the Present*. Christiansted, St. Croix: Willocks, 1995.

Wolf, Naomi. *The Beauty Myth*. Toronto: Vintage, 1990.

Yano, Christine R. *Crowning the Nice Girl: Gender, Ethnicity, and Culture in Hawai'i's Cherry Blossom Festival*. Honolulu: University of Hawai'i Press, 2006.

INDEX